AUTOBIOGRAPHY OF LUTFULLAH

AUTOBIOGRAPHY OF LUTFULLAH,

A MOHAMMEDAN GENTLEMAN;

AND
HIS TRANSLATIONS WITH HIS FELLOW-CREATURES

INTERSPERSED WITH REMARKS ON THE HABITS, CUSTOMS, AND CHARACTER OF THE PEOPLE WITH WHOM HE HAD TO DEAL

EDWARD B. EASTWICK

GYAN

Published by

Gyan Publishing House
5, Ansari Road
Daryaganj, New Delhi-110002
Phone: 011-47034999, 9811692060
E-mail: books@gyanbooks.com

Distribution Network
gyanbooks.com
India, USA, Canada, UK, Australia

ISBN: 978-93-7447-214-9 (PB)

First Published, 1858

2nd Impression 2026

Printed at: Gyan Press, Delhi.

AUTOBIOGRAPHY OF LUTFULLAH
Author: EDWARD B. EASTWICK

AUTOBIOGRAPHY

OF

LUTFULLAH,

A

MOHAMEDAN GENTLEMAN;

AND

HIS TRANSACTIONS WITH HIS FELLOW-CREATURES:

INTERSPERSED WITH REMARKS
ON THE HABITS, CUSTOMS, AND CHARACTER OF THE PEOPLE
WITH WHOM HE HAD TO DEAL.

And one man in his time plays many parts.—SHAKESPEARE.

EDITED BY
EDWARD B. EASTWICK, F.R.S., F.S.A.

[THIRD EDITION.]

LONDON:
SMITH, ELDER, AND CO., 65, CORNHILL.

1858.

TO

COLONEL W. H. SYKES, F.R.S.,

ETC., ETC.

LONDON.

DEAR HONOURABLE SIR,

With due respect I place before you my humble work, in the shape of journal, about which I talked to you ten years ago, when I had the honour of waiting upon you in person at your own house.

I do not pretend to say it is worthy of the perusal of a learned scholar like yourself; at the same time, I am confident that the unvarnished truths contained therein, if cleared of grammatical errors by your able pen and published under your auspices, will not fail to teach experience to those who want it and afford satisfaction to readers in general.

I beg to observe that, being self-tutored in your most difficult language, I stand far beyond the reach of critics, who will surely pardon me, when they are fully acquainted with my circumstances, by going through this book.

With due respect,

Dear Honourable Sir,

I remain,

Your most obedient and humble servant,

LUTFULLAH.

Sûrat,
24*th November*, 1854.

PREFACE.

As this volume contains the genuine sentiments of a native of India on many matters connected with the Government of that country, it will, perhaps, be read with some interest at the present crisis. The Author is known to be one of the least bigoted disciples of Islám; yet his bias towards his own sect, and the leaders of it, is most evident. If any one is disposed to think that the English are beginning to be regarded otherwise than as aliens by the inhabitants of Hindústán, a perusal of this book will probably lead his convictions the other way. In short, we may take it for granted that there is scarce a Sipáhí in our army, or other native of India, whose dislike of what Europeans deem progress does not equal that of the writer of this work. The majority are certainly much more opposed to it.

To some peculiar notions I would have willingly drawn attention by notes, but the great object being to condense as much as possible, I have for borne from all remark, and cut down the original as much as could be done without leaving out any fact or sentiment of importance. Indeed, my chief editorial task has been to compress; but, except with this view, I have altered the MS. as little as possible. Some stories, however, more suited to Oriental than to European taste, have been altogether omitted. The quotations and scraps of Latin are all of Lutfullah's own insertion.

When the slender advantages of the writer are considered, the reader will no doubt accord to Lutfullah some praise for composing so long a work in the, to him, foreign English language, with so much general accuracy.

THE EDITOR.

HAILEYBURY,
June, 1857.

PEDIGREE OF LUTFULLAH.

1. Adam.
2. Seth.
3. Enos.
4. Cainan.
5. Mahaleel.
6. Jared.
7. Enoch, or Idrís.
8. Methuselah.
9. Lamech.
10. Noah.
11. Nyám.
12. A'ramjád.
13. Sálah.
14. Ghábir.
15. Fannaa.
16. Arghun, or Húd, the Prophet.
17. Asroch.
18. Najúr.
19. Turij.
20. A'zur, or Tárak.
21. Ibrahím.
22. Ismaíl.
23. Kídar.
24. Jumaila.
25. Salmah.
26. Yáshab.
27. Mughráb.
28. Alsa.
29. Arwad.
30. A'ad.
31. Oad.
32. Adnán.
33. Maad.
34. Názar.
35. Madar.
36. Elias.
37. Madrak.
38. Hassan.
39. Kannanah.
40. Nassar.
41. Málik.
42. Fákhar.
43. Ghálib.
44. Laví.
45. Kaab.
46. Murra.
47. Adí.
48. Farat.
49. Abdu'lláh.
50. Zerrah.
51. Raial.
52. Abdu'lazíz.
53. Nofail.

54. Khattáb.
55. Umar.
56. Abdu'lláh.
57. Násir.
58. Ibrahím Adhan, of Balkh.
59. Shekh Isház.
60. Shekh Abu'l Fath.
61. Wáiz Asghar.
62. Wáiz Akbar.
63. Shekh Abdu'lláh,
64. Shekh Sultán Masaúd.
65. Shekh Samán.
66. Shekh Sulaimán.
67. Shekh Nasíru'd-dín Nasímí.
68. Shahábu'd-dín Farrukh Shah Kabulí.
69. Shekh Muhammad.
70. Shekh Yúsuf.
71. Shekh Ahmad.
72. Shekh Shuaib.
73. Shekh Salmán.
74. Shekh Jamálu'd-dín.
75. Shekh Faridu'd-dín Masaúd or Shakar Ganj.
76. Shekh Nasru'lláh.
77. Shekh Baiyazíd.
78. Sháh Kamálu'd-dín Maulví.
79. Shekh Bábáu'd-dín.
80. Shekh Mughís.
81. Shekh Khojú.
82. Shekh Ahmad.
83. Shekh Daulat, or Shekh Kalai.
84. Shekh Núru'd-dín.
85. Shekh Niamatu'lláh.
86. Shekh Faizu'lláh.
87. Shekh Abd'ul Kádir, or Shekh Kalai the 2nd.
88. Shekh Abd'ul Ghaní.
89. Shekh Muhammad Akram.
90. Shekh Lutfu'lláh.

CONTENTS.

CHAPTER XII.

CHAPTER XIII.

CHAPTER XIV.

AUTOBIOGRAPHY

OF

LUTFULLAH.

CHAPTER I.

My birth and parentage—Death of my father—My mother finds an asylum with my uncle—Famine and the persecution of my cousins—My mischievous habits—I catch a Mullá napping and dose my schoolmaster—The tank of Dháránagar where my cousins attempt to drown me—Rájáram, the Good Samaritan—A new cure for dysentery—End of my childhood.

I MADE my first appearance in this world of wonders in the ancient city of Dháránagar, in Málwah, on Thursday, the 7th of Rajab, 1217 A.H., corresponding with the 4th of November, 1802 A.D.

My father was a Mohamedan of the sacred order, a descendant of Shah Kamáluddín, who was a great saint of his time in the province of Málwah, being the spiritual guide as well as modern preceptor of Sultán Mahmúd Khiljí, during a period of thirty-six years, from 1434 to 1470 A.D.* On the death of

* *Vide* Briggs' "Mohamedan Power in India," vol. iv. p. 195.

his venerated friend and adviser, this good Sultán built a magnificent mausoleum at the western gate of the city, and endowed therein a shrine to the memory of the holy man; opposite to it he caused to be raised another edifice, surmounted by a superb dome, which was intended as a resting-place for his own mortal remains, and there they still repose. Near the shrine was an ancient Hindú temple of considerable size, which, by order of the Sultán, was transformed into a beautiful mosque. To these sacred places he bequeathed in perpetuity about three hundred acres of land immediately surrounding them, the annual produce of which was directed to be employed in the occasional repairs of the edifices, and in the maintenance of the posterity of the saint. In addition to the above, he granted an allowance of one rupee per diem from the revenue derived from certain grass lands, to be applied to the same purposes. These rights were enjoyed by my ancestors until A.D. 1706, when, after the reign of Aurangzeb, the Maráthas having possessed themselves of the province, confiscated both the land and the allowance, leaving, however, from the former, about two acres, for the support of my great-grandfather. Thus was a family which, for a period of nearly three centuries had enjoyed affluence, reduced to a state verging on destitution. To use an Eastern metaphor, the light of the day was withdrawn, the shadows of night had gathered around them.

My father, at a very early period of his life, when not more than seven years of age, travelled in the country, in company with a relative of his, in search of knowledge. In the course of a few years he mastered his profession, that of a mullá (priest); and, on attaining the age of fifteen, was desired by his companion to return home. But the beauty and delightful climate of the Upper Provinces, and the pain of parting from the many kind friends who had rendered his stay there so agreeable, delayed his return for ten years more; although, when he was about twenty-six years of age, being urgently summoned by his father, he quitted Delhi for home, and nothing particular appears to have marked his course until his arrival at Agra. There, being a man of great personal attractions, with a highly cultivated mind, winning manners, and in the very prime and vigour of his life, he was offered in marriage the daughter of the person with whom he lodged. He accepted the offer, forgetting the urgent necessity of his return home, and this circumstance detained him there for four years more. It was while he lived at Agra that he received the intelligence of his father's death, a circumstance which hastened his return home, where it was his lot to remain for the future.

At the age of forty-nine, he had the misfortune to lose his good wife, by whom he had issue only two daughters. Those who are acquainted with the sentiments of eastern nations, know the intense anxiety which every man, whether Mohamedan or Hindú, feels to have a son to bear his name, and transmit it (as the English poet says) "to ages yet unborn." Such persons will be able to enter into the state of my father's feelings on finding himself, at an advanced period of life, a widower, and with the dreary prospect of descending into the grave the last male scion of his race. Had he consulted only his own inclinations, he would have been content to suffer this fate, miserable as it was, rather than endeavour to forget in the society of a second wife the severe loss which he had sustained in the death of the former partner of his bosom. But, at the earnest solicitation of his friends, he was induced, at the end of a year of widowhood, to wed a girl of seventeen, exquisite in beauty, elegant in manners, perfect in virtue and goodness, and of a family fully equal to his own, both as regarded sacred and social advantages. Reader, she was my mother; and you will, therefore, I am sure, forgive me if I display more than ordinary warmth in paying this tribute to her departed worth.

It was not till three years after he had contracted this alliance, that the tree of my father's hope became fruitful, and that I, the humble author of these memoirs, made my appearance on the stage of existence, to gladden the hearts of my fond parents and of all those who felt an interest in their happiness.

There were some, however, nearly connected with me by blood, cousins on the father's side, to whom my birth brought anything but joy, seeing that, if I survived, one half of the profits arising from the remains of Sultán Mahmud's grants must necessarily fall to my share. These profits were now miserably small; some 200 rupees, or about 20*l.* per annum. But, insignificant as they were, the prospect of losing any portion of them served to kindle and to keep alive the fire of envy and hatred in the bosoms of my unnatural relatives, abundant proofs of which I shall have occasion shortly to adduce. Leaving them for a moment, however, let me return to the more pleasing task of recording the delight of my dear parents when they beheld the blessing which it had pleased the Almighty to confer upon them. To mark their grateful sense of his kindness, and, at the same time, to commemorate the event in a manner which they considered the most appropriate, they bestowed on me the name of Lutfullah, which, being interpreted, means "the favour of God." Two years after I was born, my father had a second son, but he survived only a few months, and by the time I had attained my fourth year, my dear father also was taken from us, leaving a youthful widow, with a helpless orphan, to seek support wherever they could.

Our condition now was truly deplorable. My poor mother, wholly inexperienced in the ways of the world, and borne down by the suddenness and weight of the misfortune which had befallen us, knew not where to turn for aid or counsel. My cousins, co-sharers in the small estate before-mentioned, so far from rendering her any assistance, were unceasing in their endeavours to compass our destruction; and, to complete the measure of our misery, the country was afflicted with a famine, the severity of which has probably never been exceeded. This last calamity lives in my recollection as freshly as if it were only an occurrence of yesterday. Numbers of people died daily of starvation; famished corpses were dragged out of the city by tens or twenties, and buried in huge pits dug for the purpose, or thrown promiscuously into dry wells; but there was one case in particular, connected with this season of horror, which, as displaying the dreadful lengths to which human nature may be driven by the force of hunger, I must not omit to record. I remember being taken by my uncle to see a woman who was subjected to "public disgrace" by being paraded through the streets of the city, seated astride on a donkey. Her face, one side of which was painted white and the other black, was turned towards the animal's tail, and I, not knowing the reason of this strange exhibition, was at first highly amused by the sight. My mirth, however, was soon dispelled, by being informed that the wretched creature before me, who was an inhabitant of a

Bheel village in the district, and who was afterwards to be transported for life, had been convicted of having killed the young child of a neighbour, and, to allay the pangs of hunger, had boiled and eaten it.

But to return to my own affairs. At the expiration of the "Chihlum," or forty days of mourning, prescribed by the customs of the Moslems in India, when the memory of the deceased is supposed no longer to engross the attention of sorrowing survivors to the exclusion of the ordinary concerns of life, my mother thought it advisable to remove from my late father's house, where we were surrounded by a host of miscalled friends, intent only on accomplishing our ruin. We accordingly took up our residence with her mother and brother, by both of whom we were received and treated with the utmost tenderness. These dear relatives had no pecuniary interest, like my cousins on the father's side, to neutralize those kindly feelings which the ties of nature, when left to themselves, are calculated to inspire; and though the addition of two members of their household necessarily pressed hard on their limited means, the sincerity of their sorrow for our bereavement was attested by the liveliest sympathy. Towards myself, the conduct of my good uncle differed in no respect from that which marked his intercourse with his own children; or, if it did, it was perhaps in being more kind and tender, as if urged thereto by a sense of my utterly helpless condition; and the treatment which I experienced at the hands of my grandmother was equally characterised by real benevolence.

Under this hospitable roof we passed our time in tranquillity; but, in those days, lawless turbulence found a much larger field for display than it did a few years afterwards, when the power of the British Government was exerted for its suppression. Two or three times a year accounts would reach us of the approach of large bodies of Pindarees, who had been committing havoc in the surrounding districts; or of an intended attack by some neighbouring potentate, for the purpose of levying contributions on the city. Then the hearts of the inhabitants were filled with terror and dismay; and forthwith jewels, money, and articles of value were buried in the earth, or otherwise secreted. When the attack did take place, the situation of the inhabitants was truly pitiable. They were then literally "between two fires," from both of which they suffered nearly equal injury, the cannon balls from the citadel, instead of reaching the enemy for whose special destruction they were intended, generally falling short of their mark, and causing fearful loss of life and property within the walls of the city. This, of itself, was dreadful enough, even when the enemy failed in their object; when victory declared on their side, such of the citizens as had survived the onslaught became the victims of the most refined cruelty, in order to discover the places where their treasure was concealed. Numerous modes of torture were had recourse to for this purpose, amongst which the three following generally proved the most effectual. First, the victim was pinioned and exposed bare-headed to the burning rays of the sun, while his ears were pounded or pinched between the lock of a gun; secondly, after being pinioned, as above, he was made to stand in the sun, with a stone of enormous weight on his head, first inserting a gravel stone of the size and shape of a small grape, which gradually forced its way through the skull to the brain; thirdly, a horse's grain-bag, half filled with ashes and red pepper in powder, was tied over the sufferer's face, so as to include his mouth and nose, the consequence of which was, at first, a most violent fit of sneezing, and, if protracted to a quarter of an hour, a horrible death by suffocation. But though these, and some other modes of extracting confessions, equal in cruelty to anything which I read, many years afterwards, of the Inquisition in Catholic countries, were in general attended with success, there were not wanting instances in which a love of gold prevailed over a love of life; and I have heard of many persons who submitted in resolute and sullen silence to the most agonizing tortures, till death released them from their sufferings, and restored them to that mother-earth, wherein their loved treasure lay interred.

Our houses, however, having contained sacred families, were looked upon with reverence by all the troops of the banditti. Moreover, they always made some presents to my uncle and self when they left the city, which they considered a sanctification of their booty. People of our neighbourhood, either Moslems or Hindús, whoever had the opportunity of hiding themselves and property in our houses and thus escaping diabolical outrages, made us some presents: so we were not badly off even in such times of difficulty; but the sufferings of our fellow-creatures rendered our lives bitterly miserable.

My good uncle took our part against our other usurping relatives, and demanded one half of the produce of the landed property, and of the daily offerings, etc., to the shrine. Accordingly, sometimes they paid a few rupees: but always said they would give us nothing unless I should either personally attend every day at the shrine, as they did, to superintend the offerings, etc., or employ another person to act for me. My uncle afforded us all the pecuniary aid in his power; but then he had a large family of his own to maintain, and my mother did not like to burden her kind brother with our wants. She had jewels of her dowry, about four hundred rupees' worth, which she was now obliged to sell, one by one; and, in the course of one year, all the jewels vanished—but, luckily for us, so did the dearth.

After a few years, my pronunciation became as correct as possible. I spoke with accuracy, and tried to cheat my mother and relatives by patching up stories, which often excited their mirth. I was, besides, a mischievous young creature, and devised various plans of playing tricks, to the great annoyance of my protectors.

I caught frogs, and slyly put them into the ladies' work-baskets, which contained their needles, thread and cotton, etc. I watched the time when they finished their domestic matters, and, after breakfast, sat at their peaceful occupation: I then fixed my eyes on the basket, and just as the poor lady uncovered the lid, out sprang the imprisoned animal upon her. This caused her to scream, and sometimes faint, to the laughter of the lookers on.

At the age of five I grew more troublesome, and now it was determined that I should be sent to school. A day of good luck was fixed, and the book being placed under my arm, I was led to the place of instruction. I proceeded, of course, unwillingly, like a lamb to the slaughter-house.

I was introduced by my uncle to the master, who took me in charge, and was very glad to find, in a short time, that I learned my lessons quicker than my schoolfellows, and knew my Kur'án as well as any mullá. In the course of six months I learnt all the prayers of Islám, and was received everywhere with approbation. Whenever I happened to recite any part of the holy book in an assembly of great people, I was loaded with applause and presents.

During this period I was only punished once, but very severely, for a grievous offence against a holy man named Shaikh Nasrullah.

This good old man was a priest of the village of Hásilpur, about fifty miles distant from us, and was an intimate friend of my uncle, to whom he occasionally paid his visits, and these not of short duration of a day or so, but he stayed with him for weeks, and sometimes for months. Our means were too scanty to endure the burden of maintaining this old priest, who seemed to take no notice of our circumstances; but, as my uncle was unparalleled in liberality, generosity, and humanity, he pawned his clothes, and ran in debt, for the entertainment of his guest.

It happened that this old Shaikh Nasrullah had come as usual on a visit. He was an old man of great wit, and almost every other word of his conversation was a proverb. I remember his form and features very well: he was a tall man, of good and strong make, with a depressed forehead; he squinted much, and invariably shook his head up and down, as if he consented to everything proposed to him. He had no teeth in his mouth, but his long flowing white beard made up for all his deformity. He was so fond of talking, that he chatted on, whether sense or nonsense, whether one listened to it or not. Although speaking ill of our neighbours is a crime unpardonable,—particularly of those who are gone by, "de mortuis nil nisi bonum,"—yet I cannot help recollecting Lord Bacon's remark here—"Deformed persons are commonly even with Nature; for as Nature has done ill by them, so they do ill by Nature." In short, it was not easy for my poor uncle to get rid of him after the evening meal; he frequently fell asleep during the interminable conversation of his old guest, and did not wake to perform his nightly prayers, until roused up from his sleep. The old man—may God forgive him! (or rather forgive me for the crime I committed upon his sacred person)—somehow or other did not like me. He always checked me for something or other, and scolded me severely if I made a slight mistake, even in pronouncing a word. These unjust reprimands made me resolve to take my revenge upon him.

On Friday, our Sabbath, being free from my task, as is usual in all Mohamedan schools, I went out to the market with a few pieces of money, which I had by me, saved from my presents, and purchased a little gunpowder. The same day, after the mid-day prayer, the old man returned home, and went to sleep in an airy part of the verandah, his stomach overloaded with food, his mouth wide open, and his eyes half-shut, presenting a truly laughable picture, and his thick long white beard lay on his breast like a bundle of hay. I entered quietly, went to his side, and spread the combustible on his beard. I then went out, and, tying a match to a long rod, lighted it; I gave a touch from a distance and off it went, setting the beard on a sudden blaze. The old man started from his sleep and began rubbing his face, repeating his creed as a sign of distress, Láillah illillah,—"There is no God but one God." Presently he got up, mad with rage, and I slipped in at the door of the Zanánah unobserved by him, and looked on at the fun through the key-hole with the eye of admiration and satisfaction. The old fellow ran here and there with his staff, ready to smite even the devil himself, if he met him. His face and hands were flayed, and, what with his natural ugliness and his singed beard, he was certainly a hideous object. His shouts soon brought my uncle out of his reading place, and seeing his friend with face and hands flayed, and deprived of his beard, he cried out, "What ails you, Shaikh Nasrullah?" "Ails me? the devil himself!" replied the old man: "I am gone for ever: God has punished me for my sins; my honour is gone with my beard. Oh, my beard! my beard!" Examining well his face, and hearing such exclamations, my uncle could not help smiling, for which the old man reproved him very harshly, saying, "Have you no shame to laugh at the calamity of your brother?" My uncle begged his pardon, and inquiring how it happened, he replied, "That dog! that brute! that infidel! that little Shaitán! that learned nephew of yours, whom you call a promising young lad, has, I am sure, done this: that rod of his lying there is a proof substantial enough to have him beheaded." Hearing this I trembled, went quietly to my bed, and pretended to sleep soundly. In the meantime, my good uncle poured two or three phials of ink on his face and hands (it being the common remedy used in our country for burns), and consoled him by saying all of us were helpless against the decrees of fate, to which all must submit, and that what has been ordained by the omnipotent hand of Deity for any individual being must come to pass: we must bear it with patience, according to the saying, "Beneficiis maleficia pensare." He promised the old Shaikh that my foolish act should not go unrewarded, and that the punishment should be a severe one; which last sentence gave the old fellow more consolation than all the doctrine above preached. My uncle then came in, determined to fulfil his promise; but, being a man of very tender heart, he could not punish me, so he told my mother and grandmother what had taken place, upon which both the ladies, without asking a question, and without a judge and jury, began to use their canes on my back unrelentingly. I cried for mercy, and declared my innocence, telling them that I never burnt the beard, which last sentence, foolishly uttered, proved me guilty beyond all doubt. Fortunately, my uncle being present, I received but very few blows, and was released from the hands of my fair torturers.

My mother now swore, by the holy Kur'án that she would burn my hands with a red-hot pair of tongs, if ever I was found guilty of a similar misdemeanour again. I was very glad that I got off so easily, unaware of another impending thrashing that I had to undergo next day.

Early in the next morning I proceeded to school, with my books and breakfast. My master looked very stiff and awkward, and did not return my salutation. A young friend of mine, who sat next to me, whispered that the old Shaikh had reported my offence to the master, and that I must soon expect the consequence. The boys were then examined in their lessons of the day before, but I was required to repeat by heart all that I had learnt for the last three days, which I did with perfect fluency, and without a single mistake. We were ordered to resume our seats, and the master then asked me, "Did you burn the old Shaikh's beard yesterday?"—"No, sir," replied I, "but I set fire to it by mistake, and have suffered for my error."—"Mistake! you little brute!" rejoined he, "it was a heinous crime, in return for which, if you do not get something from me, as an additional reward, you will certainly try my beard next." I was then immediately tied to the post, and flogged most unmercifully till my back was flayed. This unexpected punishment caused me to determine on another revenge, which I took on my master, and I fortunately managed it so well as to escape detection. Moreover, his superstition led him to view the accident in the light of a punishment inflicted on him by the invisible hand, for maltreating the person of a sacred orphan, and he was confirmed in this belief by several dreams. In the course of two or three days, I took another opportunity of going to the market-place, and purchased a little Jemalgota (*croton tiglium*), the severe purgative powers of which nut I knew beforehand, my uncle having administered it to several persons as medicine. I powdered one of the nuts, and preserved it folded up in a piece of paper in my turban. My custom was to go to school before the other boys arrived. The next morning when the coffee was brought in small cups for my master and his three friends, each cup was placed before their respective seats on the floor, they being outside warmly engaged in arguing on a religious point. The attendant having placed the cups went out to inform them; and I immediately taking out the powder from my turban, put it in my master's cup, and mixed it with my finger. In the meantime, in comes a youngster, and, seeing me near the cup, cries out, "Ha! ha! stealth!" Mentally cursing him, I told him he was blind and had lost his sight, for accusing me, when I was driving away the flies with my kerchief. I then asked him to come in my place and act my part, as my turn was over. He readily accepted the situation, and I, resuming my seat, began to read my book with profound attention. My master and his friends now came in, still engaged in conversation, and drank their cups and smoked hookas with their usual zest. After about an hour the friends left and my master began to feel uneasy. I saw quite clearly that my miraculous dose was taking effect on him; his brown complexion became pale, his fiery eyes appeared dull and sunk; and strange qualms coming on, he told the boys to take a holiday as he felt very unwell, and that it was owing to his own imprudence, for in the entertainment of last night he had eaten beyond the bounds of moderation; and "one of such feasts," observed he, "will sooner or later put an end to my life."

We gladly received this order, and commenced folding up our books, etc. In the meantime, the master's suffering became greater; he threw his rosary on one side and his turban on another, and began to roll on the floor, embracing his large pillow and cursing the entertainment and its author. When we prepared to leave the house and saluted the master, he was seized with severe vomiting and other painful symptoms; so leaving the poor old man in this state, we rushed out, each of us taking his own way.

For my part, I bent my steps towards home, with the tear of sorrow in one eye and the light of satisfaction in the other. To say the truth, although my revenge was appeased, yet I could not help thinking my horrid vengeance had exceeded the punishment I had received; that one quarter of the cursed quantity I gave him was quite sufficient for the poor old fellow, and that if anything worse happened to him,

I should have to carry his blood on my head at the day of judgment (according to the preaching I often heard from my uncle and others). With these confusing thoughts I reached home. My mother asked me the reason of my unseasonable return, and I explained to her the cause, viz., the master's severe illness, not forgetting, however, to mention the unlucky feast of the night before, in which he had overloaded his stomach according to his custom on such occasions. Upon this, my mother ordered me to sit at her wheel and read to her what I had learnt during the last week.

This being the mango season, my uncle had gone out to his trees in the morning, and did not return till the afternoon. On being informed of the master's indisposition, he observed that he had predicted it last night, when he saw the old gentleman at the feast. He immediately ran to his house, and finding him exhausted and nearly lifeless, gave him some cordial medicines, and leaving advice with the attendant, returned home. The master recovered the next morning, but was unfit for his duty for several days, during which period I studied with my mother and uncle.

On the master's recovery, the school became repopulated, and I resumed my visits as usual. The master's profound superstition led him to be more respectful towards me than necessary, and he told every one that his indisposition was owing to the displeasure of the saints—my ancestors—from whom he had received many warnings in his dreams. He begged my pardon for his past ill-treatment of me; so, at the age of seven, I was a little priest; everybody kissed my hand, and I was respected by all.

It was no more requisite now to instruct me in the Holy Book, as I knew it almost all by heart. I knew all the forms of prayer, and was sometimes put in the pulpit to repeat sermons on Fridays, and I remember having acted my part well.

I was soon after removed from the Alkoranic school, and intrusted to a Persian teacher. My studies now became heavier, as I had two lessons to learn, both in reading and writing, with the Persian master during the day; and, at night, my uncle was pleased to load my little head with the elements of the Arabic grammar, which last I hated, not knowing the importance of what I was learning. On the other hand, I liked Persian, having had the advantage of knowing it colloquially from my infancy, the language being generally spoken by all the members of our family, on occasions of secresy and religious discussions, etc. Besides, my new master was a very gentlemanly man, of most amiable character. He explained fully everything I asked, and proved logically all he said. He seldom grew angry, and, if ever he did, his words of anger were sweeter than the applause of my first master. His instruction was a mere matter of favour, as he was an officer of his

Highness the Gaikwár, residing there on duty, and kept no school.

At the age of eight I went through the celebrated works of the immortal Sâdi. I could write a passable hand in Persian, and thoroughly knew the elements of the Arabic grammar. During this year I met with a dangerous accident, but was lucky enough to escape from the dreadful claws of the angel of death. It happened, one Friday, that I went to visit the shrine, being requested by my uncle to attend occasionally, in order that my rightful claim to the income might remain undisputed. I was received with their usually hypocritical kindness by my two cousins, and sat for a little while talking with them. They observed I was too wise for my years, but that I passed my life in a sort of prison under teachers, and that, when I reached their age, *i. e.*, seventeen or eighteen, I should have got no knowledge of the world. To this I made no reply, but I could not help admiring their condition, compared with my own, and thought their life must be very happy, as they had no restriction of school, but enjoyed freedom, and always talked, laughed, and played, while I was confined in a dungeon, with bundles of nasty papers. At the same time, I consoled myself with this conclusion (commonly resorted to by all Muslims): it was written, in the book of their fate, to have a good and kind mother, and, in that of mine, to have a strict one; it was not, therefore, proper to strive against fate, and thus I comforted myself. In the meantime, several boys came in, and all of us joined in playing and running about for an hour. About 10 o'clock A.M. we got tired, and my cousins proposed going to a tank in the neighbourhood to bathe, so all of us proceeded thither.

This was a small but beautiful tank, built at the junction of several streams descending from hills. The deep column of water was about fifteen yards square; three sides of the tank were almost level with the ground, with steps of red stone, but the fourth side was built up perpendicularly, and here the water was deepest. The spot was lovely, covered with verdant trees both of fruits and flowers, and adorned with lofty Hindú temples at a few yards' distance from the pool. On our arrival here, my cousins and others jumped down in the water from the enormous height of the fourth side, and swam from one side to another, seeming to enjoy themselves vastly. I longed greatly to play with them; perceiving this, from my looks, they asked me to join them. I pleaded my inability in swimming, but they offered to teach me by supporting me on their hands. I willingly accepted the offer, and, stripping myself, entered the water. My cousins swam across once or twice with me, and then left me to my fate in the middle. I went down and floated up once or twice, and at last sunk never to rise again, if such had been the will of the Almighty. My cousins and all the boys (I was told afterwards) ran away, the former under the pretence of fetching some one to take me out of the water, most likely thinking that by the time they returned I should be no more. I know not how long after I was taken out. When I came to my senses, I found myself hung to a tree with my legs upward and head down, the water flowing from my mouth, nose, and eyes, mixed with foam. Opening my eyes, I saw a Brahman standing by my side and whirling me about. As the rope by which I was suspended to the bough slacked and tightened I attempted to speak, but had no power of doing so. I made signs with my hand, begging the Brahman to release me from the torture I was undergoing, and the good man did so; after which, he seated me on his right arm, and, standing up, he turned round like a top until he was tired; he then fell down with me exhausted. In a little while, regaining strength, I sat up, but was seized with severe vomiting which spoiled his clothes. The water issued from my mouth for about an hour; in the meantime, the good Brahman washed, bathed, and purified himself in the tank, and returning to me, stood at a little distance muttering his prayers in Sanskrit, all the time eyeing me with compassion. He asked me how I did? To this kind question my reply was, that I was very nearly recovered. I then saluted him respectfully, and begged to know his name. He told me his name was Rájárám, and that he was the principal warden of the temple opposite to me; that he was watching me from within the temple all the while, and when the boys deserted, leaving me to perish in the water, he was inspired by his god, Mahádeva, to draw me out, in obedience to which sacred command he had saved my life. He then asked me to make a prostration to the deity to which I owed my life. Situated as I was I could not well disobey my patron, so I made a profound bow apparently to the stone, touching the ground with my head, but, at the same time, bending my little mind to the Almighty, the only God, the Maker of the stone as well as of all creatures. As a young Muslim priest, the first thing that had been inculcated in me was to ridicule the folly of the Hindús, in worshipping stones framed and made by themselves, and other beings besides the Supreme One.

This accident, however, raised doubts in my young mind as I thought of Polytheism prevailing everywhere, and I argued with myself,—"If the Hindú shrines are stones, ours contain but dust and bones. To believe in one or the other, or believe or disbelieve in both, is a most puzzling question." On the other hand, when I afterwards came to think upon Christianity, Christians, too, seemed to have fallen into various erroneous opinions respecting the Prophet Jesus Christ (blessed be his name!). Some make him their God, others the Son of

God, and others one of the three persons of their Trinity.

Although in my after life I was a good Muslim, yet I could not shake off such confused notions entirely, until I was about thirty years of age, when my close study of some excellent works set my brain right, and then I knew what I was and how to perform my devotions to my Creator. I beg, however, to observe, that I am still ignorant of my first origin, and of what I am to be on my being transferred to the undiscovered country, "from whose bourne no traveller returns." Talking upon these subjects, even with strictness, with some of my learned friends, renders me an infidel in their estimation, to whom my general reply is the ode of the immortal Hafiz (may his earth be cool!), very nearly corresponding with the following lines of Lord Byron:—

> "Some kinder casuists are pleased to say,
> In nameless print, that I have no devotion;
> But set those persons down with me to pray,
> And you shall see who has the properest notion
> Of getting into heaven the shortest way.
> My altars are the mountains and the ocean,
> Earth, air, stars,—all that springs from the great Whole
> Who hath produced and will receive the soul."

To return to my own predicament: I had hardly finished my affected prostration to the well-formed medium of worship, when the Brahman pointed out to me the boys coming with ropes and hooks, for the purpose of taking me out of the tank. My cousins ran and embraced me, and washed my body from the dust and mud, etc., and assisted me in my dressing, and shed false tears; telling me, at the same time, that they were very sorry that I had slipped from their hands, adding, that if they could not have drawn me out of the water with the materials they had brought, they had determined upon drowning themselves for my sake. The Brahman listened to this plausible story of theirs very quietly, and looked on at their washing and dressing me; which having done, they asked me to go along with them. I got up, made my salâm to the Brahman and was about to depart, when he in an angry tone addressed himself to them. "The boy shall not leave the spot without my going with him, and you shall not take him to throw him into another well."

My cousins pretended to discuss the point, alleging that I was their brother, but he threatened to call to the neighbouring gardeners for help, and to send them along with me to the Minister of the Raja, and report their infamous conduct to him in full. Hearing this, they were frightened out of their wits, and prostrated themselves at his feet, begging his forgiveness for the sake of the deity in the temple. They made him some present in money, and in return took his solemn promise not to allow the story to transpire.

I liked this arrangement, dreading that the betraying the secret would bring on me a severe punishment. He entered into the agreement with them in every respect, except as to delivering me over to them, which he declared he would never do for anything in the world.

After mutual promises my cousins left the place, and Rájárám led me behind the temple, where he spread a few bundles of grass under the thick shade of a tree, and desired me to go to sleep.

I recollect that my sleep at that time was as sound as that of eternity, and, to this day, I have never had a slumber so refreshing. When roused by the Brahman, I got up; it was dark night, and I found my clothes and the grassy bed all wet with the moisture which issued from me during my rest. I felt my head heavy, my limbs benumbed, and my mental power stupified. The Brahman made me wash my hands and face, and then asked me where I resided. I mentioned to him the name of the quarter and that of my uncle,—the mere mention of whom caused me, on a sudden, to burst into a violent flood of tears. The Brahman then held me by the hand, and led me to the direction I pointed out. He asked me where my father was? "He died long ago," replied I. As we proceeded, he put several questions, regarding my station in life, means of livelihood, and relatives, etc. I told him everything I possibly could, and the poor man seemed greatly moved with compassion at my distressful condition. He made me a present of two rupees, and advised me never to go to bathe, or trust my cousins again.

At the gate of my house he left me and departed. My mother, uncle, and others received me with delight after their long anxiety. My uncle was ready to start in search of me, when I arrived. I was asked the reason of my long absence, and, in reply, I pleaded indisposition; and, after taking my meal, I was put in bed.

Five or six days after, my uncle was informed of the accident by some of his boys. He explained it to my mother, and this time all the members of the family took pity on me, instead of visiting me, as usual, with reproof. Rájárám was sent for, and sincerely thanked by all. My good mother, especially, with tearful eyes appeared before him, against all the laws of morality of Mohamedan ladies; she thanked him most sincerely for having saved her only son's life, and offered him a pair of silver bracelets and ten rupees in ready cash as a humble reward, declaring that was all she then possessed in the world, and that if she had ten lacs of rupees she would have given all to him with pleasure, still considering his service had far exceeded in comparison the amount. The poor, but honest, Brahman said he took the offer to be the very act, and that he would not deprive the poor lady of a small sum on any account; however, he took one rupee out of it to please her.

After this, I was not allowed to go anywhere, except to my school. Misfortunes do not come singly: about two months subsequent to my being thus saved from drowning, I was seized with dysentery, which tenacious and trying malady fed on my flesh for seven long months. I was reduced to a mere skeleton. All sorts of medicines were tried on me, most abominable in taste and appearance, but without any effect. I was allowed nothing but rice and dál, which food to my palate was worse than medicine. In short, I was given up by all. The poor Brahman often called on me; he comforted me in my presence, but, on turning his back, he shed tears at my orphanage, poverty, and mortal disorder.

As the time went on, the month of Moharram—or the anniversary of the death of our most sacred king of martyrs, Imâm Husain, the son of Ali, by the daughter of our blessed prophet—arriving, a sort of fair was held in the city for about ten days. I had little or no strength to walk without another person's aid, and asked my uncle to help me out as far as the gate of our house, where he seated me on a small bench and returned. Looking on the thoroughfare of the people, and their playing with warlike weapons, etc., I could not help envying their healthful condition, and had the mortification of reflecting that my time was over, and that it was no use thinking of the world, where I had to stay for only a few days, or, very likely, a few hours. I was seized with despondency and despair,—ignorant of this, that I had still many vicissitudes to encounter, and many years more to breathe upon this terrestrial globe of wonder; and little thinking of the unlimited power of the omnipotent divine Providence, which shows its miraculous effects where all human powers fail.

During my stay at the gate, my attention was drawn to the cook-shop, adorned with several kinds of cakes and some pastry of mince-meat, etc. I asked my uncle to give me some money that I might purchase some of it, as I felt my desire irresistibly strong to have it; but the reply was a usual one,—"You shall not have any of it; for meat is indigestible, and poison for those who have dysentery; you are sure to die in case of tasting even a particle of it." For my part, I did not like this advice, but was obliged to submit to it. The next day I stole a few pieces from my mother's work-box, and prepared in the evening to buy some of the pastry. My desire was so great that I would have it, and cared not if it cost me my life. The evening came, and I took my staff, and walked out to the gate supported by it. Taking my seat, I called to the cook, and, giving him the pieces of money, I obtained the object of my ardent desire. But now, it was another difficulty, almost unsolvable, where to eat it undiscovered by anybody? My experience, however, soon suggested a secret place, where I went and devoured the large quantity—I think about one pound in weight—and then going to my bed, I slept; concluding, from the advice of my good preceptors, that the venom would have its full effect on me during my sleep, and that I should never rise to suffer any more distress from dysentery or other misfortunes. The next morning, to my own great surprise and that of all the family, I found myself quite recovered. The venom, in my opinion and that of my friends, acted as an antidote. I began to gain strength every day, and in about two months I was altogether as healthy as possible, excepting that my stomach still remained exorbitantly protuberant, but without any sensible pain. To remove this unnatural deformity some of my advisers desired me to smoke the hooka; this I readily acceded to, and the expected result gradually followed: I quite recovered, though I thus became addicted to a bad habit of smoking, and now I conclude this chapter with the expiration of the eighth year of my age.

CHAPTER II.

Political state of affairs about the year 1810—Rumours respecting the new race of foreigners called the Feringees—Bheel robbers—Mode of executing them—Visit to Baroda—First rencontre with Feringees—Rite of Circumcision—Reflections —Visit to Ujjain—My mother's second marriage—Plunder of my step-father's house by Sindiah's soldiers—An Eastern story.

At this time, rumours of war were heard in all directions. The kingdom of Delhi received a mortal blow at the death of Aurangzeb, A.D. 1706; but the dynasty was, in fact, extinguished by by Sháh Alam, who, after a life of sensual enjoyment, was blinded by Ghulám Kádir Khán, one of his nobles, in 1788, expired in 1806, and was succeeded by his son, Akbar the II., who was placed on the throne by the Maráthas. Observing the kingdom in such a state, the governors of different provinces assumed independent power.

Amid these changes, the most interesting news to us was the following:—About sixty years previously, during the reign of Mohamed Sháh, some foreign adventurers, wonderful in their character and manners, appeared in the country, where they began to establish themselves, taking the advantage of the emperor's weakness, and of the universal discord amongst the nobles and governors of the provinces. Strange things were said regarding this wonderful people, who, it was affirmed, had no skin, but a thin membrane covering their body, which made them appear abominably white. They were perfect in magical art, which made them successful in all their undertakings. They did not believe in our blessed Prophet, and they called themselves Christians; but would not act upon the laws of the sacred Anjil, which holy book they had changed in several places to serve their worldly purposes. Most of them still worshipped images, and they ate everything, and particularly things forbidden by the holy Moses, and this in spite of the order of the sacred Anjil (St. Matthew, v. 18 and 19); nay, they did not spare human flesh when driven to extremity. They had made three Gods for themselves instead of one—the only Omnipotent Supreme Being—contrary to their first commandment; and, most absurd of all, they attributed to the Almighty God the having wife and children; and by the same token they called their Prophet and themselves Son and children of God. Such reports were the topic of almost all conversations, and many other things were said against them, and only one in their favour — that they were not unjust; but in the administration of justice, they never deviated from the sacred book of the ancient law of Solomon, the Son of David, etc.

These and similar accounts not only amused us, but sometimes excited us to a fit of fanaticism. Such were the tales that spread abroad in India at that time. My uncle and myself wanted particularly to see some of these extraordinary people, and to question them on their erroneous religion. But as they had not visited our city yet, and we had never seen a European face, our zeal remained untried. The morning of good luck, however, now began to dawn upon the people of our district, for they in those days were not molested by the outlaws, the Pindarees being engaged with their enemies. But the hill Bheels still infested the roads, and occasionally paid their nocturnal visits to the town, to rob at the risk of their life. They were sometimes apprehended, and then rarely escaped, and that only by bribing the ministers and giving large presents to the Rájá himself; and if not, they used to be punished and executed in most cruel fashion; such as by being tied to the foot of an elephant to be dragged through the town, or being split by one of those huge animals. In the latter case, the elephant, directed by the maháwat, puts one of the legs of the poor victim under his foot, and, seizing the other with his trunk, splits him in a second by a pull, when the leg pulled comes off with the covering of the stomach and very nearly half the skin of the body. The next mode is breaking the head: this horrid punishment is inflicted by putting the man horizontally on one side with his head on a flat stone; a ball of stone is then put on his upper temple, and the executioner, asking permission of the officer three times, inflicts a fatal blow with a large wooden hammer on the small ball, which smashes the head at once, and the brain is dashed out. Other modes are, throwing down from the high wall of a castle; beheading with the sword; and, lastly, blowing from the mouth of a cannon. I have often been an eye-witness to these horrid executions, and beg my reader to avoid them to the best of his power.

Returning to the subject of my own life: our circumstances now became miserably straitened; we sold all we had, and sometimes starved for a day or so, after which we obtained but sorry food through our own hard labour. All the females either worked with the needle or the spinning-wheel from morning till midnight; and my uncle wrote copies of different books, and I assisted him in reading and comparing them all day long. But the price of our labour was insufficient for our livelihood. My uncle at last, tired of the sufferings consequent upon poverty, resolved to go to Baroda, where resided several wealthy disciples of his own and of my late father; and our visit to them would, we fully trusted, relieve us from the misery of want, at all events for some time.

Our journey being determined upon, my uncle, mother, and myself made the required preparations to start with the first caravan of opium carts, took leave of all the members of the family, and left the town. We were received by the cartmen of the caravan with great respect; all of whom, being Moslems of the Oilmen caste, regularly worshipped us. They prayed five times a day with us, and made comfortable places for us in the carts. They gave us better food than what they ate, and sheltered us from the sun and the dew. This was my first travel, and the curiosities of nature filled my little mind with uncommon amusement; the sweetly-fragrant breeze of the jungles, in the morning after prayer, refreshed my brain; the views of lofty mountains of various shapes, of rivers and clear streams, and the beauty of the trees clad in green and covered with flowers of different hues, afforded an admirably new landscape to the sight; and the most sweet and melodious voices of the birds enchanted my ears. At such times my uncle generally cited the beautiful verses of the immortal S'adí of Shíráz,—"Each of the green trees, in the eyes of the wise, is a book that will teach you the knowledge of the infinite power of the Author," etc., in the same sense with William Shakespeare,—

> "And this our life, exempt from public haunt,
> Finds tongues in trees, books in the running brooks,
> Sermons in stones, and good in everything."

We travelled on comfortably enough in the carts at the rate of thirteen or fourteen miles a day, and reached our destination in the course of twenty-one days. On our arrival we were received by our disciples in a manner most hospitable. Five days afterwards my uncle and myself unfortunately caught the jungle fever: my sufferings ended in a short time, but those of my uncle were very severe, and his fever terminating in diarrhœa, rendered him very weak, lean, and miserable; and our return to sweet home was soon determined upon in consequence. We got about three hundred rupees, subscribed by our good hosts, and another caravan of carts was most anxiously looked for to convey us back.

Previous to leaving the city, I will give my reader some account of it. The town of Baroda, originally Barpatra (or a bar leaf, *i.e.*, leaf of the *Ficus Indica*, in shape), was the first large city I had seen. It bore no comparison with my poor miserable town, which was hardly equal to one-twelfth part of Baroda. The inner city is enclosed with walls, irregularly towered, extending about two miles and a half in circumference, in height from sixteen to twenty feet; but the outer is only nominally walled. It has a lofty and great quadrangular public building in the centre, called Mandavee, under the roof of which there are about one hundred shops of retail dealers. This place has three high gates on each side, and the four angles stretch forth, in direct lines of shops and houses, down to the inner wall of the city; so the town divides itself into four equal parts, the roads crossing each other at the central market-place. The palace is meanly built in the usual Marátha style, more like a dungeon than a palace. The population of the city at that time was estimated to be something more than one hundred thousand.

The Government of Baroda was then held by a Marátha Rájá, of the Gaikwár or cowherd caste, named Anand Ráo, the sixth Gaikwár from Pílají, the founder of the dynasty. These Rájás being an illiterate race, were much under the influence of designing ministers, who perpetrated all sorts of enormities, and introduced disorder and confusion into every department of the State in order to veil their own wicked acts.

Anand Ráo was succeeded by his brother, Syají Ráo, who, being a person of economical character, amassed a large treasury, and had eight sons and several daughters. The eldest son, Ganpat Ráo Gaikwár, commonly called Ráo Sáhib, having been already acknowledged as heir apparant, by his late father, put himself on the *masnad* immediately on his father's death. On all occasions the father had acted the part of a minister to his son, except in business with the British Resident, who, I believe, would not recognise him to be the heir apparent. Amongst the population I saw, for the first time, two classes with the eyes of amazement. They were the English and the Pársís; of the former I gave my reader some account in the beginning of the chapter, according to my then knowledge, founded upon the information I received from good authorities. I will add something here, which struck at me the time, concerning the English. One morning as I was walking in the city to divert myself, I saw four men, two of them on horseback, and the other two walking along with them; to my great curiosity I found their complexion corresponding with what we had heard. I heard them talking among themselves, and their jargon sounded harsh and wild to my hearing. Their dress tightly fitted to their bodies, without any skirt to screen such parts as the law of modesty has taught man to conceal. I felt inclined to accost them; but thought myself too young to venture on such an intrusion in a foreign city. I raised my hand, however, to my forehead, in token of salutation, without uttering the sacred sentence, "As salámun alaikum," to which my mind whispered none were entitled except true believers. They returned my salutation very kindly, which civility greatly softened my prejudices against them.

I was much amused at Baroda with a tame rhinoceros, kept at one of the gates of the city, known by the name of "the animal." It is the most powerful animal on the face of the earth. I was so fond of looking at the creature during my stay at Baroda, that I spent many hours of leisure in sitting with the keepers, and staring at the animal.

In the course of a few days a caravan of empty carts being ready to start to our district for the purchase of opium, the cart owners, some of whom were the same individuals who brought us to Baroda, readily agreed to take us back. Our disciples went along with us for two or three miles, and then, after they had paid their last and profoundest respects, we bade adieu to each other, and proceeded on. Our marches were short; but being unintermitting, we soon reached home in safety. My uncle recovered from his distemper during the journey, without any medical aid; and we concluded that the same air and water in a jungle which at one time produce disorder in a person, at another are the best antidote for his recovery.

In short, our journey being ended in success, we had the pleasure of seeing our kind relations. I cannot express the sense of happiness I felt in embracing my old and dearest grandmother and others. In this world of accidents no happiness can be equivalent to that of seeing one's friends after a separation. All of us lived in peace for some time, returning our thanks to the Almighty God for the satisfaction we enjoyed. I was now a boy of some weight in the family, having gained a little experience by travelling, and being attentive to my studies.

Another year of my life passed away, as if in the twinkling of an eye, during which scarcely anything occurred worthy of notice, with the exception of the antique Jewish ceremony, strictly attended to by all the Mohamedans except the royal family of Delhi. This was very painful and provoking to me, and confined me to my bed for more than one month.

Here I must express my wonder that Muslims are so strict in adhering to this hurtful and sometimes fatal operation, though the sacred Kur'án is entirely silent upon the subject. Common-sense should teach my good people not to deprive a son of Adam of any part of his body bestowed on him by nature: "hæc membrana data est pro preservatione sensationis peculiaris et procreationis." Notwithstanding this scrupulousness in a rite which our sacred book has not made binding on us, most of the true believers in general at this time neglect many strict orders enjoined by the Kur'án,—such as prayers five times a day, fasting thirty days annually, the bestowal of alms to the extent of a fortieth part of one's property annually, and pilgrimage to Mecca once during one's lifetime, if it can be afforded. True believers are prohibited from making use of any inebriating thing, and from receiving or paying interest on money. These, and many other religious duties, I am sorry to find are very loosely attended to by the Muslims of this time in the world.

Prayers and fasts are observed by very few of the religious character only, and the prescribed charity by one among a thousand of the rich. Pilgrimage is performed by very few people of affluence; it is resorted to, in general, by the poor wretches who either find or render themselves useless to the world. Those who abstain from intoxicating drugs, or liquors, do not exceed one in five thousand; and those that are clear from the crime of usurious transactions are, I may safely say, absolutely none. The mysterious secret of producing or destroying any religion rests with the only omniscient Supreme Being: His acts must be full of wisdom, and unfathomable by philosophers of highest rank. Let me, therefore, be silent upon the subject. leaving things to run their own course at His mighty pleasure, and let me be guided by the law of His blessed Prophet. A mortal like myself should not deviate from a path followed by twelve crores (120,000,000) of people for the last more than twelve and a half centuries. As the English poet well observes :—

> "Thyself but dust, thy stature but a span,
> A moment thy duration, foolish man!"
>
> PRIOR.

In a few months, the stock of our money again being exhausted, my uncle made another preparation for a new journey to the ancient city of Ujjain, taking a few MSS. along with him for sale; my mother and self, being his best companions in travelling, accompanied him at his earnest desire. We hired a vehicle, and proceeded on at the rate of four or five miles a day, halting at every village that contained some houses of Muslims, where we preached the sacred commands and prohibitions, and in return were treated with every respect, and great reverence. At length we reached our destination. The suburbs of the city were most charming, and afforded an excellent view of the edifices and domes of the ancient Hindú temples, and the minarets of mosques, rising above groves of fresh and verdant trees at the side of the river Sípra. We entered the city, and put up with an old friend of my uncle.

After our arrival here I was highly pleased with the town, and upon inquiry about it, I was informed that the city had stood, according to the Hindú legends (or Puránas) for many ages. It is held in great veneration by the Hindús, on account of its having been the place where the Rájás Karan, Bhartrí, and the most celebrated Vikram, once sat on the throne of Government, aided by invisible spirits. The death of the illustrious Rájá Vikram, which occurred about 57 years B.C., is the principal epoch of the Hindús throughout the whole of India. The city was first conquered by Mohamedans in 1229 A.D., and it fell into the hands of the Maráthas during the imbecile reign of Mohamed Shah; and ever since has been enjoyed by the Sindhiah family. The population in 1810 A.D., amounted to about 120,000 persons.

During our few days' stay in this city, several offers of a second marriage were brought to my mother. To some of them my uncle gave his silent assent; seeing that, though his sister was twenty-seven years of age, yet her beauty was still more exquisite than ever. Presently he began to speak to her seriously, telling her that it was a sin to keep unmarried for the sake of mere name—which was a sin against our law; besides, it was sheer folly and a great pity to put a restraint on nature, in attempting which many pious persons naturally fell victims to heinous crimes. To this my mother made a very angry reply, telling him that she knew she and her son proved cumbersome to him, but, in future, she would take great care to live separately upon her own industry; and, as for a second change in the state of her free life, she would rather go to hell than submit to such nonsense again. My uncle pacified her, explaining many things concerning the vicissitudes of man's life in this world, and affirming, at the same time, that we were of great assistance to him and far from cumbersome, and that all his happiness consisted in our welfare and prosperity. In fine, my good parent, listening to the advice of her brother, accepted an offer, and was married to a soldier of high rank in the service of His Highness Daulat Ráo Sindhiah's mother, named Mynábee. He was a man past forty years, and of great experience; and the lady in whose service he was, had entrusted all her public and private matters to his care and superintendence. She would not do anything without his advice. The discord between herself and the Prince, her son, was owing, I was told, to his bad advice. He was a tall man of large stature, well-made, but with a semi-oval enormous paunch before him. His complexion was dark, and his mind was darker than an infidel's heart, for he was illiterate and completely given up to worldly matters. I did not like the unsuitable alliance for some time, but the man having no male issue from his former wife, began to regard me as his own child. He ordered his people to teach me horsemanship and the use of arms. Two servants waited on me, and I went out in the morning to the courts of the nobles in the city; and in the evening with my suite, led by vanity, perhaps, to show myself to the people. Matters went on thus for about two months, when the old lady, our employer and protectress, departed this life, and the counsellor under whose protection we were, began to tremble for his safety, as he was not on good terms with anybody in the court, and under the displeasure of Sindhiah.

Ten days after the death of the old Princess, one morning at about four o'clock, our lodging was unexpectedly surrounded by a strong party of matchlockmen, their matches lighted and their swords drawn. They fired a volley at our peaceful abode, which put us in great consternation and peril. My stepfather was in inexpressible alarm. The doors of the house, however, being very strong, the assault of the soldiers had but little or no effect upon them; but much on the minds of the inmates. The poor master of the house, collecting his scared senses, performed his ablution and had recourse to his prayers. My mother, with her female slaves and attendants, thinking the approach of death near, fainted outright. As for myself, I felt firm enough, believing that there was no chance of my being killed, as I felt conscious of my innocence; and, further, that even if they put me to death I should die a martyr, and would, in consequence, go to heaven, where I was sure to enjoy a better life in the palaces of rubies and diamonds, fed with nectarious food, and associating with Húries —instead of this miserable life. In the meantime, the door of the yard was broken open and in rushed the ruffians. The morning now began to dawn, and the great luminary to send forth its brilliant rays over the world: I felt as if I could not keep myself within the house any longer, but presented myself to the unwelcome visitors. I found them busy in pillaging everything they could lay their hands upon. They had already saddled and despatched the horses, sent away the palanqueen and the carriage, I know not where; suffice it to say that the outer apartments were swept clean in a few minutes, but they dared not enter the house—law and custom being impenetrable barriers against them. One of them happening to see me at a distance, standing with both my hands in my pockets, cried out to his comrade in Maráthí (which, on account of my natural avidity for languages, at this time I began to understand), "Seize the young rascal!"—"Make haste," called out another, "and tie him to the post, torture him a little, his screams and lamentations will soon fetch out the Súbahdár, to secure whom is the final object of our expedition." Hearing this, I boldly advanced to the commanding officer, who knew me previously and often talked and joked with me, warning the guard, at the same time, not to touch one whom they would find ready to go to the loaded cannon's mouth if they wanted him. As for torturing, I cared not; and I swore I would not utter one word, even if they tore my flesh off with pincers; but if they used me fairly, I considered it in my power to bring out the old Súbahdár and all his property too. The officer heard my bold speech with admiration, and said, "Touch him not; he is a brave little soldier; let him come to me; he is my friend, and hath nothing to do with this rotten affair." This encouragement, of course, emboldened me more; I greeted the officer for his kindness, and thanked him; he was greatly pleased with me, seated me by his side, and observed that he was reluctantly put on this important duty by the Minister of State; and his orders were to confiscate all the property that he could find in the outer apartments, and keep the Súbahdár under strict surveillance until further orders from his Highness the Mahárájah at Gwálior, but that in case the old man should not give himself up, or should show any resistance, his party then might enter the private apartments with naked swords, take possession of all the property that might be found there, and secure him, *nolens volens.* I replied I would go to my stepfather and explain to him the orders, and do my best to persuade him to show himself; should I fail, I told the officer he might execute his commands as he chose. He agreed to this plan, and I, as a little politician, returned and spoke to the old man, telling him that it was the best thing for himself and the family to surrender, and that it was of no avail to kick against the pricks, or, as the Asiatics say, to strike the hatchet upon one's own foot. The old man hearing me with patience, embraced me and kissed my forehead with his eyes full of tears, but he was too fond of his life to give himself up so easily. "Ill conscience can never be fearless." He told me that if the officer took his solemn oath, by pouring water on a cow's tail, declaring that no harm was intended to his person, he would appear; otherwise, he would escape, breaking through the roof of the house, and that he would be off with all speed; and, "as to the females," quoth he, "let them devise the means of their own safety in the best way they can." Charged with this cowardly message, I turned my back and cursed the old fellow for his cowardice. I recollected some of my lessons in the Persian Book of Examples and found them verified. "A lion in appearance may turn out to be a jackal on trial, and *vice versâ.*" I will here insert the fable related under the proverb in the same book for the perusal of my reader.

"There were in ancient times five ladies of exquisite beauty residing in the city of Samarkand, intimately connected with each other both by friendship and consanguinity. Four of them had been married, but the fifth would not, on any account, exchange her state of freedom for that of matrimonial bondage. On one beautiful evening in spring, as they sat conversing among themselves, one of them said that her husband's love towards her was unequalled in the world; the second, in her turn, observed that her husband was the handsomest man in Persia; the third remarked that her spouse was the bravest man of the time; and the fourth added that her husband was unequalled in liberality: thus, each of them praised her own lord to excite the envy of the unmarried lady, whom they then addressed,—'Madam, have you nothing to talk of this evening?' She replied, she had many things to say to them, but would examine first into the truth of the commendations they had bestowed on their consorts, and see if they were deserved. She then asked the first beauty, 'if her husband had ever seen a beautiful woman besides herself.' The reply was, 'No!' 'Then,' said she, 'try him first, and then you will certainly know whether he loves you or not.' Of the second she asked, 'Madam, has your handsome husband got his manly ornament, *i.e.*, the beard?' 'No;

not yet,' replied the other. 'Then wait until he is bearded, and then you will be able to tell whether he is handsome or not.' To the third she said, 'My young lady! has your lord been wounded in a battle?' 'No, Madam, not yet,' was her reply. 'Then,' returned she 'you cannot tell yet whether he is a brave man or not, so wait till such an accident occurs to testify to his valour.' She then interrogated the fourth, inquiring 'whether her lord was liberal upon wealth obtained by himself, by his own industry, or otherwise?' She replied, 'Upon the estate left by his late father.' 'Then,' said the virgin, 'term his liberality extravagance and prodigality until he is liberal from his own riches.'"

At first, the gaudy military appearance of my step-father, led me to believe that he was a man of courage; but, on this trial, I found him to be worse than a jackal.

Bearing, however, the above message, I came down, and, returning to the officer, I told him that the Súbhadár had armed himself; that he had his blunderbuss loaded with bullets to the mouth, full cocked, in his hand, and as soon as the guard attempted to enter, he would act in his self-defence. I added, he was determined to hold out to the last; that he intended to destroy his females, and then he would break through. "Thus," said I, "you will see several murders in cold blood in your presence, and for these I know not who will have to atone; and, after all, it is not so safe for the guard too. Who knows to whose share the bullets of the blunderbuss are to fall, before the Súbahdár is captured, dead or alive? But," added I, "there is only one way for a peaceful conclusion left, that is, if you take your solemn oath upon the cow's tail that no treachery will ensue so as, in any way, to endanger the person of the old gentleman; if he were sure of this, he would come out and surrender." Thus I delivered the cowardly message, with the addition of a few touches of my own.

The concluding proposal of mine was immediately agreed to by the commander. A Brahman and a cow were soon produced; and the Brahman, putting the tail of the animal in the commander's hand, poured down some water upon it, and uttered some words in Sanskrit, which caused the poor man to tremble at their solemnity. The Súbahdár, observing this through the keyhole, immediately descended; and the commander's party surrounding him, the officer read his order to the Súbahdár, and asked him to give up his arms. This he did with some reluctance, and resigned himself to the decree of fate. In the evening, he gave a bag of five hundred rupees secretly to the commander as a bribe, which dumb coins made him and his party, not only dumb, but enslaved them all to us; and though we were their prisoners, yet they made themselves ours.

Two long and tedious months elapsed in this

unlucky restraint. The poor governor, during the day, sat at the door of his zanánah. At night two men always sat by his bed; and if he walked he had them at his elbow. For my part, I was free; I entered the house, and went out anywhere I liked, without any sort of obstruction whatever. At last, the orders arrived from Gwálior directing our release, and they were duly executed. A robe of honour was given to the old man in the Durbár, to make amends for his sufferings; and a long speech, in the high Maráthí language, was read out by the Minister, to give consolation to the poor weak-minded old fellow. He took all this very coolly, and, on his dismissal, he asked for the restoration of his live and dead stock, confiscated by the Government officers. To this, the deputy replied, he could not give anything back, as the orders were silent on that head. "Had it been otherwise," added he, "I would have had much pleasure in restoring them, and would have added something from myself."

CHAPTER III.

My step-father imputes his calamity to shaving on an unlucky day.—Astrology and superstitions of the inhabitants of Hindústán.—We visit Sindhiah's Court at Gwálior.—The Prince pays our losses with a smile—enlists my step-father in his service.—My cruel treatment.—I fly from Gwálior.

THE old gentleman, after his imprisonment, appeared quite satisfied with his lot, attributing the misfortune partly to destiny, and partly to having his head shaved on an unlucky day.

I will here give some idea of the superstitious rites prevailing all over India, among all castes. Although the law of our blessed Prophet rejects every kind of superstition, whether founded upon astrology or Arab traditions of the Dark Ages; yet, even Mohamedans in general do still follow the errors of the false religions. Upon almost all undertakings of importance they will consult astrology. Marriages, going on a journey, the birth of a child, the commencement of a building, venesection, and even shaving one's head, are all occasions which require an astrologer to be consulted, and lucky days and hours are appointed for such acts. Six days in every lunar month are considered unlucky; to find out these, count on the tips of the fingers, beginning from the little finger to the thumb and repeating the same for the thirty days, and the days that come on the tip of the middle finger are avoided; they are as follows, 3rd, 8th, 13th, 18th, 23rd, and 28th.

Mohamedans are particular in shunning the performance of business, or going on a journey, as forbidden by the Prophet himself, during the moon's rotation of about fifty-four hours in the sign Scorpio. The rule to find out this time is a very simple one. Take the dates of the lunar month, double the same, add five, and divide the amount by fives, allotting each five to each one of the signs, commencing from that which is the mansion of the Sun at that time, and the last five must be that sign in which the Moon then performs her course. Should there remain any number less than five, such a residue is to be multiplied by six, and the product is the number of degrees which the planet hath gone over in that sign: *e.g.*, this day is the fourth day of the lunar month Jamádu'lawal, corresponding with the 20th of April, 1847, the time when the Sun is in the sign Taurus. Take the number of days in the lunar month, four; double the same, add five — total, thirteen.

In the number, thirteen, there will be two fives, so the moon must be in the second sign from Taurus, *i.e.*, Gemini; and the residue, three, multiplied by six, will produce the number eighteen, which is the number of degrees she hath passed in that sign this day.

The following table exhibits good and bad luck for an undertaking:—

Days of the week.	The Planets assigned thereto.	Successful for.	Unsuccessful for..
Saturday...	Saturn ...	Traffic	Cutting or putting on new clothes, bleeding at the arm, and shaving the head.
Sunday ...	Sun	Taking medicines, employment, cutting, and putting on new clothes.	
Monday ...	Moon	Building.	
Tuesday*...	Mars	Warfare..............	Beginning with a building or marriage, bleeding at the arm.
Wednesday	Mercury	Study and scientific undertaking	Performing obsequies.
Thursday	Jupiter ...	Marriage.	
Friday......	Venus ...	Journey.	

The seven planets, viz., Sun, Venus, Mercury, Moon, Saturn, Jupiter, and Mars, have dominion assigned to them by astrologers over the seven days of the week; and, then, each of the twenty-four hours of the day has been allotted to a planet dominant during that time. The times of the planets Saturn and Mars are considered unlucky, and those

* A new-born child on the day or hour of the planet Mars, is considered to become crafty, greedy, unjust, and hypocritical.

of the remaining five planets are thought good, except Thursday. On this day, though not an unlucky day, a visit to a sick person, inquiring after his health, or taking medicine, is strictly forbidden. Wednesday, governed by the planet Mercury, is appointed for commencing study; but to begin with any other business is prohibited.

The dominant planets of the twenty-four hours are found by the following rule. For example, take Monday. The first hour of this day, beginning from sunrise, belongs to the Moon; second, Saturn; third, Jupiter; fourth, Mars; fifth, Sun; sixth, Venus, seventh, Mercury; and eighth, again to the Moon; and so on, in the above routine through a whole week.

Another superstitious rule, strictly adhered to by all Mohamedans, and considered by Hindús a part of law, is the observation of invisible spirits that are believed to perambulate the eight directions of the globe, on particular dates of the Hindús' lunar months throughout the year.

In undertaking a journey, or any expedition of importance, or game of chance, the direction haunted by these spirits should be behind the undertaker to ensure success; not opposite, which is considered very unlucky, and ill success must follow. These spirits are called by Mohamedans, "Rijalulghaib," by Hindús, "Jogní," or "Dissásul." The following diagram will point out the directions of the "Jogní," and the dates counting from 1st to 15th, and then again from 1st to 15th, the last 15th day standing for the 30th.

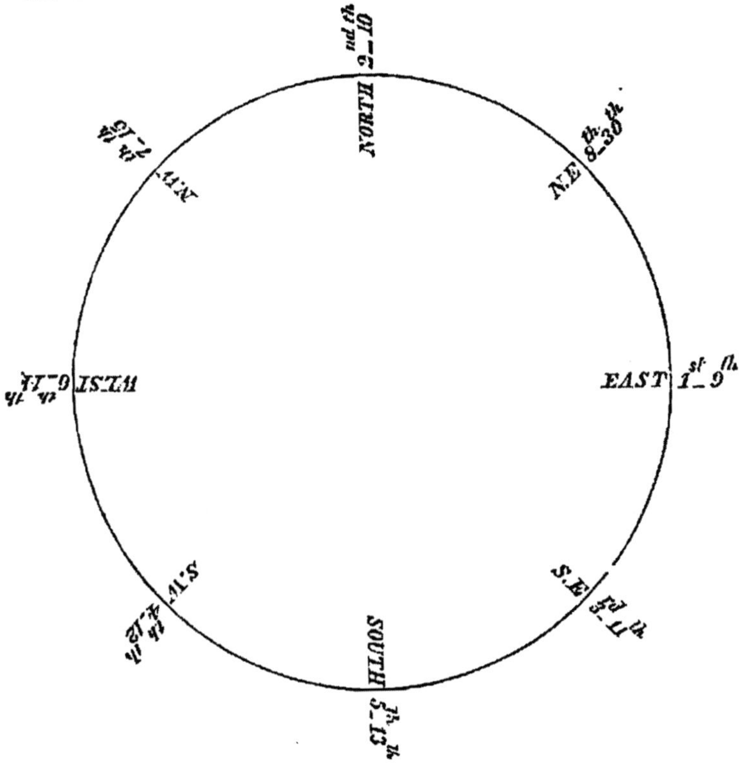

Auguration also is not left unpractised by the natives of India in general. For instance, a cat crossing the road of an individual on his way, will surely retract or prevent his going at the time. In the same manner, a sneeze in his opposite direction will deter him from going to any place, or undertaking any business: a sneeze heard at the right-hand side will prove to be of a contrary effect. In the same way, flights of birds, sight of a herd of deer, and many other things, are good or bad omens.

Not wishing to take up my reader's time any more with astrological nonsense, I will return to my step-father, where I left him at the beginning of this chapter, quite satisfied with his lot. He thought proper now to proceed to Gwálior, and lay his case before His Highness the Mahárájah Daulat Ráo Sindhiah. He purchased several horses and camels, and left them in charge of his brother-in-law (his former wife's brother) with some diabolical instructions, which hereafter will be mentioned.

A lucky day having been fixed, we left the city in company with a nobleman of Sindhiah's family, who was likewise proceeding to that court, after visiting his family at Ujjain. The character of my step-father being that of a real timeserver, he soon ingratiated himself with the nobleman; so much, that during our journey they were intimately leagued in friendship. We marched every morning till about four o'clock P.M., and then halted. I was now really transformed from a young priest to a nice little soldier. I rode a beautiful mare, ornamented with my glittering arms, sword, shield, and a small spear, all proportioned to my stature, except the mare, which was large, but a very nice animal; her name was "Bark" (lightning), and she was as quiet as a lamb, that is to say, when I rode her quietly: but if I spurred, or raised my hand by chance, she was as swift as her name; and, after all, so good-natured was the animal, that if I fell down she stood by my side to let me mount again.

In the course of about one month we reached Sindhiah's camp at Gwálior, which was, in fact, no camp but a regular city, consisting of houses built with soft red stone and mortar, with a large and magnificent palace of His Highness in the centre. The population, at the time, was estimated to amount to three hundred thousand persons, of which armed soldiers amounted to one-third. There were two hundred elephants and three hundred cannons ready for action. We pitched our tents upon a respectable site appointed by the officer of His Highness, and lived for two months unnoticed by any person of consequence. My step-father, however, did his best to enter into intimacies with men of rank and dignity; and at last succeeded in obtaining admittance to the Court by distributing one thousand rupees amongst the members of it.

A day being appointed, we went to the audience; His Highness, seeing us, stood up on his seat (a cushion of valuable brocade, set with jewels), as a mark of politeness, and stretched forth his right hand to honour us, touching which respectfully with our fingers, we kissed them. His Highness's conversation was so graceful, civil, and fascinating, that my step-father seemed stupified, and could not speak of his complaints: however, he did not fail to give some hints respecting them. His Highness pretended not to notice them, but comforted the old man by observing that he had given orders for him to be paid his arrears up to the end of that month; that he might consider himself in His Highness's service from the death of the old queen; and that His Highness had already enrolled him amongst his most favoured courtiers. This filled the old man with an uncommon pride, and locked his mouth, and rendered him unable to utter another word, except thanks; but he kept on making saláms and profound bows. Immediately upon this, at a signal from an officer in the assembly, atr, pán, rosewater, and dresses of honour were brought out for us. At the time of our dismissal, His Highness inquired smilingly as to who I was? "He is my son," replied the old man; "but let the young man answer for himself." Hearing this, I respectfully joined my hands and said—"The Súbahdár may be believed, if it please your Highness, since parents are the best authorities to speak about their children." This reply, though a simple one, excited the mirth of the Mahárájah to a great degree, and he was pleased to put playfully another question to me. "What is your opinion, then, regarding your own birth?"—"I am too young, my lord," rejoined I, "and not competent to give my opinion upon matters of such importance." His

Highness then asked the old fellow if I could read and write; and in reply he praised me very highly. Hereupon His Highness added to my dress of honour a very handsome MS. copy of Háfiz and S'adí, in one volume, which I have still in my possession as a meménto from a great man.

We were now settled at Gwálior, and were well off. The old Súbahdár's duty was a very slight one; he went out on a shooting excursion with His Highness perhaps three times a month, and was to sit three hours alternately as a sentry, ready armed, at the door of His Highness's bedroom, which fell to his turn only two nights a month. This was a post of great honour, and trusted to the charge of gentlemen high in rank, and worthy officers: they were called "Yakka," *i. e.*, "a single man with a single horse," and received daily in cash each according to his merit. The minimum of the salary was five, and the maximum thirty, rupees per diem; besides, they got their daily food ready dressed from the Government every day, and valuable dresses twice a-year. The number of "Yakkas" did not exceed one hundred and twenty-seven. My step-father's situation was the lowest, *i. e.*, five rupees per day; but it being very respectable, he was not only glad, but proud of it.

During our absence from Ujjain we received several letters from home, one of which informed the old man of the birth of a son, which tidings afforded him unparalleled pleasure; and he gave a grand entertainment to all the nobles in the camp, which cost him about two thousand rupees; and the congratulatory presents given to him by them on this occasion amounted to upwards of three thousand rupees. This circumstance not only rendered him independent of me, but he began to hate and abuse me now on trifling matters: he used the coarsest language towards me, which I could not possibly bear. He passed his days among his friends, and his nights with a new friend's wife, the man appearing to wear the pair of horns without any sense of jealousy. He never went on his duty, but sent me invariably in his place; besides, when at home, I was always ordered with other servants of his to stand sentry three hours every night. Being maltreated in this manner, I felt very melancholy, and wrote to my mother all the particulars of my predicament, adding that I had formed the intention of deserting the old man, and would rather commit suicide if unsuccessful in doing so. Unfortunately, this letter was intercepted, through the irregularity and neglect of the postmaster of the Marátha Government. The old man happened to call at the post-office, respecting the receipt of some bills of exchange, forwarded through that office some time before; and the postmaster plainly told him that no reply till that time had been received regarding his bills, and that the reply to his last letter, which was delivered two days ago, and was immediately going to be sent off, would certainly bring joyful tidings of all kinds. "I have sent no letter," rejoined the Súbahdár, "it must belong to some other person." Upon this, the letter being produced was recognised, opened, and read by the postmaster, at the request of the old fellow, who returned home with it, highly excited with rage.

On getting from his palanqueen, he called for me. I went in, and he rose on his seat to show a mocking honour to me, of the meaning of which I had not the least conception, but stood amazed and thunderstruck. "My good friend," says he, "here is a letter for you to read, if you please." I took the letter from his hand, and knowing it to be my own, I opened and glanced through it: though the fear of being put to death made me quite pale, yet, seeing no escape, my youthful heart soon resumed courage, and I called to mind the old Persian proverb, "Death with courage is far superior to life as a coward." I told him it was my letter, that I delivered it to the postmaster to be forwarded to my parent, and that nobody had any business to open it. This reply kindled up the fire of his anger more than before. "You young rascal," said he, "you have committed an unpardonable crime; and then you are impudent too!" Uttering this, he sprang from his place, and knocked me down with two or three blows; not satisfied with which, he kicked and pounded me with his fists until he was tired (of this I was informed afterwards); but, falling down senseless, I declare I felt nothing. When I recovered from my swoon, I found myself lying on my bed in the stable, and a horse-keeper, named Khushál, standing by. I called for water, and the poor man kindly gave me a cup of sherbet, scented with rose-water, at his own expense. Of this sweet beverage, I could take but a very little quantity, finding all the functions of my body paralyzed. I slept again very soundly for two days and nights, and did not rise until I was forced to do so. Now I could use my limbs, though still very stiff, and made a vow not to see the infernal old butcher's face again in my life, if possible. He sent me sweetmeats and other delicious eatables, as a token of his kindness, but I gave them to the grooms; and for myself, I took, morning and evening, a small piece of their plain bread and cold water, to keep up my spirits. Thus I lived for nearly a fortnight, during which I found that my severe pain had made me quite dumb, my head being overfilled with thoughts of thousand kinds.

In the meantime, the turn of the guard having occurred, the remorseless old tyrant asked me, through his servant, to act his part as usual. I replied I was unfit for duty, and would not go. Hearing this answer, he armed himself and proceeded to the palace; and I, having provided myself with one loaf, one sacred book, the beautiful volume of Háfiz, presented to me by His Highness, and my small scimitar, took my way to Agra. I left the camp early in the morning, and followed the path, or rather direction, to the town of Gohad, about twenty-two miles from Gwálior. Leaving the highway, I began to proceed through the jungle, to avoid being observed by any individual that might have been despatched to pursue and apprehend me. I went on as fast as my legs could carry me; and to my great satisfaction, for some time I met no animal walking upon two legs, except a few shepherds every now and then, resting under shady trees, pasturing their herds, guarded by their faithful dogs. At noon I took my rest under a magnificent banyan tree, by the side of a river; I made my ablution, and spreading my doputta,* or waistband, I sat upon it, with my little sword, my Kur'àn, the other books, and the loaf of bread before me. A shepherd who sat under another tree near mine, very probably being struck with curiosity, came near me with his dog. He stood at a little distance, leaning against his staff gazing at my acts. The dog also appeared to stare at me with equal curiosity, and at the same time wagged its tail, being pleased, I suppose, with the scent of the bread in my possession, of which it wanted to have a share. The cravings of my hunger

* It is a sheet that the natives of India tie round their waist, and use for many other purposes.

at this time being excessive, I took a piece of bread, a fourth of which I first offered to my flattering guest, the dog, and to the remainder I began to do justice. The kind-hearted shepherd asked me if I had any objection to have a little milk with my plain bread. On the contrary, replied I, I should be most happy to get a little, if he pleased, and would feel obliged to him for his generous and hospitable act to a stranger, and a man of different caste like myself. The liberal shepherd immediately brought me a pot of excellent fresh milk; but the difficulty now arose, how to receive it. The shepherd, being a Hindú, would not allow me to touch his pot; by his advice, however, I folded up some leaves of the tree into cups, and drank the fresh milk with my bread. The taste of this milk I found far superior to any I ever drank previously; and, to tell the truth, I never obtained milk of that flavour afterwards. The shepherd and his dog then went away satisfied, the former for his benevolent act to one of his fellow-creatures, and the latter at the liberality of a stranger. The sun now declining from the meridian, I said my noon prayers, and set off again, thanking the good shepherd for his kindness, and inquiring of him about my way to Gohad.

I travelled on with expedition till four o'clock, P.M., when I felt much fatigued, and was looking about for a solitary place to take rest for the night. I wished not to put up in a village, for fear of being apprehended; seeing, however, from afar a well situated near a village, I repaired to it to drink, intending then to look for a place for nocturnal rest. Arriving near it, I asked one of the Rájput maidens, who were busily engaged in drawing water and carrying it home for their use, to give me a little water to quench my thirst with. In reply, she asked me a question, with a lovely air, as pretty as herself, "Have you nobody else to quench your thirst with but me?"—"Madam," replied I, "I have none; but even if I had one, she could not be more than an atom before your incomparable beauty: a lamp can have no splendour before the sun." This flattery produced a smile in her fair countenance, and she held her pot to me very gracefully, telling me, "Drink till thou art satiated." Thanking her, I took both of my hands to my mouth in the form of a cup, and she kindly poured the water in a fine stream, which I found greatly sweetened with the excellent scent of her rosy hand; and I drank until I was full. I then made a grateful bow to the beauty, who, taking her pots on her head, went home.

In the meantime, a tall well-made Muslim, of about forty years of age, came up to me; he appeared to be a wayfarer like myself, by his dusty dress, etc. He saluted me very respectfully, asked me how I did, whence I had come, and where I was going to? I returned his salám, and told him I was a traveller, and was going to Gohad on business. Hearing this, he observed, his destination was the same, but he feared we could not reach it till after sunset, as it was full four miles distant yet from the spot. I liked not the man's appearance, his dull stupid eyes, and his intruding manners; but he soon familiarized himself to me during our march, and put me off my guard by his conversation to a great degree. We went about two miles when the brilliant traveller, the sun, reached the horizon. At this time we came to a river, at the bank of which there was an old mosque standing, but no population to be seen in the vicinity. I told my new companion that I could walk no longer, and would make my halt in the mosque for the night, and that he might proceed on to Gohad if he pleased, where the next day I would have the pleasure of seeing him, *inshá Alláh ta'ála*,—"if it pleased the Almighty God." Hereupon he observed this was a place infested by both robbers and wild beasts, and he would recommend my proceeding on, instead of staying in that dangerous place. But I told him I cared not for both kinds of the savage animals: as for the first class of them, I did not think they would injure me, for I had not a particle of the precious metal about me; and to guard against a frightful visit of the second class, I thought would not be a matter of difficulty, as I was a son of Adam endowed with reason, with which they were not favoured by the Deity: I would collect some pieces of firewood and make a fire in the middle of the entrance, and would remain inside without any apprehension. My new companion, "Jum'a" (such was his name, meaning Friday), heard all this with attention. He examined my person with searching looks, again and again, and then replied, "Very well, sir, do as you please." I then undressed myself to perform ablution for the evening prayer, and to wash my body from the dust of the road. I told Jum'a to take care of the bread, that no dog carried it away, and to watch the dress, etc., whilst I washed myself. He readily accepted the charge, and carefully searched my small luggage, the cloth in which my two books were wrapped up, and my pockets, etc. Finding nothing in them that might have satisfied his brutal cupidity, he sat in silence watching me, very likely to see if I had any money or jewel about me; this expectation of his also proved to be in vain. Coming out of the water, I wiped my body and performed my sunset devotion to my most sublime Creator, whilst Jum'a sat looking on, and sometimes smiled, perhaps at the acts of prayer, which of course are curious to the vulgar eye.

The night came on, and we entered the mosque; Jum'a and myself brought some firewood and made a large fire at the entrance to guard against the wild beasts. We made a supper upon a piece of bread, each from his own possession. Jum'a offered me some of his own bread, but I declined the acceptance, and told him he might take a part from my bread if he liked. Now I felt myself excessively fatigued, and so sleepy, that I could hardly keep my eyes open; but it was the pleasure of Almighty God to save me from an injury or heinous crime from my evil companion, Jum'a, who opened a horrid conversation with me, telling me that he had already found I was no more than a mercenary like himself, and even, in my young days, had no friend in the world; that, if I swore to him by the Holy Book never to divulge the secret about to be delivered to me, he would take me as one of his pupils; that his profession was so excellent a one as to render the follower of it a man of great fortune in one moment, etc.

The conversation of Jum'a charmed me much; and, being a young imprudent creature, I swore to him by the Book without thinking, though I regretted it afterwards. Jum'a then remarked that he had seven pupils in the country, who were all faithful to him. I then asked him to tell me the secret, upon which, making me swear once more, he said he was a *Thug*, and that he killed travellers very easily, and made his fortune by doing so. Opening a long bag from his waist, and undoing its mouth, he poured down gold mohrs from it to enchant my eyes and fascinate my mind. These precious coins amounted to 112, being counted afterwards. When I heard this appalling announcement, instead of being pleased I was horrified at the sight of the infernal Jum'a, and still more at the coins. However, I did not forego my self-command, and asked him very coolly how he could destroy a man so easily as he said, since, having been an eye-witness to some executions, I found it no such slight affair to put a human being out of the world. "Never you mind that," said he, "I could teach you that in one moment by my performances; but be you careful never to mention my name in any town or village, for I am a man of great name: keep this secret, and there are chances that to-morrow you will be as rich as myself; but remember, you must pay one quarter of the gain to me and one quarter to a handsome maid of ours, whom we shall see to-morrow at the gate of Gohad." Although exposed to such danger, I could not get rid of my inclination to sleep, which attacked me more and more every minute. To keep awake, I, under the pretence of lighting my cheroot, went to the fire and purposely burnt the tip of my ring finger, and, lighting the cigar, I returned to the seat. Jum'a now being satisfied of my fidelity, began his diabolical instructions to me, telling me that it was not difficult to put an end to a man's life, but it was difficult to delude him and to get into a little confidence with him for the performance of the act. "We adopt various modes," said he, "in making ourselves familiar with travellers, by appearing to them as mendicants, by engaging to be their guides, and even by acting as pimps for them. The woman I mentioned to you is for the last purpose: she attracts a traveller's attention immediately; and, fascinating him in her enchanting conversation, she leads him apart from the road, and then, pretending to be tired, she sits under a tree, takes out a tinder-box from her bag to strike fire for smoking; in the meantime one of us arriving there, the traveller naturally dislikes such an intrusion, but the woman pacifies him by telling him 'he is my husband (or brother), and will soon go away about his business after taking a little fire, and then we will smoke and talk at leisure.' During this talk, if the traveller is not enough off his guard, in smoking and talking, etc., she, as if by accident, removes such a part of her dress as naturally very soon attracts his whole attention; and then any one of us throwing a handkerchief like this (exhibiting a long silk handkerchief with a knot) over his neck, gives him a pull, which brings him down senseless: he, however, shakes his hands and legs a little, which are instantly silenced by giving one sound kick upon his scrotum. His person is then searched, and immediately interred at the same spot, and we pursue our way separately, engaging to meet again at a certain place on a certain day."

Listening to these abominable narratives, my ears became deaf, my eyes motionless, and my blood thrilled in my veins. My self-possession, however, I still maintained, and asked him another question with the same indifference as before. "Do you not relent at all when you commit this act?"—"No," replied he, "we are accustomed to it; a butcher is never moved when he kills his goat or cow. In the beginning one always feels compassionate a little, but practice renders everything easy: upon such occasions we must think of the people's unkindness, selfishness, and remorselessness. For example, they would not give us a rupee were we dying with starvation, and they would not be moved at all if we were punished to death; so they must be treated similarly by us. In the commencement of the profession, I myself was once very much disgusted at it.

"It happened that once I followed an old priest for about thirty miles from Kota, in the direction of Udepur. In the course of the first day's journey with him, I could find no opportunity to finish him. In the evening he put up with some of his friends, where I could not possibly intrude. The next morning very early, he marched, and I accompanied him, sometimes following, and sometimes preceding him. When the first quarter of the day had elapsed, he took his breakfast near a village, and seeing me in a wretched condition, he gave me a piece of bread, which I received from him with an apparent eagerness, and thanked him, but never tasted it, thinking that eating his salt, and then killing him, would be an unpardonable infidelity in me. I told him I was going to Udepur to look for a situation, and he replied, "May your undertaking be prosperous!" He proceeded on after his breakfast, and I after him till noon, when the time of his prayer, or I may say his death, approached. He asked me if I knew any place nigh where water could be found for his ablution, if not, he might purify himself with the sand, and pray. I told him there was a stream of water running about a quarter of a mile thence, but it was a little apart from the road: he asked me to show it to him, and I made him follow me to the water, where he performed his purifications; and spreading his cloth, began his prostrations, and rising up, heedless as he was, in the latter act of his devotion, I strangled him. He soon gave up the ghost, and to my great despair, on searching his person I found only one "pice," or farthing, with him in ready cash, a rosary, and some pieces of dry bread. The body, however, I interred immediately, and returned. The next day I came to the village, where I had previously appointed to see my old mother, and found her there. I mentioned to her what had taken place, and my being moved with compassion, and my determination of giving up my profession, telling her that I would rather starve to death than be obliged to stain my hands in future with innocent blood for such trifling gains. She did not like this unmanliness of mine, and, taking the farthing from me, she proceeded to the market-place, whence she returned with a bundle of about one pound in weight of small fish or prawns: placing the bundle before me, she said, 'Can you count these small animals my son?'—'Yes,' said I, 'but it will require one whole day to count them, without any use.'—'Then,' returned she, 'you foolish boy, do you not see how many lives are destroyed here for one farthing? and you, like a stupid, cowardly, relenting fellow, seem concerned at the death of an old priest, who had one foot already in the grave. If a lion,' observed she, 'feels remorse over his prey, it is quite clear he must starve to death.' This wholesome advice of the manly old woman," continued Jum'a, "restored my mind to my favourite profession, and I never afterwards felt foolish remorse for my deeds."

Midnight had already elapsed by this time, and the cursed Jum'a now told me that I must be very sleepy and might go to sleep for two or three hours; during which time he would keep awake, and then he would awake me to watch in my turn. "My friend," remarked I, "I have accidentally burnt my finger, and the pain thereof will not allow to sleep; go thou to sleep, and I will watch and awaken thee when I feel sleepy." At this he laughed, and, accepting the offer with great pleasure, he slept, and began to snore like an unclean animal. I feel it impossible to express to my reader the torture that my mind was undergoing at the conversation and sight of this devil in the disguise of man; but it was quite clear that I was helpless. In escaping from bad, I was involved in worse: my finger now became inflamed, the pain was excessive; but the pain of my mind surpassed it. I thanked Heaven that I had nearly stripped before the beast in my evening ablution, which act assured him of my being moneyless, otherwise I should have been strangled like others ere that. I had a great mind to cut the throat of the unmanly wretch with my small but sharp scimitar, and send him at once to hell from his slumber, the door whereof, I thought, must be open for him, and "Malik," the keeper of it, would with much pleasure receive and put him into the eternal fire. On the other hand, I felt disinclined to kill him with my own hands, for fear of my being liable to be prosecuted on suspicion of cold-blooded murder, perpetrated for the money on his person. In such troublesome thought the long and tedious night at last came to a finish; the chirping of the morning birds conveyed the glad tidings of its approach to my anxious ears. I rose from my place very quietly, and getting out of the gate of the mosque, without making any noise, instead of going to make my morning ablution, which was my first intention, I ran in the direction of Gohad, doing the two miles in about twenty minutes. I often looked behind to see if Jum'a was not in pursuit of me. Just as the gate of the town was going to be opened I reached there, and the doorkeepers and the guard, seeing me out of breath, inquired the reason. In the fit of my excitement and fear (forgetting my oath, I must confess,) I uttered "Jum'a the Thug," in an inarticulate manner; but the name of the rogue was quite sufficient to rouse all the guard. The question then arose where he was, and I pointed out the place. I was asked to accompany them and show the place; but pleading my inability, I stayed where I was. Caring not for me, they ran to the spot. In the meantime I was sent for by the Minister of the State, a young Hindú of very respectable appearance. I was informed afterwards that this young nobleman was the son of the Rájá's Minister, and acted as Governor. He examined me very narrowly upon the subject, but before the examination was finished, to my great satisfaction, I saw the brute Jum'a brought into the presence of the Minister, pinioned in a condition befitting his black acts. He was thrashed, beaten, and even pierced and cut with swords all over his body. The Minister and the people present recognised him, as he had escaped from their prison once before. All of them spat on his face, and his person then being searched, the money found thereon was taken by the officers, and without any further inquiry or delay, he was tied to the mouth of a large cannon, and in a second blown into atoms, and all his hopes of committing murders in future were in one instant at an end. Thus his abominable existence was terminated: I took my way to the gate, and thence to a well, where, having performed my ablution, I offered my thanks to Heaven for this narrow escape, and sincerely demanded forgiveness of the Deity for the crime of breaking my oath.

Finishing these humble supplications, I kindled a little fire to parch some fresh grain for my breakfast, which having done, I sat comfortably chewing it. This day it was my intention to make a long march; I was now shy enough of strangers, and determined to proceed on as fast as possible. Just as I was preparing to start, I saw, to my great alarm, one of the guards coming up to me: his appearance filled my mind with a double apprehension. In the first place I thought somebody might have come from Gwálior to catch me, or very likely I was to be accused of having been a partner of the damned Jum'a, in which case I must have to share his fate, or be made a prisoner. But all such fearful thoughts left me soon, when the man, coming nearer, saluted and kindly told me that the Minister wanted to see me: I accordingly returned with him to the Darbár, and was desired to be seated. The Minister thanked me in the assembly for having been the cause of the destruction of the impure bloody robber, who had destroyed many lives, and would have taken more had he lived. He then ordered his treasurer to pay me twelve gold mohrs from the amount of one hundred and twelve, found on the person of the guilty. I made a respectful bow to him, and got the money from his man; but counting them I found only ten, and looking at him to express that the number of the money was incorrect, he said he had deducted two for his fee: I made no farther dispute about the shortness of the money, and pursued my course.

Having now ten gold mohrs in my possession for the first time, the feelings of pride, vanity, and self-confidence, began to take their seat in my little brain. The pure sense of being altogether resigned to the will of the One real Provider of everything to every individual creature, began to leave me. The "yellow slave," as it is termed by the immortal Shakspeare, soon evinced its noxious effects upon its possessor. Notwithstanding all this, my fears, too, were aggravated; formerly I was only fearful of a pursuer, but now my life was endangered by keeping gold about me. The base metal being the object of everybody's love, there are in this world a thousand kinds of plots laid for its attainment, and the human frames, formed by the omnipotent hand of the Deity, are destroyed for the purpose of its impure acquisition. I was obliged to travel by the general road, and to seek some company, for the safety of my newly-obtained riches, which I kept on my person with all possible secrecy.

In short, after seven days' hard work and circuitous travelling, I had the pleasure of seeing the vicinity of the ancient city of Agra. My bread, I may say, had the blessing of Jesus Christ, that during the week I lived upon three quarters of it, and had still one quarter of it left; but to tell the truth, the green grain of the fields, which I plucked and parched every morning, was my wholesome breakfast throughout the journey. It affords me the greatest pleasure now to think of the freedom and happiness I enjoyed in this short travel after bondage. The remembrance of my morning walks, my ablutions in the pure limpid springs of water, my noon prayers in the still jungles, under the shade of the finest tree that I happened to select, on the emerald carpets of verdure supplied by nature, whereon I took my rest after the prayers, still enrich my memory with delight and joy.

Arriving near the city, I made my halt under a fine shady tree, and sat for a while admiring the ancient lofty buildings, raising their heads from the verdant cloaks of the trees. In the afternoon, I entered the town, and searched for the house of my late father's relative, and was glad enough to find it. I called at the door, and a female slave asked who I was. I told her I was the son of the late Molví Mohamed Akram, who was first married in this house. The effect of this message was soon shown by the entry of an elderly man of very respectable appearance, whose countenance betokened his scientific mind. When the lock of silence was removed from his worthy tongue, he minutely examined me regarding my step-sisters and the names of my ancestors, which he seemed to compare with a piece of paper in his hand; and finding my tale to be a genuine one, he embraced me heartily, and took me into the house, where I was surrounded by an assembly of the fair sex, and was introduced to the old lady, my step-grandmother, who kindly took charge of me at once. I was obliged to repeat my history to every new friend that visited me, and I contrived to abbreviate it to a few sentences to save trouble.

I must acknowledge I am infinitely obliged to this noble family, and most heartily thank them for their hospitable protection and kindness to a stranger, as I was to them, for the principal cause of my relationship with them was removed by the demise of my step-mother. The old gentleman, being master of a school, kindly took charge of my education: my punctuality, perseverance, and love of knowledge, soon rendered me his favourite scholar. On Friday I was left to myself to select any amusement I liked; but instead of going to play, I went out to see the ancient gardens and edifices in company with my friends.

The ancient city of Agra is handsomely situated

on the south-west side of the famous river Jamná, one of the three sacred streams with the Hindús, *i.e.*, Gangá, Jamná, and Saraswatí, supposed to run under ground. The confluence of these rivers at Prág, or Allahábád, is called Tribeyní (that is, three braids of hair), and is considered by them to be a place of great sanctity, and ablution therein is said to wash away all the sins of the performer; whereas, bathing in the river Jamná here, frees him from one-third of the sins at least. Agra assumed the title of Akbar-ábád from the time of the great Emperor Akbar, who much enlarged it, and made it his capital. The houses of this city are in general lofty, consisting of several stories; but the streets are very narrow and complicated, not unlike to those of Grand Cairo, except one that leads to the Mathura gate from the fort. A great part of the town in those days was in ruins. About five miles to the north, at Sikandra, is the mausoleum of the wise Emperor Akbar—may his memory be blessed! Should the reader feel inclined to know the history of this great king, I beg to refer him to the "Akbar-Námah," or the "Annals of Akbar," by his learned and able minister, Abulfazl, where he will find in detail the account of his wisdom and benevolence, and his incomparable political energies, etc., from the time of his youth. When he was only thirteen years of age, he took the reigns of the great and vast empire of India in hand, and held them unshaken up to his sixty-third year, when he left the kingdom of this world for the next and a better one, where he must be in the eternal enjoyment of the blessings of palaces and húrís.

Agra is renowned as the birthplace of the celebrated minister, Abulfazl, and his brother, the learned Faizí. To the latter, the world is indebted for a translation of several famous Sanskrit works, such as the Gítá Mahábhárat, and Rámáyana, etc.; and to the former for his energetic political administration of the affairs of India, and for the composition and production of the law institutes, such as the Ayíní-Akbarí, etc.

I beg to draw my reader's attention, in this place, to the wonderful character of the Emperor Akbar, whose reign of fifty-one years was, and ever will be, considered a blessing to India. Had his successors been half as wise as himself, it would not have been the fate of the country to be under the rule of foreigners. The enormous weight of the kingdom was placed on his shoulders when he was a boy of thirteen years. It must be borne in mind that to sway the vast continent of India is not an easy thing for a boy of that age, when, in this peaceful time, three able statesmen of the enlightened land of England, aided by members of council, find it an irksome and difficult task to govern. Whereas, in the beginning of his government, he found the whole country in a state of confusion; but the young ruler, as the historian says, being endowed with the following three accomplishments by nature, viz., courage, benevolence, and foresight, he proved to be an incomparable warrior, reverenced monarch, and a pre-eminent statesman, and consequently managed affairs in such a way as to procure all his subjects' and friends' love for him: and he is loaded with praises, not only by all Asiatic historians, but by Europeans too, and, lastly, with all the eternal showers of mercy from his Creator.

The fort of the city is strongly built of red stone, such as is taken out of the Gwálior quarries; the depth of its ditch is considerable, the ramparts double, with bastions situated at equal distances from one another.

Amongst the famous edifices of Hindústán is Mumtáz Mahall, here vulgarly called Táj Mahall. It is a most remarkable work by Indian artists, built of pure marble, decorated with Mosaics. Its materials are uncommonly rich, its design chaste, and its effect most brilliant, attended by solemnity. In beauty, it surpasses all the edifices of India, and in solemnity, those of the whole of Asia.

The founder of this wondrous building was Shah Jahán the Great, who erected it for his favourite queen, Mumtáz Mahall Begam, who was an able woman, and, also, queen of the beauties of her time: it is her mausoleum.

The number of inhabitants in Agra at this time, I was informed was about eighty thousand. The district was surrendered to the English army, under Lord Lake, in 1803, by Daulat Ráo Sindhiah.

I lived here under the protection of this noble family for a period of five years, until the beginning of 1817. My education being considered complete in that school, I was left to myself. The old gentleman then sent a message to me through a friend that my acquirements under him had already qualified me for a man of business, and that he had some interest with the British functionaries, whose Government, a few years since, had been established there, which he would be glad to use in my behalf if I liked; also, he would be happy to get me married, too, amongst some of his relatives.

In reply to this kind message, I returned my most sincere thanks to my noble protector, adding that I should never, during my life, forget his kindness towards me, and that, although at that time it was beyond my power to do him any service in return for the protection I had received, yet I hoped I should be able some day to serve him, if it pleased the Almighty God. As to the marriage and employment, I pleaded inability to accept such offers, being desirous of seeing my mother at Ujjain once more by the first opportunity.

CHAPTER IV.

My service with Hindú Ráo's physician—I visit Delhi—Return to Gwálior—The cobra's bite cured—Once more at Ujjain—Filial love stronger than the astrologer's threats—Sir T. Hislop's army—Battle of Mehidpur—I weary of Ujjain—My luckless rencontre with Musá the Afghan—Strange wanderings in the jungle—The secret unveiled—Nádir, chief of the Bheels—Am promoted to be thieves' secretary—A Bheel banquet and strange horrors—My flight—The old Sheik once more—My mother's death.

In the month of February, 1817, Hakím Rahmatullah Beg Khán, physician to Hindú Ráo, the brother-in-law of his Highness Daulat Ráo Sindhiah, came to Agra on his way to Delhi on business. Having had the honour of knowing this good old gentleman previously at Gwálior, I called on him, and was received very warmly. I begged, if I could be of any use to him, to be allowed to accompany him in his present travels. He kindly took me in his service as superintendent of his medicines and his household, on a small salary.

Favoured by unexpected success in this object of my desires, I returned home with the good news, and communicated it to my benefactor, who, with all the members of the family, were excessively sorry to part with me, after being domesticated with them for a period of about five years. On the day of our departure, the ten gold mohrs, with a few rupees that I had in my possession, I placed at the feet of my benevolent instructor, and begged him to oblige me by the acceptance of such a trifle. He granted this request with some reluctance, to my great satisfaction, and then he called on the physician in person, and spoke to them a great deal about me and in my favour; and, giving my hand into his, he bade us *khudá háfiz*, "God preserve thee," and a good journey.

Early on Thursday morning we took our leave of our friends, and bade farewell to the city of Agra. It must be well known to those who have visited that part of the country, that travelling from Agra to Delhi, is no more than walking in gardens for pleasure; and we completed this interesting journey in a week. On the morning of the eighth day, the very splendid view of Delhi, the ancient capital of rájás and emperors, presented itself to our eyes. The first look of this grand city reminds the reflecting traveller that this was the central seat of empire in India, whence orders and prohibitions were issued and executed throughout the whole of the provinces; that this was the place, the sight of which filled the mind of many princes of high rank with terror and awe; that the heads of many delinquent nobles and princes used to be hung at the gates in retribution for their misconduct, while others passed through in triumph.

On our entering the city gates, some few clerks

and peons of the English Government, to our great annoyance, searched our luggage and examined us, questioning us very minutely respecting our intention and cause of coming to the city, which being directly replied to, we were left to ourselves. The physician took his temporary abode with a nobleman, a descendant of Nawázish Khán, residing at Chándní Chauk in a grand mansion, furnished with everything requisite for the luxury and vanity of man. Here, after the fatigue of the journey, we lived very comfortably for seventeen days, during which period I had very little to do. In the morning only I had a few prescriptions, written by the doctor, to enter in the book, and sometimes gave some medicines as he directed to some of the patients from the chest in my charge; and then, after breakfast, having all the day at my own disposal, I passed it delightfully in walking through the city and its environs

The ancient city of Delhi, entitled Indraprastha in the mythological annals of the Hindús, lies in mounds of ruins, to the south of the modern town. Several marks of the ancient palaces and mansions, etc., are still in existence; and some few of them, such as the old gates of the town, mosques and mausolems of the Emperor Humáyun, etc., the fort of Sher Sháh and other small citadels, stand unshaken up to this time. Their form and structure seem wonderfully strong, even at this time. The first Mohamedan invader of India was Sultán Mahmúd of Ghizní, who took the capital about the end of the the year 1110, A. D. But, according to his political liberality, he restored it to the Rájá, and replaced him on the throne as a tributary to himself.

The modern town was peopled by the Emperor Sháh Jahán, in about 1631 A.D., on the western bank of the river Jamná, and he entitled it Sháh Jahán-ábád, bestowing his own name upon it. The population at the time of my visit was estimated to be about two hundred thousand inhabitants. The city seemed to be in a ruinous condition, having suffered much during the Marátha wars. The city walls, with numerous bastions, and seven gates, are built with red-stone. There are many edifices here worthy of notice, some in good condition, others falling to decay. Of the former class are the college of Ghásiuddin Khán, situated near the Ajmeer gate, the palaces of Alí Mardán Khán, Kamru'ddín Khán, and Kudsya Begum, the mother of Mohamed Sháh, and many mosques. But the loftiest of all, and most elegant, is the Jám'i Masjid, or great Mohamedan cathedral, built of the red-stone lined with pure marble, and situated in the middle of the city. This venerable place of worship was begun by the Emperor Sháh Jahán in the fourth year of his reign, and completed in the eleventh.

The people are generally polite and well-behaved, and the climate seems healthy. After about three weeks' sojourn in Delhi, my employer ordered preparations for his return to Gwálior, which being made in a short time, we left the old metropolis of India, and in about another week reached our destination in safety, with the exception of one accident to a peon of ours. It happened so, that on the fourth day of our march, as we halted under a tree by the side of a small village to take our breakfast, this poor Hindú, feeling thirsty, was the first person to descend into the well (near which we had halted) with his pot of water. After having gone down a few steps he was bitten by a large black snake, that was lying under the stepping-stone of the same colour. As soon as the man saw his mortal enemy, and felt the pain of his bite, he took his pistol from his girdle and fired at it. The sudden report of the firearm instantly brought us to the well, and what did we see but the man engaged in separating a piece of flesh from his heel with his sword, and the noxious animal writhing about two yards from him with a hole in his hood that the pistol ball had made. We carried up the poor man, who fainted from the loss of blood; but our master, the kind physician, immediately ordering a large knife to be made red-hot, cauterized his foot below the ankle, and having washed the wound he put a quantity of common salt upon it. I believe the smarting of the salt roused him from his deadly swoon, and he asked for water; but the doctor gave him a copious draught of English brandy instead of water, which soon brought him down to sleep.

In the meantime a multitude of the people of the village were collected near the well. They thanked us for the destruction of the monster, which they said had put an end to the lives of two men and one woman of their village during that year. The snake, being brought out and measured, was found something more than two yards long; and its stomach being opened, a frog and a sparrow were found in it. Of the former there was only a small part remaining, but the latter was nearly whole. The poor peon, being tied on a camel, was carried during the remainder of the journey, and recovered from his severe illness after about six weeks, when His Excellency Hindú Ráo (the brother-in-law of His Highness the Mahárájah), in whose service our noble physician was, hearing of the man's courage, promoted him from his peonship to the cavalry, on the salary of a rupee per day, and dresses, etc.

Upon our arrival in the camp, the old Súbahdár, my late protector, or rather oppressor, called on the physician, and begged of me to forget and forgive what had passed between us; and remonstrated with the doctor, asking him to allow me to come with him. The doctor said he had no objection in case it was my wish to go. He then turned towards me to hear my consent. I remarked, "I had already forgiven what had taken place, and would also forget it if I could; I would wait upon him with pleasure when I had time, but would never leave the service of the doctor to stay with him, or on any other account than my finding a caravan proceeding to Ujjain; then would I beg my dismissal to repair to see my parent." This determination of mine silenced the Súbahdár, and he went home.

I stayed with the doctor about six months, during which period, being constantly engaged in medical occupation, I began to take much interest in the profession, and learnt something of that most useful science. The practice of this doctor was very simple and easy: he seldom had recourse to medicines, but generally prescribed change of diet. His employer, Hindú Ráo, had great confidence in him, though his salary was only five hundred rupees a month; but the presents he received amounted to more than double that sum. I recollect an instance of his practice. Once His Excellency Hindú Ráo went out hunting for two or three days, to a distance of about thirty miles from the camp, where he was seized with constant and severe hiccup. He had two medical men with him, who tried their best to remove this troublesome malady from His Excellency, but to no purpose. One of them wanted to take some blood from the arm, but this was objected to by the patient himself. His Excellency, not being able to suffer any more pain, returned to the camp immediately, and then my master, being ordered to attend, prescribed merely a few small pieces of sugar-cane, sprinkled with rose-water, to be chewed and smoked. This being done, the patient was instantly relieved, and our doctor, before leaving the palace, was well rewarded. His Excellency took from his own neck a necklace of large pearls, and presented it to him, with a pair of very handsome shawls.

Whenever I had leisure I visited the Súbahdár, and sometimes dined with him, and found him always civil. In August, Khande Ráo, the nobleman in whose company we came to Gwálior, obtained leave to proceed to Ujjain to visit his family, and the Súbahdár managed to be ordered to attend him until his return. On the day of their departure I obtained my dismissal from the service of the doctor, who was unwilling to grant it, observing that if I stayed with him for four or five years, he would make a good doctor of me, and then I should become an independent gentleman, or master of myself. But, anxiety to see my parent blinded the sight of my reason, and my prejudiced ear would not listen to his wholesome advice. He paid my arrears, and very liberally added a sum of money and dresses to them as a reward; so I found myself again master of upwards of a hundred rupees.

About the middle of August we left the camp, and proceeded on our journey by long marches. We started about seven o'clock every morning, and marched till four in the evening. Our travel was not so pleasant, on account of the rainy season.

Every river and stream detained us for hours, and sometimes for a day and night. On our halting near Bundí the rains began to fall in torrents, and continued all night, and the next day never ceased even for a second. At night the waters, breaking through the trenches of the tents, rose more than two feet above the level of the ground, and caused our beds and pillows to float. Our horses and camels stood trembling, and ourselves were in no better condition than the poor animals; besides, the pain of hunger crowned our misfortune, and we were obliged to halt here for five days.

At the end of the first week in September we at last reached our destination in safety, and glad was I to see Ujjain again, after an absence of more than six years. Khande Ráo, as also the Súbahdár, would not enter the city for a week more, it being unlucky, according to the astrological calculations. As for myself, I was so anxious to see my mother that no astrology could possibly keep me a moment longer in the camp, and, previous to the prohibition being proclaimed there that nobody should enter the city until next week, I was in the house of my parent, with the tears of joy running over my face. I was glad to see her in a state of perfect health, and her son, too, a fine healthy boy. I was more surprised to see her house filled with all sorts of furniture, drapery of several kinds, valuable spices, and copper vessels, etc. Finding these articles beyond the income of the Súbahdár, I asked my mother whence they came? To this she gave me an evasive reply; but, not being satisfied with her answer, I made further inquiries about it, and found out, from other members of the family, that all the riches were plundered property, unlawfully obtained by the brother of the Súbahdár's former wife, who all the time during our absence, acted agreeably to his orders as a freebooter, and used to go on his diabolical excursions with his horses and camels, and bring these articles home.

I lived with my dear parent for a period of three months, and a few days, very quietly. About the middle of December a force of about ten thousand of the English army, headed by Sir Thomas Hislop, arrived there, and halted at the other bank of the river Sípra. My whole attention was taken up by their excellent uniforms, their cannons in beautiful order, and all their warlike materials. Every day, after morning prayer, I went to the camp to see their extraordinary manœuvres, exercise, and processions, on parade. I contracted friendship with a white soldier, who was very civil to me in his manner, but he could not speak my language. We expressed our thoughts to each other by signs and a few words of bad Hindústání that he knew. He took me to his tent and seated me by him, and all his friends received me with kindness, and asked me to drink some of the forbidden liquor, which they seemed to enjoy. I declined the offer, and took a piece of bread and milk to please them. This was the first time I heard the English language spoken, and I felt an irresistible desire to learn it. In this society, of only three or four days' duration, I learnt thirty-seven words, which I wrote down in the Persian character; the list still remains with me in bundle of my notes.

One morning as I repaired to the camp, to my great surprise, I found it gone. The site, being crowded with crows and kites, appeared horrible, but there were a few camp-followers left behind, and they too appeared to be in great confusion, engaged in pulling down their tents, and loading their provisions, etc., on the back of a poor camel, that seemed to have been overworked, as its lamentable cries denoted. From these people I learnt that the army had proceeded to Mehidpur, where they expected to have a battle with Holkar's forces. Hearing this I returned home in despair, considering myself very unlucky, not being capable of participating in such affairs.

Híra Khán, the Governor of Ujjain, and almost all the chiefs, got ready to plunder the English baggage, the owners of which they considered would get a good beating and be defeated. Also parties of the mercenary vagabonds, who had nothing to lose, but everything to gain—and who sojourned in the city, in expectation of such an opportunity of executing their evil designs—appeared in singular excitement. My old Súbahdár and his former wife's brother, a notorious robber, seemed particularly so, anticipating a disaster to the English. There would have been a host of about ten thousand armed men to destroy the foreigners had they lost the battle; but all these hopes were frustrated by news of a contrary nature, which appeared to them incredible at first, considering the strength of Holkar. Little did they know that Nuwáb Abdulghafúr Khán played the part of a traitor to his master, and deserted the field of battle with the force under his command, just at the moment when the English were on the point of losing the battle through the loyal and gallant exertions of Roshan Beg, the Captain General of Holkar's artillery. The stain of this disgrace clung too firmly to the name of Abdulghafúr, as long as he lived, to be effaced by his great liberality towards the poor and others: and his son Ghází Mohamed Khán is not unreproached by the natives of India for his late father's misbehaviour, though he enjoys the district of Jaora, assigned to the family through the favour of the British authorities in India.

I stayed with my good parent in the city until the end of December, 1817, and then began to feel very dull, being tired of a monotonous life. Besides, I did not like to eat the Súbahdár's bread so unlawfully obtained, and I found my mind in a state of excitement, hearing the news of wars in the Dakhan, and the overthrow of Bají Ráo, the last representative of the family of the Peshwá, whose vanity and short-sighted policy had lately rendered him odious to two formidable castes, his benefactors, viz., Mohamedans and English, forgetting that through the aid of the former he was put on the throne, and through that of the latter, he retained it. He incurred the dislike of the Mohamedans by prohibiting them from appearing in his sight till ten o'clock in the morning every day, in order that his eyes might not be defiled by seeing them.

Moreover, he issued a proclamation prohibiting all Muslims of whatever rank or station from even passing through those streets which were overlooked by his palace. The wise and powerful Christians, although they were treated alike, yet cared not about his folly in such matters, but were greatly incensed at his vacillation and disregard of their advice.

In the beginning of January, in the year 1818, hearing talk of the war in the Dakhan, I burned to proceed thither, thinking I should find there a ladder to ascend to the terrace of distinction. Infatuated with this idea, I wandered about in the city in search of a caravan or any kind of a companion through whom to accomplish my design. One day as I rambled about I saw some twenty stranger Afgháns, and a Jamadár, apparently a well-behaved man of good temper, who was lodging in the shop of a Banian.

As I passed by, I saluted them according to the established custom of the Mohamedans, founded upon the tradition of the prophet. The Jamadár Músá Khán (such was his name, as I found out afterwards,) kindly returned my salutation, and asked me to sit and smoke with him, to which I agreed with pleasure; and, to my great satisfaction, I found from the conversation, that he was on his return to Púnah, whence he had obtained a few months' leave to visit his family at Rámpur. I inquired as to the time when he intended leaving the city; "for," said, I "I was also thinking of proceeding to the Dakhan, where I might get employment." The Jamadár replied, he was to leave the place next morning after prayer, and would take me into his service if I liked, on a salary of ten rupees per month, and that I should eat and drink with him free of charges; he would also furnish me with clothes, and I should keep the accounts of his twenty-five Patháns, and might leave him when I got a better situation: but I must make up my mind and be quick. I readily assented to the above terms, and promised to be with him the next morning as early as possible with my luggage. "No luggage," replied he, "as we have none, except our small carpets and arms; but, if you have any, recollect that you will have to carry it on your own shoulders." Thinking I might easily put up with such an inconvenience for a short journey, I told him I should be as light as possible, and perhaps lighter than his men.

I returned home delighted, and packing up all my things in a box, gave it in charge to my mother, retaining the key in my own possession. I kept my intention a profound secret, knowing that, if divulged to anybody, my going would surely be stopped. My future prospects having filled my brain, I was so busy all night in building castles in the air that I could not sleep for a moment; not having the least idea that I was precipitating myself headlong into an abyss of misfortune worse than death; but the lines of fate prescribed by the mighty hand of the Supreme Being are entirely unintelligible to the eye of our limited reason. Who can tell what is to become of him to-morrow? Hearing, at last, the first crow of the cock, I got up, and, performing my ablution, said my prayers; and putting my small carpet on my shoulder, and pen, ink, and paper into my girdle, I repaired to my new friends, whom I found preparing to start. They unanimously received me with an acclamation of joy. "This is the first day of your employment with a gallant party of real men," said Músá, "may your days be prosperous: you are very welcome us." He then asked me if I had said my prayers, and if so to sit near the bonfire and look over the arms, etc., until their return. On my taking charge of their things, all of them repaired to the nearest Mosque, and performed their devotions; and then, returning to me, they rehearsed their salutation, as it is the duty of Muslims to salute each other after prayers, and when they come near one who is seated. They then accoutred themselves in a few minutes, and unanimously repeated the following prayer, to be said by all Muslim travellers and warriors at the moment of their starting on an expedition:—*Nasrum minalláh, fathun karíb wabashshiril mominín, Fallâhu khairun háfiza wahuwa urahmánu'r ráhimín,* viz., "Assistance from God, and a speedy victory, and do thou bear good tidings to the true believers. God is the best guardian, and He is the most merciful of those that shew mercy" (chap. lxii., ver. 12, Alkur'án). Having done this we started off, and were out of the gate of the city by the sunrise.

We went south-west from the town, and leaving the city of Indúr on the left, we proceeded by long marches from morning till evening every day, avoiding to put up at any of the large towns that were in the way, for reasons unknown to me. We halted at small villages at nights, and, purchasing our provisions, dressed them by turns. We took our dinner at about eight o'clock in the evening, all sitting together; and then one loaf and a little quantity of onions, or coarse sugar, was given to each man to take care of for his breakfast the next morning. My time passed very pleasantly in the society of my new friends, and Músá Khán particularly seemed always very anxious about my comfort. On the evening of the sixth day of our departure from Ujjain, we halted at a small Bheel village, situated at the foot of the enormous chain of mountains in this part of the world, extending east and west along the valley of the Narbadda River, which on the other side forms a natural boundary between the two extensive provinces of Málwah and Khandesh. On inquiring the reason for our coming to this dreary and difficult part of the mountain, instead of going through the celebrated pass of Jámghát, I was informed that this pass, named Jámanya, though very difficult, having only a footpath, was preferred by Músá Khán as being the shortest road to Mandaleshwar, where the Narbadda is always fordable.

The next morning, about two o'clock A.M., we set off and entered the mountain. Our progress was very difficult—"dark before, and dangerous voices behind;" but, at the same time, it was very fast. Músá Khán, and the other Afgháns, seemed to be as well acquainted with the giddy ascents, dangerous precipices, and fearful ravines of the mountains, as a citizen with the winding streets and narrow lanes of his own native town. At daybreak we halted near a clear fountain, and, performing our ablutions, said our prayers. The cold this morning was so intense that our teeth involuntarily chattered. The Afgháns seemed indifferent to it; but, for my part, I felt my extremities benumbed and my whole body chilled. After prayers, however, Músá ordered a bonfire to be made and pipes to be filled. We obeyed the order with alacrity, and in a moment pieces of fire-wood, of which there was no deficiency, were collected into a large heap; and one of the Afgháns, taking the *chakmak* (steel and flint) from his girdle, struck fire and soon kindled a flame, to our inexpressible comfort. In the meantime, the great planet rising from the eastern horizon rendering us independent of the fire by his rays, we took our breakfast, and soon concluded it with another smoke. Thus, being well refreshed, we set off again at a more rapid pace than the night before. The road was very difficult and complicated: the footpath that we followed often became traceless. Sometimes we penetrated through the thick forest, and at others we caught hold of the roots of trees and corners of rocks to sling ourselves over a precipice or craggy peak.

Thus we went on till about five o'clock in the evening, when all the Afgháns joyfully exclaimed, "There is the end of our journey; thanks to God! we have at last reached our destination." Seeing no trace of habitation, or the expected ferry of the Narbadda, I felt greatly surprised, and asked Músá where we were? In reply, he pointed out to me a wide valley, thickly covered with trees and dotted with huts, situated at the distance of about a musket shot from one another. "There," said he, "that is the place I was so anxious to reach, and there is to be my home for one year, and then I shall return to my native country." He added, that in the same valley resided his lord and master, the chief of the

Bheels, by name Nádir, who always had about five hundred of his tribe ready at his command; and they, with the party of Afgháns I had joined, plundered caravans and travellers, and infested the passes and roads of that moutain. The booty was brought to Nádir and divided into three shares, two of which were taken by the Bheel chief, and the remainder by the Afgháns. After telling me this, Músá consoled me by observing that I had nothing to do with their excursions, and might stay at home and take care of their baggage, etc., during their absence, and that their accounts would not engage my time more than half-an-hour every month.

I was actually horrified at this unexpected address, and my vexation was so great that it nearly burst forth in angry words, when, no doubt, I should have been murdered on the spot; but, on reflection, I perceived the necessity of having recourse to a hypocritical policy, and, with a feigned smile, I inquired, "Are we not, then, to go to Púnah, after all?"—"No, never," rejoined he; "what is the use of going there when we can acquire here the object of our desire?"—"Well," replied I, "as I am joined to you by the decree of fate, I will try and make myself useful in your service for the fixed time of one year, and then I shall see if fortune casts her favourable eye upon me." At the end of this confabulation we arrived very near the den of our host, and three muskets were fired from our party as a sign of our arrival. The report echoed and re-echoed in the valley, and was followed by the wild cries of the Bheels in reply, and in a few minutes we were surrounded by a host of them, naked, save a narrow strip of cotton round the middle, but armed with bows and arrows. Their bows were made of a strong piece of bamboo string, with a thin slip of the same material, and the arrows were not unlike those used in sport by more civilized nations. One of them, advancing furiously forward, cast his red fiery eyes upon us, and addressed the party in a wild, threatening tone, as follows:—"Who are ye that voluntarily rush into the jaws of death?"—"Dost thou not know me, Kaliya?" cried Músá. The Bheel recognised the voice of the Jamadár, and advanced towards us, shouting at the same time to the others, *Re Músá re apno Músá rip nahín*, *i. e.*, "It is our own Músá, and no enemy." Upon this all of us were intermixed with the native robbers; and old Kaliya's friendly talking with Músá Khan demonstrated their former intimate acquaintance with each other. As the evening began to set in we reached a cave, at the mouth of which we beheld a black well-made man squatting on a four-legged frame interwoven with fibres of wild creepers. He was also naked as the others; but a pair of thick golden bracelets on his wrists, and a sword placed before him, in addition to the usual bow and arrows, and a chafing dish with live fire at a little distance, encircled with several squatting Bheels, clearly showed that he was the chief of the banditti. Músá, looking at him, saluted and said, "There is Nádir Bháí, the good prince of the wilderness; make your respects to him and go home; I will be with you after a little while." So all of us raised our hands to our foreheads to the Bheel, who got up from his seat, returned our saláms, and desired Músá to approach, which he did, and sat near him on the ground, leaning against one of the feet of the rude throne. Our party now walked to the place of our future stay, which they knew too well to require a guide. It was only about half a mile off; but abhorrence, disappointment, and despondency having expelled all my eagerness and ambition, I felt going over this little distance equal to a fatiguing journey of a hundred miles. At length we arrived at a place near the side of a hill, which, like a natural wall, formed the back of our dwelling. Adjoining this hill was a spacious shed built of trunks of trees, and the three sides walled with strong bamboos, leaving a large space in the middle of the front side to serve as a door. There were two compartments, and about thirty rooms in each, partitioned off with split bamboos. This last march had much fatigued the Afgháns too; so, immediately on our arrival there, all of them hung their matchlocks to the walls of the hall, and each taking possession of a room for himself, flung himself down on a rude frame, the only furniture there. I followed the example of my friends, and, stretching myself out, attempted to close my eyes in sleep, and thereby relieve my exhausted limbs. But, instead of sleeping, I began to reflect, "Why did I accompany this murderous gang without inquiry? I might have waited another month with my kind parent and looked for a better convoy. It is my want of experience, nay, my folly, that always pushes me into the abyss of misfortune. It is true, Músá acted treacherously towards me; but an outlaw considers treachery a joke. Why did I allow myself to be imposed upon? Being nearly eighteen years of age, I ought to have judged for myself." Feeling utterly helpless (as is natural with man), I betook myself to the last and unfailing resource. I lifted my eyes and hands towards heaven, and prayed thus: "O Almighty and glorious God, how long wilt thou keep me in calamities? Am I doomed to be dishonoured, and destined to live with murderers, robbers, and outlaws? O Lord of earth and heaven! am I born to be a disgrace to the name of my ancestors? If so, my most gracious Lord, I beseech thee to put an end to my being in this world. Amen." As I repeated this, the tears flowed over my cheeks incessantly, and then an opposing train of thoughts made their appearance in the mirror of my brain to exonerate me from blame. I began to reflect as follows: "I do not deserve these severe accusations, for I must submit to the decrees of my fate in the same way as man, wise or fool, whether endowed with the philosophy of Plato or the stupidity of Khozíb, whether with the crown of royalty on his head or the wallet of misery over his shoulder; I knew not the character of the former Súbahdár, nor that of Jum'a the Thug, nor was I acquainted with that of the present Jamadár. My outward senses clearly showed that they were men; and if they turn out inhuman, I am not to blame."

In the meantime, about eight o'clock, P.M., Músá came home. He called to us, and the whole party ran to him immediately, when, to our great delight, we saw several Bheels along with him, carrying pots of water, milk, sugar, and wheaten cakes, more than our appetite demanded. These articles of indispensable necessity at this moment were considered a great blessing: Músá was loaded with thanks from all sides. We then performed our ablutions, and said our evening and night prayers at once. Due justice was then done to the meal, and everybody retired to repose, except two sentinels, one of them posted in the hall, and the other upon a lofty tree. Being well tired by the hard labour of the day, all of us were soon asleep; for my part, I think I was more soundly dormant than the others. In the morning I did not get up from my deep sleep until I was shaken by the shoulders.

I soon felt the necessity of putting up with all my troubles and torture of mind without murmuring, and began to familiarize myself with the place and its original residents. I often sat alone under trees in meditation, and sometimes conversed with the Afgháns, friends of mine and foes of the public, or rather bitter enemies of mine too, having imposed on me with success. The system of robbery and rapine was, meantime, constantly carried on under the guidance of the notorious Nádir, the Bheel chief, whose detestable followers not only infested all the passes of the mountain, but very frequently attacked the neighbouring villages and towns. When one of their own party happened to be disabled by wounds from keeping up with them, they immediately cut off his head, which they buried or burnt to avoid being recognised, and to prevent the secret being divulged, as the individual, being tortured, might confess, and bring on a general misfortune.

Our arrival caused a great acceleration to the current of black deeds systematically perpetrated under the diabolical superintendence of the black chief. Twice or three times a month a detachment of about fifteen of the Afgháns used to be ordered to go on an expedition with a band of the native robbers, and if they found no travellers in the passes, etc., worthy of attack, the Afgháns generally proceeded to the civilized part of the neighbouring country, stationing the Bheels in ambuscades, where they awaited the return of the former, with travellers decoyed by them and persuaded to engage their escort to the fatal spot. A signal from them then drew the Bheels to the point, and a false conflict taking place between the banditti and the Afgháns, the latter were of course defeated and driven to a distance; and the poor travellers were then stripped of everything in their possession, even to the clothes they wore. A piece of rag about one foot broad and three feet long was generously given to every plundered individual to cover himself, and he was sent away. Any mark of resistance on the part of the poor travellers was sure to bring upon them severe blows or cuts, or even loss of life. Such were the horrid scenes, the accounts of which were brought and faithfully related to me by my comrades, to my secret disgust. Thanks to heaven I was never an eye-witness to these horrible affairs; but the descriptions were quite sufficient to inflict wounds upon wounds on a heart unaccustomed to cruelty. On the fourth return of our party, three heads of our own people were brought back with the booty; two of them belonged to the Bheels, and the third was that of a young Afghán named Dárá Khán. These three individuals were so badly wounded in their legs by the defending escort of an attacked caravan, that they were unable to walk; so, severing their heads from their bodies was considered expedient by their friends. We interred the head of poor Dárá according to our usual mode, and he was never thought of any more.

My annoyance, indignation, and horror were indescribable; but my safety depending upon my feelings being kept concealed, I still hypocritically preserved a smiling countenance with my companions. I got up early, at about four o'clock every morning, and proceeded to a solitary fountain, where I made my ablutions and performed my prayers. I returned home after sun-rise, took my breakfast with Músá and others, conversed with them for an hour or so, and then, with a pellet-bow, a kind present to me from an old Bheel, I repaired to the jungle, where I passed my time either in shooting small birds, or sitting in solitude lamenting my deplorable condition. Very nearly four months—as tedious as four years—passed in this state, and I thought eight more must be completed before the tree of my hope could bear the fruit of release.

The eighth expedition of our detachment was so lucky, and so abundantly lucriferous, that every Afghán of the party returned loaded with gold and silver, coin and jewels. The division of this booty took place during the next night, and the Jamadár and all his party became at once in possession of large sums. Two pair of silver anklets, one golden bangle, and thirty rupees in ready cash, altogether amounting to the value of about four hundred rupees, fell to my lot in the distribution. I thanked the Jamadár for this unexpected boon, and buried my riches in my room, unperceived by all. The charm and beauty of the gold tried to allure my thoughts in vain, for the possession of this plundered property could not afford me that genial pleasure which one feels in well-earned and lawful gains.

The Afgháns having obtained their object, were now anxious to take their leave of the Bheel chief for a few months to visit their home; and Músá, waiting upon him for the purpose, the request was readily granted. The chief told Músá that as he and his party were to leave him for six months, he would not allow them to depart without giving them a grand feast in about three days. Saying this, he ordered his people to make the necessary preparations for the appointed day. Músá returned to his followers, and mentioned to them the result of his visit, which delighted them to a high degree; and I must say these tidings, as they involved my liberty, rendered me happiest of all. Opium and henbane, both plain and in confection, and sweetmeats in plenty, and fat sheep, were sent to our quarters to feast us. The Afgháns, considering themselves relieved from active duties, had recourse to the nourishing and intoxicating articles, and thereby made themselves as happy as possible. They sat up till late at night to look at the wild dances of the Bheels, and to hear their songs. Thus my friends were deluded, or blinded, by the order of the chief, for three days and nights, and on the fourth day they expected to have the grand feast which had been promised them.

On the morning of the feast I got up from my sleep earlier than usual, and repaired to my frequented fountain; and, after performing the unavoidable duties of a good Muslim, I sat down and began to think upon the happy subject of my return to the civilized world, and freedom from the society of freebooters and thieves. Strange to say, such thoughts, instead of delighting my heart, rendered it more heavy; I knew not why, but the dawning of the hoped-for morning, instead of cheering the heart, seemed to be clouded with gloom. I took little notice of these ominous forebodings, and at daybreak began my return to the shed. As I neared the place, and came within sound of the voice, my senses were terrified with yells and screams, attended with the slashing noise of cutting instruments, as if a butcher's hatchet descended upon an animal's flesh and bones. Then came cries of distress, ending in groans. Here reason, again making its timely appearance, stopped me to think over the matter. "It may be the sheep are being butchered for our feast," said I to myself; "but what then can be the cause of these dreadful squealings?" Whilst engaged in this soliloquy, my feet were naturally forced backward instead of forward; and suddenly, to my great terror and dismay, what did I behold but an Afghán running away, with his head bleeding, and his dress covered with gore! Running up to him, "What is the matter, Ibrahím Khán?" inquired I. To this he replied, "We are undone; all the Afgháns are assassinated by the Bheels. I have lost these three fingers in parrying a cut aimed at my head. My wound is not a bad one; but, feigning death, I have escaped. Don't follow me—I may be overtaken—run as fast as thou canst to save thy life."—"Adieu, Ibrahím," said I; "may God protect thee!"

Saying this, I ran with the speed of a swift horse for more than two hours in a northern direction, without looking back, making hair-breadth escapes over the precipices, rugged heights, and deep valleys. Sometimes I climbed where I saw the clouds under me spread like an ocean; at others I went down as if to the lowest region. Three hours' run, however, rendered me quite exhausted; and not being able to move on any more, I dropped down under a tree to refresh myself. Hunger and thirst advanced their demands to be satisfied; I knew not where I was. The slightest shake of the dry leaves of the forest by the wind or an animal was sufficient to scare me; I trembled at the thought of being overtaken and murdered by the assassins. Recovering myself in about half an hour, I resumed my journey, but was unable to perform it with the first speed. I went, however, on through the wilderness of the mountain and the thick forest till sunset, making several halts to regain strength whenever I found myself unable to walk through fatigue. Often I gathered a quantity of wild figs and berries, with which I tried to satisfy the cravings of hunger; but they could not well answer the purpose. Fright, I suppose, having deranged my stomach, it could retain nothing. The pellet-bow and tinder-box fortunately remained with me; with the former I tried several shots at small birds, but without success.

The dusk of evening now came on, to my great satisfaction. "The darkness of night," thought I, "will be a good motherly veil to protect me." But the danger of being torn to pieces by some ravenous beast, and loneliness, were sad companions. There was no sign of habitation anywhere to be seen. I travelled all day without meeting a footstep, or even a footmark, and knew not where I was. "Where is a bed for me to repose upon? where friends? Is there no one to aid me in this solitary condition? Can I think of being so fortunate as ever again to reach civilized society?" Involved in these thoughts I stood gazing about on the side of a ravine. Hope did not forsake me even in this condition; but my fears were far stronger. Horror of either being murdered, or becoming a prey to wild animals, haunted my brain; and, to avoid these evils, I climbed up a large high tree, and rested myself upon a branch of it in deep contemplation. A dead silence reigned, only disturbed now and then by the howlings of the wild creatures of the place. When my eyes turned up, they were fascinated by the clear azure sky, ornamented with innumerable brilliant stars, the wonderful works of the omnipotent Creator: these common phenomena filled my unscientific mind with awe. In the meantime the beautiful orb of the moon began its welcome rise from the eastern direction like a mountain of pure gold. A flood of brilliance quickly extended over the surrounding mountains, and the objects therein situated. The scenes around me began to assume a different form. Steep sides of mountains with hillocks and uneven plains in their front, covered with verdant trees, represented palaces and grand mansions, with handsome gardens before them. These deluding phantoms in the clear moonlight, and the refreshing breezes, impregnated with the delicately-sweet scent of flowers and the shrubs of the forest, had such a tranquillizing effect that I was immediately transported to the region of sleep; and the active mental and corporeal powers being at once suspended, I walked in my dreams in these fantastical gardens amongst Húris and nymphs, when a sudden dash, severely felt by my back and head, soon restored me to my senses.

> "He dreams of riches, grandeur, and a crown;
> He wakes and finds himself a simple clown."—ROWE.

Thus I was made conscious who and where I was. I found myself lying under the tree, for a moment unable to move; but I soon recovered. Luckily, my tree was situated in a sandy part of the place;

so the shock was, although a great one, in no way injurious. I re-climbed the tree, and then fastening myself to the bough with my turban, I slept as fast as a horse merchant after the disposal of his horses.

The reader here will observe the superior advantages of the graceful Asiatic garb over the patchful light pieces of dresses of the Europeans, which can only be used for the one particular purpose of covering the body closely. On the other hand, our convenient long coat may be gracefully put on to command respect; and the same will serve as a bed if we chance to have no other. Our *dopatta*, the waistband, is a zone on respectable occasions; it is a sheet to cover one at night, if required, or may be erected as a small tent to protect one from the burning sun. The turban is the most useful part of the Asiatic attire, far superior to the European hat in every respect: it is a handsome ornament to the human head, and repulses the severity of the sun; the hat, on the contrary, attracts it. The turban is the best means to save the life of a thirsty traveller in the deserts and jungles, where there is no water to be had except in deep wells. In such a crisis, the precious liquid can be drawn by the aid of the turban with great ease. A silken turban's softness guards the head from the cut of a sharp sabre better than a helmet; it can serve the purposes of bandages for wounds on important occasions, when surgical aid is wanting and not at hand; and many other advantages can be derived from it, which, if described, would take up time and space unaffordable here.

The most beautiful chirping of the morning birds awoke me from sleep, when I felt myself much refreshed; but I found the joints of my limbs stiff and reluctant to move. Coming down, however, from my elevated place of sleep, I performed the usual duties of a good Mohamedan to his Creator, by the side of an elegant spring of water near to my tree of rest, and then I resumed my march in the northern direction. Although I had not now the elasticity of the day before, yet I had scarce walked half a mile when the stiffness left me, and the spark of vigour kindled the flame of power anew in my veins. Reader, I should tire you with the difficulties of my progress, without a road or path, or even a spot appearing ever to be trodden on by a human being, the sight of which would then have given me inexpressible delight; but you will understand me if I say that my egress was a hundred times more difficult than the ingress already described to you.

To shorten the account of my misery, I travelled on four days, guided by the sun only, and for four nights I slept upon trees, tying myself with my turban to the boughs. My food for this period was wild figs and berries; I shot only three sparrows and one parrot during the whole time, and, I must confess, they were very palatable. The last-mentioned bird, although forbidden by our law, the compulsion of hunger would not allow me to spare. On the morning of the fifth day, from the summit of a hill, I had the happiness to discern, at a distance of more than a mile, several poor Bheel women and men with bundles of firewood on their heads, which clearly denoted that they must go to some habitable part to sell them. I ran towards them with all possible speed, and overtook this half-starved party about nine o'clock A.M., whilst they sat by a well to refresh themselves. The ungovernable love of man for his fellow-creatures felt when alone in a wilderness, involuntarily attracted me to these children of Adam, forgetting that these were of the race inimical to the civilized; and, although they were in a miserable condition, yet their number was sufficient to put an end to my existence if they liked, for a snake, though lean, is still as poisonous as ever. But having already arrived near them, it was now too late to hesitate. "Inquiries as to where and how far was a village," thought I, "might induce them to take me for a wandering dupe, and thus being placed at their mercy, they will surely injure me to any extent they choose." So, shaking off all timidity, I was obliged to put on a grave appearance, and I sternly inquired the price of their bundles. Each of them, mentioning a very trifling sum, asked me if I would buy them on the spot or at Hásilpur? The name of the village of poor old Shaikh Nasrulláh, noticed in the first chapter, revived me as if from death. I spoke to them with an affected firmness, to command their respect, and said that a party of my friends I had left behind would require some firewood, and I would buy when I got to the village, if they went with me.

Upon this, the party started with me; and, after marching for about three miles, ascending and descending several hills, I had the happiness of descrying the environs of the village. I shall never forget the inexpressible joy I felt at that moment. I ran to the village, leaving my humble escort far behind; and it was about eleven o'clock in the morning when I reached the cottage of the old Shaikh, whom I found sitting at breakfast with the members of his family; a large trough, filled with the coarse flour of the Indian corn boiled in water, being in the middle, and a cup of sour milk before each of the assembly. The old Shaikh recognised me from a distance, and ran and embraced me with great warmth and pleasure. I attempted to offer my humble thanks to him, and to inquire after his and his family's health, but the power of articulation was lost. The old man then told me that he had heard of my return from Gwálior, and of my subsequent disappearance. "Tell me, where have you been, young man?" said he. But, instead of a reply from the mouth, he had it from my eyes. He was astonished to see the torrent of tears which burst forth at his question. He tried to offer consolation, and inquired again if I had been maltreated by anybody. "Tell me, my friend, what is the matter?" he asked, but in vain. I made no answer, and my tears flowed incessantly. The old Shaikh then ordered a goblet of cold water to be brought, with which he made me wash my face, hands, and feet; and, by this simple remedy, I found myself quite recovered from my hysterical fit.

After this, mutual compliments and inquiries having taken place, I was requested to partake of food with them. Hunger lent charms to the trough of plain and sorry gruel and sour milk, and I joined them with eagerness, and devoured a very large quantity of it. I also mentioned to the old Shaikh my miserable circumstances, which, moving his sympathy, caused him to shed tears of pity and compassion over my misfortunes. The enormous quantity of food I had eaten, a feeling of safety, and the sense of excessive pleasure at my escape, soon brought on drowsiness. The old Shaikh, perceiving this, showed me a room to take my rest, where I slept very soundly for about eighteen hours—being the remaining six hours of the day and the whole of the night. Early next morning, the old Shaikh aroused me from deep sleep, and after prayers we entered into a long conversation. He gave me news that made me uneasy; it was about my stepfather at Gwálior, the Súbahdár—that he had resigned the service of Sindhiah, and had engaged himself, along with his brother-in-law (his late wife's brother) and a few horsemen, in the service of Holkar, at Indúr, to which city he had removed with his family. Shortly after his arrival at Indúr, there ensued a quarrel between him and his brother-in-law, and excitement on both sides rising higher and higher, words were changed into blows, and blows into sword cuts. The latter, being a young and smart swordsman, inflicted several fatal cuts with his sharp scimitar upon the former, and disabled him from any further movement. Seeing that he had finished his adversary, he next made a desperate attempt to escape, in which he wounded several persons that happened to be near; but the noise of the scuffle having attracted a multitude of people to the spot, many pursued him and shot him dead. The Súbahdár also died of his wounds the next day, and the Government seized all the property, under pretence that they died criminals—having disturbed the peace and taken the law into their own hands.

This sad news brought another cloud over my head. I felt sorry for the Súbahdár, but I felt extreme distress for my mother. What had become of her I knew not. My stay with Shaikh Nasrulláh was, in consequence, of only three days' duration.

On the fourth I left him against his will, and proceeded to Indúr. I reached the city in two days, where fortunately I soon found out the place of my dearest mother's residence, who was the sole object of my love. Our mutual happiness at meeting is beyond my power to describe. She told me all the particulars of the fatal quarrel, and the unlawful steps taken by the Government in pillaging the house and property afterwards. My own chest that I had left with her, containing my things and the small sum of money lawfully earned, escaped the ransackers, its shabby appearance attracting no attention. Inquiring earnestly after my mother's health, which did not appear to me good, I received a sad answer, which, on a sudden, like a Tátar's arrow, pierced my breast. She simply said she had a low fever attended with slight cough and diarrhœa, for which she cared but little; but she felt her vital powers gradually sinking. Knowing the nature of her seemingly mild, but fatal, indisposition, my alarm was great. I kept, however, my self-possession in her presence; and, affecting indifference, I told her that she would recover very soon, if it pleased Almighty God, as the distemper was not serious. At the same time I recommended change of air, saying it would prove beneficial to her, particularly if she returned to her native town, and saw her dear mother, brother, and other members of the family. To this she willingly agreed, and taking a bracelet off her arm, asked me to sell it for the expenses of the journey. But I objected, telling her that I had some money in my chest for such and other expenses, and that, thank God! we had not been driven to such extremities as to think of disposing of a part of the few jewels that remained to her untouched by the plunderers, who dared not infringe the rule of respect towards ladies of rank, on such occasions of injustice perpetrated under Government orders.

I hastened to the market-place and made all the preparations in a short time. On the next day, early in the morning, we left Indúr, and, by the blessing of Heaven, reached our native town on the third day without any accident. When we entered our humble abode, we were received by all the members with very sincere joy; and surprise and astonishment at our unexpected arrival seemed to prevail everywhere in the family. It was a day of real happiness to all except myself: the anticipation of our impending evil day did not allow me to participate in their pleasureable feelings. I informed my uncle, in secret, of the mortal disease of his sister; but the paleness of her complexion, slow cough, and depression of spirits, having already told him the same fatal tale, his grief and despair were great. At the same time he comforted me, observing that I should exhibit no sign of grief to the patient or anybody else, and rather seem pleased and satisfied in my conversation with her, for such were the rules of treatment in such maladies; and that I must not suffer myself to be overcome with despair, for life and death are the mysterious secrets solely in the omnipotent hand of Providence; and that it is unwise to fear death on the two days, *i. e.*, the day that is doomed and the day that is not doomed for our death, because, in the former as well as in the latter case, fear must be folly.

We observed the above rule very strictly, and used all the remedies in our power; but to no purpose. The disease made progress every day, and the sufferer's strength changed into utter weakness, and in about twenty days she was reduced to a mere skeleton. Perceiving, at last, that her days were nearly finished, she gave me her last injunctions as follows: "My son, be virtuous, and guide yourself by your reason and conscience in the world Take care of that orphan boy of mine, who is only in his sixth year, and has no one else to look to; treat him with brotherly affection, and may God be your protector wherever you are: as for me, I am now perfectly sure of being obliged to return to the same region whence I was obliged to come." Saying this, she fell into a deep swoon, and I could no more restrain the flood of tears that was every now and then ready to flow for the impending eternal parting. All the bystanders, my grandmother, uncle, and others, melted into tears and followed my example in the tragical scene. Thus we continued for about half an hour, when, to our great joy, she returned to her senses and called for water; and then she began to appear more composed and firm in reason, as she comforted us and particularly enjoined us not to grieve. The next day she appeared to be quite recovered, and, to our extreme happiness, we saw her walking a little, assisted by a staff. But, alas! this sudden recovery could but retard the fatal result: it was something like a sudden blaze emitted by a lamp when about to go out. So on the following day she became worse than before; and, in the afternoon of Friday, the 24th of April, whilst her head rested on my bosom, her pure and sacred soul took flight to the blissful region of eternity. May the blessing of the merciful God shower upon her for ever and ever. Amen.

CHAPTER V.

My mother's funeral—A friend obtains me the postmastership at Dharampur—My sojourn there—Sudden dismissal—The night march—The tiger's spring—Sir John Malcolm—No refusing a great man—I become Munshí to the Bheel agent—I am transferred to Lieut. Hart—The expedition to Nagar Parkar—A Marátha horseman's impudence—Decision of the Native Magistrate—Egyptian version of the story of Shylock.

I BEING the only person now to be consulted as to the funeral ceremonies, I directed them to be performed, poor as I was, in a dignified style, and defrayed the charges liberally. My funds were, however, nearly exhausted, as I had to bear all the expenses of the obsequies, of the alms to the poor, and of entertaining relations and friends, who paid their visits from far and near to condole with the family. I disposed of the few jewels left by my mother, but even then there was not enough to defray all the charges. I began to think of some pretence of deserting the town, where my further stay seemed likely to be both disagreeable and hurtful to my reputation; for the creditors, of whom I had borrowed small sums, already began to importune me for repayment.

A friend of mine, named Munshí Najaf Alí Khán, a very respectable gentleman from the upper provinces, at this time resided at Dharampur, as native agent of the British Government. I frequently visited him, and was treated with much kindness, as I was useful to him in supplying information. Finding an opportunity, I imparted to him my distressful circumstances with tearful eyes, which moved this honourable man with compassion; and he not only prevented my fall into the abyss of impending ruin by his generous aid, but used his exertions to promote my interests, in getting me employed as a district post clerk in the Honourable Company's service, upon a small salary of fifteen rupees per mensem. On the 18th of May I received the order, bearing Sir John Malcolm's seal and signature, from the head-quarters at Mhow, purporting that I was taken into the service of the Honourable Company, and that, if I proved a loyal and faithful servant, my rise would be certain. At the same time I was instructed to proceed to the village of Dharampur with seven harkáras (or runners) under my command, and, stationing myself there, to act as postmaster and despatch all packages from the Sindúa Pass to Mandleshwar, and *vice versâ.* With the Mandleshwar post I was ordered to write a letter containing all the news of the place, and daily transmit it to the address of Mr. Bell at Mhow. Having received my instructions, I made preparations for the journey, and proceeded forthwith to the station with my harkáras. I reached my destination on the 22nd, in three days, and put up in a large Hindú temple with my small party. I was the first British officer that ever had been stationed there, and was respected by all the people in consequence. The governor of the place at this time, on the part of the Dhár Government, was a Bráhman by caste, and by name Nathú Bhái. He was a man about fifty, of black complexion, thin, and an opium eater, very tyrannical to the people of the village, and of very peevish and disreputable character, his deeds well corresponding with his outward form. In appearance, he treated me with great respect, furnished me gratis with all the necessaries of life; but, inwardly, he hated my presence in the town, seeing that I exercised my authority, and his subjects were more submissive to me than to him. Nathú Bhái, of course, was obliged to put up with this, bitter as it was to him. It being quite clear that his master's power, in comparison with that of the British, was as an ant to an elephant; and I being a representative of the latter, a handsome young man of the high governing caste, in appearance far superior to his withered person, he allowed matters to take their course.

Dharampur, a large town about twenty years ago, but now reduced to a small village, almost all in ruins, with only a hundred houses, and these inhabited by people in indigent circumstances, became the seat of my government. The people having greatly suffered from the oppression of remorseless governors, similar to Nathú Bhái, and from the depredations of robbers, seemed extremely anxious to have a ruler over them endowed with equity; and, being informed that the justice of the British Government was unparalleled in the world, they were ready to throw themselves under its protection at the first opportunity. Dharampur, though in ruins, as I have already observed, is excellently situated on the right bank of the river Narbadda, lat. 22° 10′ North, long. 75° 26′ East. The sight of the pure limpid water, flowing on the gravelly bed of the river here, is a very charming one. Both banks are adorned with many Hindú temples, built by the cebrated lady Ahilya Báí, who ruled over the extensive possessions of the Holkar Government during the years 1769 to 1795, A.D., with talent, energy, and despotic power. Her moderation, impartial justice, masculine courage, and pious liberality will perpetuate her name for many ages.

The river here abounds with water-fowl of various kinds, and the country, though its forests are not very thick, swarms with game of all sorts, and is infested with ravenous beasts. These animals were dangerously troublesome to the people of our village, whose kine and goats were carried off by them once or twice a month, even from within the enclosures; and my undoored residence, the temple, consequently was a frightful place at night. I strictly ordered my runners to keep the fire alive all night as a safeguard against these nocturnal visitors. Shortly after my arrival, a detachment of the Madras Native Infantry, headed by a very handsome Englishman, arrived and was stationed here, to the highest satisfaction of the people and myself, and to the great annoyance of the governor, Nathú Bháí. The Englishman, hearing all I had to say, left his party under the command of his native Súbahdár, and himself, with a Náik, and three Sipáhís, proceeded to Mhow early next morning. My position and authority now became stronger in the village: the time I passed here was the happiest I recollect. The performance of the Government duties did not occupy me more than half an hour; the rest of the day was my own. During the day I bathed in the pure water of the river, and caught some water-fowl by means of fish-baits, and played at chess at home with the native officers of the detachment; and, at night, I held a regular Darbár in the temple, attended by the head men from the village, and the officers above mentioned, till midnight.

Two months afterwards another Englishman, an engineer officer, named Mr. Dangerfield, arrived with his distance measuring-wheel, etc. He took down the census of the place from my mouth, and put several other questions to me, which, having answered, I retired. This poor man appeared to be very sickly, and his illness seemed to have rendered him harsh and irritable. During my stay with him, a fly having repeatedly settled on his mouth, he did not only curse his attendant, who stood fanning him, but tried to inflict a blow on his face, though without success, the man having parried it well. This excited his master more and more, until the poor fellow was obliged to leave the tent in self-defence, and would not come back, though strictly ordered to do so. At this I could not help smiling; but there appeared no sign of mirth on the face of the master.

I continued here unmolested for a period of about four months. In the beginning of September the post ceased coming to my station, without my being able to account for it; but during the latter end of the same month an order from head-quarters surprised me, like a shot striking a bird, as it announced my dismissal from the service. The translation of it was as follows: "You have conducted your duties to the satisfaction of the sublime government. H. H. the Peshwa having lately been captured, and the country being settled, there is no further need of your services, so you are hereby dismissed. Please render your accounts in your next communication, which send, with the seven footmen under your command, to Mhow. Receive the amount of forty-five rupees from the bearer, your wages for the ensuing month, and two months pay as a reward. Consider these injunctions to be strict, and act upon the same."

This final order I was obliged to carry into effect

immediately on receipt. Again I was in possession of some little money to get on with in the world; but all my hopes of rising in rank, and becoming a person of consequence, were at once frustrated, and the castles built in the air for a period of more than four months suddenly vanished.

The next day I took leave of all my friends of the village, and the native officers and men of the detachment. The nights being moonlight at this time of the month, we started at about six o'clock, in the cool of the evening. A Náik of the detachment, by name Mahiu'ddín Sáhib, accompanied me for about a mile, being an intimate friend of mine, with whom I generally played chess, and he was a man well versed in that art. I had the pleasure of seeing Mahiu'ddín Sáhib again at Surat in 1840, after twenty-two years, in religious garb, with a long flowing white beard. He appeared an entirely different man from what I had seen him. I am sorry to add that his change in life did not improve his circumstances, though he set himself up for a Saiyid.

I left Dharampur, with my seven footmen, and the bearer of the bad news of my dismissal, at about five o'clock for Maheshwar, where I intended to separate myself from these people; whence they might proceed to Mhow, and I with a caravan to my native town. We proceeded on our march, sometimes talking with each other, and sometimes hearing the song of the bringer of the black tidings, who sung very well, and was asked every now and then by the party to oblige them with his excellent music. The darkness of the evening, on account of the cloudy weather, came on with rapidity; and I advised that each man should, alternately, lead the way, with a burning log of wood in his hand to scare off the ravenous beasts, as was usual when charged with the post. Being out of the service, my words were not only disobeyed, but actually had no longer any weight with them. They ridiculed my fears, and said, "Pray come on quietly, if you wish to accompany us; if not, you may return and do as you like." This was the first insult that pierced through my heart, and I never spoke to any of them again.

It was about eleven o'clock at night when the fatigue of the march and the cool of the night rendered my brain heavy, and my feet unwilling to move; but I strolled on still with the people. The moon sometimes extended her calm splendour over us, and sometimes was overshadowed with dark clouds. Suddenly, upon the left side of our road, a crackling was heard among the bushes: all of us were alarmed, and, in an instant, a tiger, rushing out of the jungle, pounced upon the one of the party that was foremost, and carried him off in the twinkling of an eye. The rush of the animal and the crush of the poor victim's bones in his mouth, and his last cry of distress, "*Ho hai!*" involuntarily re-echoed by all of us, was over in three seconds; and then I know not what happened, till I returned to my senses, when I found myself and companions lying down on the ground, as if prepared to be devoured by our enemy, the sovereign of the forest. I find my pen incapable of describing the terror of that dreadful moment. Our limbs stiffened, our power of speech ceased, our hearts beat violently, and only a whisper of the sam "*Ho hai!*" was heard from us. In this state we crept on all-fours for some distance back, and then ran for life with the speed of an Arab horse for about half an hour, and fortunately happened to come to a small village of about fifty huts, into which we rushed, heedless of the barking of the dogs, which roused the inhabitants, who, taking us to be a gang of robbers, hooted and shouted with all their might to drive us away. Not caring for the shouts, we entered the Chaura, or miserable police hut, which had a small fire in front. The poor old police Bheel, who sat by the fire, soon found out, by instinct, that we were no robbers, but robbed, and he pacified the inhabitants by telling them his opinion. Being out of breath, we could not utter a word for some time; but, soon recovering our senses, we found that one of the footmen, named Rámá, was missing, and told our tale to our suspicious hosts. They reproached us for our folly in travelling at night through that dangerous part of the jungle without fire, and said it was no wonder we met with a fatal accident. They brought us then a large pot of sour milk, diluted with water, and a large draught was kindly served out to each. It was taken with great avidity, and thankfully drunk to the good health of our hosts. After this every one of us was attacked with fever, attended with shivering, in which deplorable state we remained till morning, when we proceeded to Maheshwar, about five miles from this, guided and escorted by two Bheels, kindly lent us by the good villagers, and reached the place at about nine o'clock, A.M. Here, leaving the Government footmen to shift for themselves, I put up with the Kází, or judge, a namesake of mine, who was also distantly related to my family.

I passed about a week with the Kází's family, and was hospitably treated during my stay; and then, with a good caravan, I returned home, where I passed some months in peace, but dejected in consequence of my unexpected dismissal from the service. By the blessing of Heaven, at this time, even after liquidating my small debts, I had a sum of money sufficient to allow me and my brother to live for a year or so. It happened that Sir John Malcolm at this time visited the shrine, and made a handsome present in money to us, the sacred attendants of it. He also took a fancy to a large slab of black marble, about two feet and a half square and four inches thick — fixed upon the seat of the pulpit of the mosque—on account of its being completely inscribed with a Hindú legend, in excellent order, in ancient Sanskrit. He asked us to give it to him for a sum of money, which we did, after considering over the question. We knew that it was improper to have one of the relics removed from the place of worship, where it had been placed by the mighty hand of the king, who changed the temple into a mosque. Taking this view of the case, we could not at once comply with the request. On the other hand, we thought it was inexpedient to reject the demand of the great man, whose one word to the Rájá upon the subject might dispossess us of the stone without any remuneration whatever; so we allowed the general's people to take it for him, on the plea that the Pagan inscription must have been fixed in that holy receptacle by mistake, and that the sooner it was removed from the sacred place the better. The stone was taken away, and the place soon repaired by the general's people, who was highly pleased with his acquisition. He called us into his tent, and finding me only (and not my cousin) fit to be conversed with, he approached so near to my person that I found my head reached only to his bosom. He then addressed himself to me, and most amiably talked much, in good Persian, in praise of the stone and our family, etc., which pleased us more than the coins.

I soon began again to look for employment, and, according to the Arabic proverb—" a seeker is a finder," I obtained the object of my desire at last, *i. e.*, got a situation with an English gentleman by name Lieut. B. Mac Mahon, the Bheel agent at Nálcha, as Persian teacher to him. It happened that he, in company with Lieut. C. F. Hart, came to our town on a shooting expedition, and put up at our Mosque near the shrine for two or three days, and spontaneously made an offer of the situation under him, which I accepted without hesitation, and accompanied him to his head-quarters at Nálcha. Lieut. Mac Mahon, now perhaps colonel or higher, was a tall thin young man of great talent and ability, endowed with an excellent gay humour and mirthful temper. His knowledge of the Hindústání language deserved high praise, and his imitations of the Bheels' cries of danger, revenge, and happiness, were perfect. He also spoke their jargon uncommonly well; suffice it to say, that if he had been placed behind a curtain, or had been painted black, with a langotí and a bow and arrows in his hand, he would have been taken, or rather mistaken, for a Bheel.

I lived under the generous protection of this young man for about four months and a half, residing in an ancient palace, when, unfortunately, being taken ill with the jungle fever, he was obliged to proceed to the Presidency for recovery, and thence, I was informed afterwards, to his native land. On his departure from Nálcha, I was made over by him to his friend, the aforesaid Lieut. Hart, to be his instructor in Hindústání; and from this time, up to the year 1835, I regularly held the profession of a teacher of the Persian, Hindústání, Arabic, and Maráthí languages to the new comers from England, from time to time, and place to place, as their duty obliged and caprice induced them to go. Upwards of one hundred pupils studied with me during the above period, and none of my scholars returned unlaureled from the Government examination committees. I have a book of most flattering certificates in my possession, and I may say that I was better off than many by following this profession.

About three months after my being employed with Lieut. C. F. Hart, he was ordered with his detachment of pioneers to proceed with a part of the Málwah Field Force, under the command of Col. Barkly, to Nagar Parkar, for the chastisement of one of the predatory Bilúchí tribes of Khôjas, commonly denominated Khossas. I was obliged to accompany my pupil, and we left the comfortable cantonment at Mhow in the early part of this year for the Parkar districts, the refuge and resort of the marauders. Our force proceeded by slow marches, *viâ* Baroda, where being joined with another detachment, we had to march on to Rádhanpur, whence we had to cross the desert Ran, about forty miles, which surrounds the insulated district of Parkar, a tract of land about forty-four miles long, and ten, twelve, fifteen, and twenty miles broad, environed by the Ran desert and sand-hills. Each of its villages has not more than ten or twelve miserable huts, except Vírawaw, which has about four hundred; and the capital town itself contains about six hundred wretched hovels.

After leaving Mhow, Lieut. Hart rose both in rank and in the estimation of his superiors: he was made Major of Brigade. His treatment of me was brotherly; he ordered his servants to consider me his equal, gave me a separate tent, and appointed one of his best horses for my riding. My duty of teaching him the language recurring only once or twice a month, I felt an earnest wish to do something for him, at least, in return for the salt that I ate and kindness that I experienced; so I took voluntarily upon myself the charge and care of his domestic affairs, and managed them well, not only to his, but to all his friends' satisfaction. In marches, I had his tent erected first of all; and at halts, I caused the pilfering hand of his servants to be paralyzed in robbing him. Such acts of zeal and good will cemented the fabric of our intimacy more strongly and firmly every day for a length of time.

On our arrival at Baroda, a few days' halt was announced in the camp, for the purpose of giving rest to the people, procuring provisions, and preparing large leather bags, to be carried by camels, filled with fresh water, an indispensable supply for the men and beasts of the army required during the impending long marches across the Ran. In the meantime I enjoyed the morning and evening ride in the town. On the morning of the day before we left Baroda, I was greatly teased by a foppish Maráthа horseman during my ride throughout the city. He frequently manœuvred his horse across my way and behind me, in such a manner as to show that he derided me and the noble Arab steed I rode, whose value, I believe, far exceeded that of him and his beautifully caparisoned horse. Sometimes he made menacing gestures towards me with his long spear, as if he was going to pierce me with it through the heart; and sometimes he retired at full speed, and whilst galloping, he threw his handkerchief and picked it up again. I felt excessively excited at these causeless provocations, and, having an excellent pair of pistols in my holsters, I made up my mind to shoot the man dead in case I received a slight touch of his lance. Curious to say, my noble charger seemed cooler and more careless at the transaction than I. I now thought of cantering homeward without taking any notice of the scornful conduct of the man, but no sooner did I begin to do so than the fellow made his appearance again with renewed energy, and, on his turning close in the rear of my horse, his animal having accidentally stumbled, slightly touched the tail of mine, upon which the noble Arab under me kicked the horse at once with all his might, which threw the horse and the rider about three yards off from me, apart from each other. I was greatly astonished at this action of the animal: it appeared as if revenge lay buried in his mind, awaiting only a spark to explode. Immediately after the fall, the horse, leaving his rider to shift for himself, followed an unfortunate rider on a mare, who happened to pass by at the time, through the market-place, with all the ferocity of a low-origined animal, and raised a great disturbance. The poor horseman's sword, in the act of his being separated from the saddle, coming out of the scabbard, slightly grazed his left arm from the elbow to the wrist, from which part an abundant flow of blood took place; and, in consequence, I was accused of being the cause of the injury, and arrested by the police to answer for it. The affected hero, the rider, perhaps never having seen blood in his life, beholding his own wound, turned pale, cried like a woman, and fainted. "Where is your horsemanship?" cried one of the crowd, the expression used in taunting a soldier. "These bragging upstarts," added an old soldier that stood at a little distance, "are only fit to be shown in the city market: like ladies of pleasure, they are no men of courage, but a disgrace."

Thus, leaving the hero in the field of battle, being requested by the police to attend at the magistrate's office, I proceeded thither, and found in the middle of the hall a stout corpulent Bráhman seated upon a silk cushion, leaning against a large pillow, attended by three writers and several peons. On my arrival there, I tied my horse to a pillar of the hall; and myself stood in front of the magistrate and made my salám, which he returned with an air of pride, raising his hand scarcely as high as his chin, instead of his head. I disliked this form of extorting deference and awe to his office; but began to think it was my evil day. He then ordered one of his clerks to take my depositions, and the man commenced wielding his pen as fluently as I did my tongue. No sooner did the court learn who I was and in whose service, than its aspect was changed. The name of Captain Hart, the Brigade Major, electrified the assembly at once, and the magistrate's assumed awfulness instantly changed into the smiles of kindness. He asked me to sit down by him; but I thankfully declined the honour, pleading inability on account of having boots on, as respect prevented my treading upon his carpet. Upon this, a chair being immediately ordered for me, I made a bow and sat upon it. In the meantime, the wounded hero, the rider of the mare—bitten in several places on his back by the vicious horse of the former—and the horse were brought before the court. As soon as my deposition was finished, the rider of the mare, who was a clown from the country, represented his deplorable case to the court; and then the braggadocio, now as quiet as a lamb, stated his in a few words, his whole attention being taken up by the wound, which still kept on exuding blood from the bandage. The court then weighed and considered the subject for a few minutes, and the worthy magistrate pronounced sentence as follows:—"Krishnají Holkar (such was the name of the cowardly horseman) in a period of fourteen months, now for the fifth time being brought before the court, having in the former four instances quarrelled with respectable citizens, was let off by the court on consideration that he would amend his character in future. It appears now that the leniency towards him was *mal à propos.* In this present instance he has insulted an officer of the British Government without any provocation on the part of the latter. It is a very heavy crime and an unpardonable one, for such behaviour of our subjects and servants might produce the displeasure of a powerful government against ours. The Holkar, therefore, shall be dismissed from the service of His Highness the Mahárájah, his property confiscated, and himself transported beyond the river Rewrâ, out of His Highness's dominions; and the British officer, in compensation for the mental injury sustained by him, shall receive the Holkar's sword and apology, and the Patel his horse, to make amends for his corporeal sufferings." A letter, then, containing a summary of the charges and this arbitrary sentence, was dictated by the magistrate, and forwarded to the Bakshí or Generalissimo; and I, having received the sword and the apologies from the man, and compliments from the tribunal, was dismissed, and returned home with the prize in my hand and satisfaction in my heart.

Being absent from home till noon, Captain Hart had become very anxious about me, thinking that I must have met with an accident; and, on my appearance at the tent, he ran out of it bareheaded, shook hands with me with the warmth of a real Englishman, and in the ecstacy of his pleasure, forgetting that I could neither speak nor understand his language, "What made you so late, my dear Lutfullah?" said he to me. Instinct, however, dictating to me his meaning, in reply, I explained to him what had happened, which made him laugh heartily.

The sentence of the despotic magistrate does not seem to be dissimilar to the judgments passed by the ancient Kází Ratalbúk of Egypt, such as the following:—

As civilization began to dawn, in the third century of our blessed Prophet, about the time of Edward II., the martyr king of England, Asiatic fables mention that there was a Cázi (or judge) in the city of Cairo, by name Mansúr Bin Músía.

His affection of humility was so great, that he even made a ridiculous alteration in his name by dividing it into several monosyllables, and substituting words of humbler meaning, of which he compounded a new name. It being Man Súr Bin Mú Sía (*lit.*, Victor, son of Moses), he divided it into the following five syllables:—

Syllables of the original name.	Meaning.	Substitutes.	Meaning.
Man...	Name of a heavy weight consisting of 40 lbs., or two Ratals or pounds in Persia...........	Ratal ...	Pound (lb.)
Súr	A large trumpet	Búk ...	Smallbugle.
Bin	The son	Abd-al .	Slave.
Mú	Hair	Pashm...	Wool.
Sía	Thirty (Persian)	Pánzdah	Fifteen.

So the third column forms his name,—"Ratal Búk Abd-al Pashm Pánzdah," Small-Weight-Penny-Whistle-Slave-of-Wool-Fifteen, instead of Heavy-Weight-Trumpet-Son-of-Hair-Thirty.

During the time of this extraordinary functionary of justice, there lived a military man in poor circumstances, who had a very pretty young wife; also in his neighbourhood resided a wealthy Jew, naturally characterized by habits of extreme usuriousness, unbounded meanness, and greediness. This son of Israel, having more than once clandestinely obtained a full view of the incomparable wife of his poor neighbour, conceived a passion for her, and to this degree that, having lost the command of his heart, he impatiently watched an opportunity to seduce her. He tried every means to accomplish his criminal desire, but invariably failed; for a mind once properly fortified with virtue can never be conquered by vice. The poor veteran, being without employment for a long time, had been so overtaken by indigence, that he and his wife actually starved sometimes for two or three days. The pangs of poverty at last being insufferable, the wife suggested a plan to the husband of bettering themselves, telling him that idling was the source of all miseries; and he must therefore buy a hatchet and ropes, and, repairing daily to the forest, bring a bundle of fire-wood, which certainly would sell for something. On the other hand, she would take to her needle, and thus they would try to make themselves as comfortable as possible in the world.

The man approved of her suggestion; but said he to her, in a submissive tone, "I extol your plan highly, but I find it even difficult to procure the preliminary means to begin. At least a hundred dirhams are needed to purchase some linen and silk for your needle, and a hatchet and rope for me." To this the wife replied that the sum might easily be borrowed, and the Hebrew neighbour would certainly lend it if a prospect of good interest was held out to him. The soldier thought the matter over, but demurred at going to the mean Jew to solicit his aid. "No," said he to himself, "I would rather starve to death than be scornfully looked upon by a faithless Jew." But again he thought he must submit to the dishonour, rather than see his lovely wife on the verge of the grave.

So, with mingled fear and hope, he betook himself to the Jew, to whom he represented his case in his soldier-like sincere but unpolished language. The Hebrew was delighted to think that he had nearly won the game, and that, by sacrificing a piece, he would certainly circumvent the queen. So at first he impressed upon the mind of his customer the importance of money in the world. He then said he was very sorry that he had no money of his own to lend him; at the same time he could not deny having certain small sums in the house, but he dared not touch them for his life, "they being," observed he, "the deposits of other individuals of power and authority."—"Then am I to return disappointed?" asked the veteran.—"I cannot help it," returned the Jew; "I will not stake my life and property for others; so pray be gone, and never trouble me again with such affairs. Don't be angry," added he, "but suppose I lend you from the deposit which I am obliged to produce to the depositor for his satisfaction after two months from this day, and suppose I cannot do so, do you think my head will remain on my shoulders?"—"But it will not be in any way jeoparded," rejoined the veteran, "if I promise to pay you back in seven weeks."—"But how can I believe you?" quoth the Jew; "what security can you afford?"—"As for security, I can offer you none," replied the poor man: "but I can assure you that I shall be punctual, and I can attach my signature to any penal bond you may be pleased to draw out."—"Very well," said the Jew; "then in that case, will you engage, as a matter of mere form, of course, to give a pound of your flesh from your body in case you fail to fulfil your promise?"—"With all my heart," rejoined the poor man, considering that he and his wife would work night and day, and would certainly be able to liquidate the debt before the time prescribed. Upon this understanding the bond was formally written out, attested, signed, and delivered, and the money paid to the poor man. On the other hand, the Jew was happy in thinking over the matter: "The bait," said he to himself, "is swallowed, and I must have patience for seven weeks, when the game will be won. On further consideration, he bethought himself that, in the case of the man's being able to produce the amount at the time promised, which appeared to him more than improbable, he would manage to steal a part of the good coins and mix up some counterfeit ones in their place; and thus he might easily render him unable to pay his debt, and, besides, might accuse him of cheating. So, the horror of such criminal charges being brought to the notice of the court of justice, and the impossibility of his submitting to be maimed, would certainly cause the tree of his hope to be fruitful of success.

As for the poor veteran, he, on the receipt of the sum of money, purchased the materials of industry for his consort and himself; he also bought some provisions and necessaries of life for the time being, and both of them set to work to release themselves from the torturing chains of poverty. They strained every nerve in working to make up the amount within the given time; but, so far from it, they could not even save half the money required. When the time was finished, the Jew made his unwelcome appearance, seated himself at the door of the poor man, and, in most violent terms, demanded payment. The poor veteran entreated very humbly, soliciting forgiveness, and telling him he was very sorry that all his labours to make up the sum were fruitless, and begged him to accept very nearly half the amount in ready cash, and to grant him more time for the remainder; if not, he might take the money and the materials, by selling which he might get something more than he demanded. These supplications, instead of doing good, provoked the Jew's indignation, and he angrily shouted, "Frivolous excuses will not do with me; the time agreed upon has expired, so be brief; remember the penalty written down by yourself, therefore produce the money or prepare to stand the consequences." Upon this, the argumentation on both sides, being carried on for some time, terminated in a regular scuffle, and the Jew, getting the better of the poor man, caught hold of his collar and dragged him towards the court of justice; but the poor man, releasing himself somehow or other from his grasp, took to flight and the Jew followed him. In swiftly crossing the first street, he came on a sudden in contact with a pregnant woman, who, being knocked down, unfortunately miscarried; and a relative of hers, seeing this breach of manners, followed to apprehend him. A little further, a horseman standing in his way, he struck the horse to clear the road, and the blow unluckily put out one of the horse's eyes. This enraged the horseman, who likewise accompanied the two pursuers to catch the man and hold him responsible for the loss. The poor man, by his quick turns and swiftness, got out of the city, leaving his followers some distance behind; and, seeing a stone quarry in front, he determined to leap into it and hide himself. With this resolve, exclaiming "*Bismillah*, "In the name of God!" down he jumped. Now, where he leaped there was a shed, under which an old man was lying; and, as he precipitated himself down upon the shed, its weak rafters gave way, and he, coming down upon the old man, not only killed him, but sprained his leg and hurt himself so much that he could move no farther until his pursuers, joined by the old man's son, whom he had accidentally killed, came up and seized him. They beat him soundly, and, tying his hands behind him, dragged him to the Court of the Kází Ratalbúk. As the culprit reached the Kází's gate, he beheld some shops wherein forbidden liquors were publicly sold, and an old reverend gentleman with a long white beard staggering about, shamefully intoxicated. Presently there passed a living man tied in a bier, and carried to the graveyard to be buried alive, his lamentable shrieks being utterly disregarded by the remorseless bearers. The sight of these horrid scenes enacted at the Kází's gate, and evidently by his decree, filled the poor soldier with terrible forebodings.

He was soon, however, dragged into the Court, and trembled at sight of the Kází, whom he positively looked upon as a deputy of the angel of death. In the middle of the hall was a cushion backed with a large pillow, upon which squatted a diminutive fat person with a very small head and long black beard. He held a rosary in his hand, and kept moving his head in token of assent and dissent to the assertions of the persons about him; and a few peons stood here and there in respectful postures, with instruments of torture in their hands. The new parties being conducted to the edge of the carpet, were struck with awe, and stood trembling. The charges made by the Jew, the relative of the pregnant woman, the owner of the horse, and the son of the old man, were then taken down by the clerks. As for the soldier, he told his unvarnished tale, adding, at the same time, that he had been very severely maltreated by his adversaries subsequent to his apprehension.

The matter then was thoroughly discussed by the lawyers in presence of the Kází, who listened with profound gravity to the arguments on both sides, and ultimately pronounced sentence as follows:—"Let a sharp knife, a pair of scales and weights, be brought forward, and let the peons seize and hold fast the soldier. Jew, there is a knife; cut off the man's flesh, who has only himself to blame for having so foolishly signed the bond." The Jew gladly took the knife in his hand, thinking that he would have the merit of inflicting a mortal wound upon an enemy of his faith, whose wife would then fall an easy prey. Just as he was going to lay his hand upon the poor man, the Kází called out, "Hearken to me before you use the knife; the pound must be exactly one pound of flesh, without any skin or bone, etc., and you must sever it from his body in one cut, no additional torture to the man by plurality of cuts having been agreed upon in the bond. You must, therefore, neither exceed nor come short of one pound; if you do, you must abide by the law of retribution according to the sacred Kur'án." The Jew, hearing all this, clearly saw the impossibility of the act being performed without endangering himself, and offered to give up his claim. Upon this, the Kází imposed a fine of five pieces of silver on him for his unreasonable prosecution, and dismissed him.

The Kází next maturely weighed and considered the case of the pregnant woman, and gave his decision as follows:—"Let the woman be made over to the defendant, who must first employ a good physician to cure her, and, after her recovery, must keep her with him in his own house until she is in the family-way, and then she must honourably be restored to her former husband." The plaintiff, shocked at this sentence, begged to give up his suit if such were justice. But the Kází observed, he should not be permitted to do this unless he paid a fine of ten pieces of silver to the Court for having taken up its time.

The horseman next being summoned, urged his claim, stating that only a short time ago he had, by a very cheap bargain, purchased his noble horse for two hundred pieces of gold; and it had been seriously damaged by the loss of its eye, "So that the whole price," represented he, "should be paid me, when the soldier may take the animal, or compensate me for the blemish by paying a moiety of its value"

Upon this his lordship duly considered the case, and decreed as follows:—"Let a pair of sawyers be sent for to divide the horse longitudinally, from the middle point of his head to the end of his tail; and, when this is done, the uninjured part shall be retained by the complainant, and the part with the injured eye be given to the defendant, who must pay one hundred pieces of gold, being one-half the price to the plaintiff as compensation for the damage." The owner of the horse, seeing that the loss of his animal would be greater than the compensation, begged to withdraw his claim, which was granted to him with some difficulty, on his agreeing to pay a fine of twenty pieces of silver to the Court.

Lastly, the son of the poor old man appeared, throwing dust over his head for the unnatural death of his venerable father, the cause of which he swore was the rascally veteran's fall upon him, and, therefore, in justice, he would have him impaled for the crime.

His lordship coolly heard all his excited statements, and what was said on the part of the prosecution, and on that of the defence, and, weighing everything in the scales of his judgment, pronounced the following sentence:—"Let the offender be dragged to the same shedding under which, with hands and feet tied, let him be placed at the identical spot where the old man was killed, and then let his son jump down upon him from the brink of the quarry in revenge for his father's death." Hereupon the young man, foreseeing the danger of the undertaking, refused to execute the orders, offering to relinquish his claim, and attribute his father's death to an accident; but his lordship replied that he would not allow the precepts of the law to be disregarded, or the claim to be abandoned, unless he paid a fine of forty pieces of silver to the Court, for his folly in making an unbecoming charge. The young man then paid the fine and went off, considering himself lucky in getting out of the scrape.

The hour of noon prayers by this time having

arrived, the Court was cleared, and the Kází, having compassion upon the veteran, bestowed on him a handsome present, and inquired if he was satisfied with the proceedings of the Court. The poor man, in reply, praised the Kází's justice, and said, "God bless you, my lord; I am entirely satisfied, and my acknowledgments to your lordship during the remainder of my life shall be unceasing."

Having said this, he began to leave his lordship's presence with some hesitation, which being observed by the judge, he asked him if he had anything to say; and the veteran answered he had something to represent, but it being beyond the bounds of respect, he would not do so unless permission were granted. "You should not be backward," observed his lordship, "in satisfying yourself about the law; for if you leave the Court in suspense respecting any verdict, it may cause others to be misled, and the mischief may become too serious to be remedied." The veteran then humbly stated that he could not reconcile with his lordship's fair justice the forbidden liquor being openly sold at the gate of the Court, where he found a venerable man drunk, nor the fact of a living man being carried to the grave. "I am glad," returned the Kází, "that you have asked me these questions, as my answers to them will quiet your conscience. Pray hearken unto me with attention. The liquors privately sold are adulterated with poisonous substances by the sellers to strengthen their effects, and have consequently proved injurious to purchasers who require strong drink as medicine, or as a narcotic after mental labour. Drinking is a crime certainly punishable by our blessed law; but the same law strictly observes, 'Forbidden things are lawful in cases of necessity;' so that by this toleration I have abolished a heinous crime, and have appointed a venerable man, of unquestionable honesty, to test the spirits that are brought here for sale; and the tasting, which is his lawful duty, may have disguised him a little. As to the person carried alive to the grave, that has been legally ordered by me, because six years ago his wife had been married to another man according to the decree of the law, two witnesses of a very respectable character having certified his death at Bagdad. The man, however, came before the Court this morning, pleading that he was not dead, and advancing a claim to recover his wife. I ordered the two witnesses to re-appear, and they proved beyond doubt, by other evidences, that they had attended his funeral at Bagdad, where he was buried in their presence. From this circumstance it is easy to conclude that the man cannot be a real one, but the ghost of the former, and must therefore be laid to put an end to all future disputes respecting the woman." The veteran upon this, dissembling his misgivings, praised the Kázi's justice and retired.

CHAPTER VI.

The Ran desert—Colonel Miles—Charles the Twelfth's music somewhat too close—Thoughts of Makka—Captain Bagnold—Mandaví —Philosophic meditations and dogmatism disturbed—Study English at Khaira—Infanticide—The pirates of Dwárka—The Fort taken—Wanderings in the hills of Kattiwar—The Aghori—Gogo—Súrat—The Pársí cemetery.

To return to my own adventures; on the next morning of my triumph over the Marátha, we marched from Baroda towards Nagar Parkar *viâ* Ahmadábád, Karrí, Sammí, Rádhanpur, and Suígám. Our marches were slow, about ten miles a day on an average. From Suígám in our first long nightly march we crossed to Narrah, a desolate spot in the midst of the Ran where we arrived at about eight o'clock, A.M., and thence on the following day we crossed to Vírawaw in another longer and more fatiguing march. All of us were so much knocked up with the fatigue, that a small party of the insurgents might have exterminated our whole force had they had courage enough to attack us at the time. The difficulties and hardships suffered by the force during the last two marches were very severe from the want of fresh water, although a good supply of it had been carried along with us upon camels, bullocks, and ponies; but soon after our arrival at Narrah, it was nearly out, and we were obliged to make use of the water of that place, brackish as it was, for the animals, and partly for ourselves too. This salt water, though drinkable, produced looseness of the bowels to many. The mere want rendered our thirst more craving, as the salt water appeared to be nearly out, on account of our free use of it; and, I am sure, if the army had prolonged its halt for ten or twelve hours more, the whole of the water of the island would have been absorbed by us. The sufferings of the Bráhman sipáhís of the regiments, whose caste prohibited them from touching water from the leather bags, was greater, for the kettles provided for them by Government held much less than what they required in two days. The good management of the officers and economy on the part of the people, were, however, the means of our safe arrival at that side of the salt desert.

The view of the Ran, *i. e.*, the salt morass, is not an unpleasant one, perhaps, because it is a curiosity not frequently met with by travellers. The Ran is a vast pathless plain, bright and level. As far as sight can reach nothing is seen but a white sheet, canopied by the sky, and bounded only by the horizon. There is no sign of vegetable or animal to interrupt the view for miles and miles. Small objects, such as dwarf bushes, are magnified by the mirage into beautiful gardens and lofty trees reaching the clouds, until you go near them, when you are undeceived. A herd of zebras, that passed by us with uncommon swiftness, assumed the appearance of gigantic horses, something like elephants flying in the air, at the distance of about three or four miles. When further off, they appeared like a hill fort suspended between heaven and earth, which, gradually diminishing in size, at last disappeared.

On the morning after our arrival at Vírawaw, I walked out of the camp in the suburbs of the town in search of something new, where I was surprised to see a European gentleman, who had already anticipated me. I found him engaged with a large slab of stone bearing Arabic inscriptions, belonging to a dilapidated mosque. As he copied it in silence without reading it aloud, I took him to be a superficial transcriber, who could not decipher the character and understand the peculiar turns in the phraseology of that difficult language. Upon this, taking out my pencil, I copied the inscriptions for myself in about five minutes, leaving him far behind in his arduous task, and then, in comparing it with the original, I read it aloud: but, finding my European friend following me very close in my reading, I purposely read out a part wrong to mislead him; but he checked and corrected me in a very able manner, which convinced me that he was a man of letters and of superior abilities. I bowed to him, and we talked with each other in Persian upon the subject of the history of Guzerat for a little while, and then, being mutually made acquainted with each other's name and address, we parted on promise of meeting again. He was Colonel Miles, the Resident at Pálanpur, and I had no opportunity of seeing him again until the middle of the year 1844, when I had the pleasure of seeing him in London at his own house. I knew him well, but he knew me not.

It was about thirty miles distance from this to Nagar Parkar, which we passed over in four slow marches. No opposition impeded our course during this short journey. One evening, however, intelligence being secretly brought to our brigadier that a band of the rebels had encamped at about forty miles distance from our camp, with the intention of surprising us, he immediately marched with a select party of his cavalry to turn their design against themselves. The next morning he overtook them by surprise, and, having killed and wounded some of them, the rest took to their heels unpursued, leaving their baggage for their vanquishers to take possession of. The next day our brigadier returned to the camp victorious. But, to our great dismay, we were afterwards informed that the party attacked were friends; they were agents on the part of the Sindh Government, deputed to co-operate with us, either in conciliating or reducing the insurgents to our submission; and thus we returned our thanks to them for their favour. It was a serious mistake on our part, and, in fact, arose through the villanous misrepresentations of a certain designing party.

During our journey from Vírawaw, some antiquarians from amongst the officers found an ample means for the exercise of their talent. Idols of fine marble and of different size, the images of the Buddhist gods, were found underground in the country, and were carefully exhumed and carried off.

On our arrival at Nagar Parkar, as the tents were going to be pitched at a little distance from the town, and a column of the regimental lines was passing by its side in proper order, the insurgents began to fire their matchlocks at us, thinking probably that they would rout the force by wounding and killing a few of us, and then attack the baggage and enrich themselves by plundering it. Our column, on being fired at, coolly turned in the direction of the enemy instead of its tents, and drove them out of the town immediately. Taking shelter in the mountain, near which the town is situated, they continued firing upon us from behind the rocks and trees in places inaccessible to us, until about three o'clock, P.M., without doing much harm. Several bullets startled me as they passed whistling and whizzing by my head. At about four o'clock in the evening the rebels vanished in the mountains and valleys, which were quite impracticable to us and familiar to themselves.

In this skirmish Captain Hart was nearly losing his life, though not from the enemy. He had taken a sipáhí's musket, and was firing at the Khójas, when, in his eagerness, he advanced too near the edge of a precipice, over which he fell, but was saved by the sipáhí, whose musket he had borrowed, and who caught him by the neck as he was falling. He rewarded the man with a liberality beyond his and my expectation, so much so that he was released from the servitude of a soldier's life at last, and able to return to his own village in the upper provinces, with an ample provision to subsist on for the rest of his life. Two years before, when he left his village to enlist, he was no more than a young rustic; but the momentary display of valour raised the star of his fortune at once, and rendered him a great man amongst his fellow villagers.

After this trifling affair our force set out on its return, and proceeded to Bhuj *viâ* Lodrání. In recrossing the Ran we encountered difficulties somewhat similar to our former hardships; but the sense of getting out of such a diabolical wilderness with laurels, rendered the labour of travelling hardly perceptible. We soon had the pleasure of entering the province of Kach, and marched on to Bhuj, the capital of the province, *viâ* Anjár, one of its principal towns, the hill fort of which appeared to have sustained a very severe injury from an earthquake, which occurred on Wednesday, 16th of June, 1819. On our arrival at Bhuj, Capt. Hart, owing to a severe attack of fever, remained in the British Residency, and the force marched on to Khaira, a small village between Bhuj and Mandaví, where it cantoned and was joined by several regiments of infantry and cavalry, and a detachment of artillery, etc., under the command of the Hon. Col. L. Stanhope, assembled to intimidate the Sindh Government.

Capt. Hart's illness was a severe one, and continued for about three weeks, during which I remained constantly at his bed, attending him like a brother. On his recovery, I found his temper very peevish, and instead of being thankful to me, he seemed to think what I had done for him was a part of my duty, so we parted from each other not in a friendly way. On leaving his service, I felt much disgusted with the world, and formed the intention of proceeding to Makka by a ship then ready at Mandaví to sail to the Arabian coast. I made preparations for the voyage, and expressed my determination to my friends, Munshí Abba Miyán, of Anjár, and Mohamed Saiyid Khán, a nobleman of Rámpur, whom accident had brought to this distant land; but both of these gentlemen disapproved of my plan, finding my stock of money too small for the trip. Abba Miyán observed that he would not for the world dissuade me from my good intention, but he would recommend my taking employment for some time until I should have gained sufficient money for the pilgrimage, and then I might execute my design.

I followed the wholesome advice of my kind friends, and the Munshí was good enough to take me to the camp at Khaira from Bhuj; and, through his favour, I was appointed teacher of Hindústání to Lieut. H. Spencer, of the 6th Regiment, N. I., and engaged to copy the history of Bombay in Persian for Capt. Bagnold, of the same regiment. Previous to my settlement at Khaira I made a trip to Mandaví to satisfy my curiosity in seeing the sea for the first time in my life. On beholding the immense body of water and its regular ebb and flow, I was struck with astonishment at the unlimited power of the one Supreme Being, before whom the whole of our universe is no more than an atom. Deeply engaged in such meditations, as I stood one evening at the sea-side, looking at the waves on which the large ships moved up and down, I began to think of the Jain tenets, according to which matter is eternal and self-existent; but, before arriving at the conclusion of the blasphemous syllogism, I was startled by a severe bite from a dog in the calf of my leg, who came slyly behind me, and, after punishing me for my crime, ran away like a shot. I followed him with my stick for a little distance to revenge the injury, but in vain; the animal vanished from my sight, and I returned home with very great pain in the leg. The next day I returned to Khaira and employed myself in the performance of my duty, in which I engaged from morning till evening. At night I enjoyed the good society of Abba Miyán, of whom I learned the English alphabet, and enabled myself to make out the words from dictionaries, and read Hindústání and Persian fluently in the Roman character. From this time until the end of 1829 I never went to bed without learning ten words of English by heart, and reading a few pages of the eminent Dr. Gilchrist's grammatical works with full attention by myself. Thus, after the hard labour of full eight years, I learnt English, the most difficult language in the world.

Before leaving Kach for Dwárka, I must say a few words with regard to the country. It does not possess that pleasing appearance which the fertile parts of India have; it has no perennial rivers of fresh water—a most invaluable blessing to the inhabitants; but there are some streams running down from the hills, which dry up immediately after the rainy season is over. In the bed of these streams springs are dug by the people, and a temporary supply of the indispensable element is thus obtained. Large wells at the towns and villages, however, make up the deficiency in quantity, but not in quality.

Signs of the wrath of God, both in former and present times, are quite visible; the surface of the earth about the hills is spread with volcanic matter, and large blocks are left, split in pieces. The recent earthquakes shattered the forts of Anjáar and Bhuj in many places, and a large number of edifices and hill forts in all the towns were transformed into ruins by the tremendous shock. Great numbers of the inhabitants remained buried in their houses to be raised on the day of the general resurrection. Although the external character of the inhabitants in general seems good, a short stay in the country will show a foreigner their want of morality, of the meaning of which thay have no idea at all. Highway robbery, larceny, and piracy are considered heroism. Adultery, fornication, and infanticide,—nay, some things more heinous—are perpetrated with impunity.

Infanticide, the most heinous crime of all—a crime unnatural and uncommittable even by irrational beings—is committed by men of this country, and that not by common people, but by the governing race of the land, who are Járajá Rájputs, originally from the Summa tribe of Sindh, who governed that part of the world in ancient times, under the title of Jám. These people must have brought this horrid custom with them from their original country. It could not, by any means, have been invented by the Hindús, who detest the very idea of the act. These Járajás think themselves so much higher than other Rájputs, that they consider giving their daughters in marriage would ruin their character. This absurd pride has hardened their hearts to the perpetration of infanticide to such an extent that, on inquiries, I found the population of Kach to be five hundred thousand souls, out of which there are twelve thousand Járajás, and of these but thirty-seven are females. The country now fortunately falling under the control of the British, the late Ráo having been deposed for his vices, his son, Ráo Desaljí, a minor remained under care of the English Government until he came of age, during which time many reforms were effected.

I lived near the camp at Khaira in the mosque for some months, enjoying the society of my friend, Munshí Abba Miyán—may God bless him for his kind attention towards me! He was my first and last master in English, as, after leaving him, I taught myself from the books of Dr. Gilchrist, etc., for a period of eight years, as I have already observed. On finishing the copy of the history for Capt. Bagnold, I was very handsomely rewarded by him. The year now approached its end, and a part of the force was ordered to proceed by sea to the islands of Dwárka and Bét, under the command of Col. L. Stanhope, for the chastisement of the rebels there. My scholar's regiment forming a part of the division, we embarked from the port of Mandaví one afternoon.

Before morning dawned we reached our destination, and the dreadful report of cannon awoke me from my sleep instead of the usually serene and sacred call of the Mu'ázzin to morning prayer. We landed at a little distance from the mouth of the river Ghúmtí, but saw the action going on with the fort quite plainly, and some of the enemy's cannon balls even passed over our heads. An English man-of-war, as if by magic, at the same time appeared in the harbour, and her guns opened at once on the fort. A party of volunteers, headed by a young officer named Marriot, scaled the wall on one side, whilst the general attack was going on at the gate. Poor Marriot, as soon as he made his appearance on the top of the wall, was cut in pieces by the garrison, and hurled back again with some of his companions nearest to him. The business, however, was not of long duration. The garrison, unable to oppose the disciplined troops, soon appeared to be in confusion, and another attack carried the place. The enemy were about six hundred in number, and, it being their characteristic not to receive or grant quarter, were soon extirpated under the English sword, except a few. A detachment of the native cavalry, headed by Capt. Solier, charged a party of the garrison issuing from the gate, who fought bravely hand to hand, and died like men. In this action, a sabre-cut from one of the enemy's party struck off Capt. Solier's fingers from the hand that held the reins, and a few men and horses were wounded. The general loss on our side was but trifling.

After our brilliant victory over the place, held most sacred by the idolators of India, a halt for a few days being ordered, I explored all the places of worship, and, to my great surprise, found the shrine of a Mohamedan saint, "Pír Patta," on the island of Amara, a light of Islám shining lustrously in the heart of the darkness of Paganism. Our regiment now being ordered to pursue and destroy the outlaw Káttís of the Kuman tribe, under Jogí Dás, in the Ghir mountains, we embarked on board a native vessel, and, after about eighteen hours' very rough voyage, landed at Surya Bandar, whence, being divided into detachments of about two companies, we hunted the Káttís throughout the whole Ghirnár mountains.

This range, though inferior in loftiness to other mountains of India, is very pleasant to sight, being fertile and verdant everywhere. It is held sacred by all the Hindús according to their legends, whence the ancient name of Rewtachal. One of its branches, extending towards Pálítánah, in Goelwár, is decorated with Jain temples of various sizes, and regarded by that class of the ancient Hindús with great veneration.

The mountains abound with game of every description, from the royal lion to the quail. Going about in this wilderness, one sometimes happens to see a Hindú monk, whose zealous austerity prompts him to give over all, and devote his life to the worship of the Deity uninterrupted by worldly people. He lives upon the vegetable productions of the place, makes fire by rubbing two pieces of wood against one another to warm himself in the cold nights, and keeps his body rubbed over with ashes, which thin cover, keeping the pores closed, renders him independent of artificial covering. After ten or twelve years' life in this state, he becomes like the wild beasts, and runs at the sight of man. The people in this part of the world have a mistaken idea that these devotees are cannibals, and devour man's flesh if they can get hold of a single unarmed person; but this is not credible.

One morning, as I marched with my scholar, we entered into a long conversation upon the subject of spirit and matter. Being deeply engaged in this very interesting topic, he left his party in charge of a subordinate officer, and desired me to accompany him a little distance from the road, to talk more fully and with less interruption. So we turned our horses to the left of the party, and walked on engaged in confabulation, taking care, however, not to lose sight of our small troop. All of a sudden we came up to a bonfire without any human being near it. The fire being alive, it seemed as if somebody must have been there. We lighted our cheroots and asked our grooms the cause of the fire in that solitary place. Their unanimous reply was that the fire belonged to some Aghorí Bábá (*i. e.*, omniverous father), and that it was dangerous for us to stay there longer. This excited our laughter, and we proceeded on without any concern about the matter. After going a little further, we came to the side of a valley enormously deep, and, on looking down, we had the honour of seeing the monk himself, the demigod of the Hindús, about a thousand yards from us, running down as fast as he could, cautiously looking behind every now and then, as if somebody were pursuing him. The poor grooms, on seeing him, were overpowered with fear, bowed to him, touching the ground with their foreheads. My scholar, with European curiosity, hailed the man, and beckoned to him as if he had to make some important communication to him; but these acts of civility, instead of producing the desired effect, accelerated the flight of our uncivil host, and the impracticable declivity altogether prevented my curious European companion from following. So having recourse to our telescope, we had a full view of him. He was a strong and powerful man, the silvery hair of his head hanging over his shoulders dishevelled, and his long beard in the same state; his eyes were quick and sparkled with fire, and his shaggy body was rubbed over with ashes. Having seen so much of him, he vanished from our sight.

Our party's destination at this time was Tulsí Shám, a Hindú monastery in the heart of the mountain, about three days' journey off, where they intended to concentrate with other detachments, and thence to disperse again in different directions in search of the outlaws. We soon reached Tulsí Shám in safety, where we found several detachments encamped already. Shortness of provisions was the general misfortune now complained of in our camp, particularly by the people of my class, who, being entitled to no bhátá like the Honourable Company's servants, suffered much. Complaints of hunger and starvation were brought before the commanding officer, who spoke to the Mahant (or grand priest of the monastery) in serious terms, telling him that if he refused his aid to our camp, with regard to both information and provisions, he would order the monastery (which he knew contained large quantities of grain) to be plundered. These threats brought the sacred old man to his senses, and he said in reply that there was no wheat or rice in that part of the country to be had; the grain in the storehouse was all bájrí (*Holcus spicatus*), which he would order to be ground. The great mill, drawn by a pair of bullocks, was forthwith set in motion; so that in a few hours a quantity of the bájrí flour was prepared sufficient for the whole camp for one day. This he distributed at the rate of about a pound a head per diem, with proportionate quantities of molasses and clarified butter, without receiving the cash that was offered in return, alleging that the articles did not belong to him, and that he being no grain merchant—the grain, etc., being delivered to him for charitable purposes—he would give them away to the same end. At all events, our need was served by this food, though it was unwholesome to those who were unaccustomed to it. I, being one of them, had an attack of diarrhœa, but soon cured myself when I got good food, which I did as follows. It happened that, during my indisposition, I was visited by a Mohamedan non-commissioned officer, named Sikandar Khán, who was then orderly of his own company (now a Súbahdár Major pensioner), and consequently was entitled to double bhátá. Finding out my circumstances, he kindly lent me some rice, which was a great relief to me and my servant. My obligation to him for this timely aid was unbounded, and we have been staunch friends ever since.

Tulsí Shám is revered by Hindús on account of a small image of Krishna, their Apollo, in the monastery, in front of which is a thermal spring divided into two large reservoirs of boiling water. Sulphuric and limy veins exist in the stratum, a strong smell of which is quite perceptible. The springs are nicely built up with stones and mortar, having flights of steps on all four sides. The heat of the water they attribute to the miraculous nature of the image, and ablution therefore in these reservoirs is considered a means of salvation.

Our stay here was no more than four days, and then we dispersed in small parties as before. During our peregrination in the hills for about six weeks, we never had the satisfaction of meeting the free-booters alive anywhere. On the morning, however, of the sixth day of our leaving Tulsí Shám, as we came near a large group of the mangoes and other wild trees, a stench, as if from a putrid carcass, became perceptible. On going a little further, we discovered four dead bodies of the outlaws hung inverted to the boughs of the trees, in a most horrid state, maimed and disfigured. This barbarous act, we were given to understand, was perpetrated three days previous to our arrival, by a party of the Gaíkwár contingent co-operating with us in the expedition. Roaming and wandering about for a period of three months in the mountains, at last we were informed of the rebels being overtaken and seized and destroyed at several places; so we had now to proceed to the village of Dhárí, to be cantoned there for the rainy season.

My scholar, being a very industrious and attentive lad, never missed his lessons, either on the marching or halting days; and, by the break of the monsoon, he made himself an excellent linguist in Hindústání. He then obtained leave to proceed to Bombay to be examined. I accompanied him as far as Gogo, where we parted with each other with a feeling of mutual esteem as good friends on the 17th of September, 1821. He gave me a handsome present in money, besides the arrears of my pay, and sailed for the Presidency with my best wishes for his success. I was soon informed of his passing a good examination, and, subsequently, of his getting the quartermastership of the regiment.

Gogo is a small town situated on the west side of Cambay; there are about three thousand houses, chiefly of Mohamedans. It is a safe roadstead in the boisterous season of the year. Tradition says that the island of Perim, near its harbour, was the seat of the Government of the ancient Goel Rájputs, when it was joined to the Gujarát peninsula by an isthmus. The island is now a wilderness, on which Government has erected a lighthouse. It is inhabited by serpents of various sizes and colours. Animal and vegetable fossils of the incalculably remote ages are found on this island by digging up the ground not very deep: many European travellers have taken away some of them as a curiosity to their country. The Mohamedan inhabitants of Gogo, being in general active, strong, and well-made, are very expert seamen. I sojourned at Gogo for three days after parting with my friends; on the fourth I went on board a small vessel, and on the fifth reached the city of Súrat. I was informed, on board, of the annoyance one is subjected to at the custom-house in being searched, though he may have no articles for sale; and, therefore, I settled with the sailors to smuggle myself and my things for the sum of half a rupee. The aid of darkness being required for the purpose, I was obliged to stay on board the vessel till evening, when two of the mariners carried my things, and desired me to follow. We landed at a place called Bádsháhí Bhágal, or Royal Gate; nominally a gate, but there was no such thing as a gate to be seen, except two dilapidated ends of the city walls, between which is this passage, a sort of ferry, whence the people carry water for their domestic use, and where small boats resort. I followed my guides in the dark for a little distance, when, unfortunately, a custom-house peon seized the men carrying my luggage, and began to abuse them for infringement of rules; he insisted on taking them to the custom-house, and said he would have them imprisoned for the night, have them fined the next day, and the baggage forfeited. At this time my fear was very great, thinking that his threats were in earnest; but the seamen, accustomed to such things, bore all the imprecations and menaces very coolly. They said I was no merchant, and had no articles of trade; besides I would willingly give him his fee. So saying, one of them gave me a pinch in the arm to signify that I should follow their advice. Upon this I gave the man the amount mentioned, and he departed peacefully without uttering another word. I put up in the nearest mosque for the night, as I could get no lodging at such a late hour.

On the morning of the 25th Zilhajj, 1236, A.H., corresponding with the 23rd of September, 1821, A.D.,

I got up from my comfortable and sound sleep at the sacred call of the Mu'azzin, and called for my servant Ismaíl: "Ismaíl, give me a little fire, that I may have a good morning smoke before I prepare myself for the Divine duty;" but, to my great astonishment and fear, I found him missing. "Well," said I to myself, "this is a very pleasant circumstance—losing in one night what I have earned in return for the servitude of four years. God is great! one must undergo the decrees of his fate." Overwhelmed with such ideas, I began to grope at the head, feet, and sides of my mattress, to which I had carefully fastened my small box, and other articles of my baggage, before I went to bed; and to my delight found everything in its proper place. The boy had run away with his own clothes, and about three quarters of a rupee in copper coins, with which he was trusted for daily expenses.

After the day had dawned, I went and stood at the door of the mosque to look for a porter to carry my things to a small house, rented to me through the kind offices of the Mu'azzin. Presently I observed Mohamedans, both high and low, hastening in one particular direction, some in pálkís and bullock carriages, and others on foot, almost all looking as if they had been struck with sorrow. On inquiry, I was informed that Nasír-ud-dín Khán, the Nuwáb of the city, had departed this life during the night, and they were going to attend the funeral. I learnt, too, that Nasír-ud-dín had two sons, but one of them, a very praiseworthy character, died eighteen months before his late father, and that the surviving son was a perfect contrast to his late brother, on account of his love for low society and bad habits, though it was hoped the English Government would recognise his right to the titular Nuwábship of the city, by which he would remain entitled to a pension of a lákh and a half rupees per annum from Government and some other rights and immunities reserved to the family.

In the city of Súrat, entitled "Báb-ul-Makkah" (or "the gate of Mecca"), I stayed four days to see the celebrated town through which almost all the pilgrims to the sacred city proceed, and through which the English first stepped into our country as trading people. Captain Hawkins, of the ship *Hector*, was the first merchant from England who landed here, in the year 1608, A.D., and after making some mercantile arrangements for his nation, and leaving some of his companions in charge of the business, he himself proceeded to the court of the Emperor Jahángír at Agra, to effect a favourable negotiation for the trading people of his country to this port. Having assumed the title of an ambassador from the King of England, he was received with attention and kindness, and by dint of some trifling presents and bribes to the king and his courtiers, he not only gained his object, but was presented with a valuable dress of honour, and a Christian lady, whose star of ill-luck had brought her as a prisoner into the seraglio.

Súrat is situated on the southern bank of the river Taptí. A brick wall encircles the suburbs in the form of a bow, the string of which, depressed in the middle, is the river. The city extends about six miles in circumference. The wall is flanked by bastions of small size at irregular distances. Its height varies from thirteen to eighteen feet, it was not originally strong, and, having had no repairs from the time it was built, it is now in a deplorable condition. It has twelve gates, with heavy wooden leaves turning on tenons: and another inner wall exists, surrounding the original city, extending about three miles in an irregular oval form, though in construction it is similar to the outer; but in condition is worse, so much so that in many places it is level with Mother Earth.

The city had no walls when, in 1512, A.D., it was sacked by the Portuguese. This grand pillage, followed by the frequent depredations of the unprincipled Christians, and the barbarous Abyssinians of the Zanjíra Island, induced the authorities of Ahmadábád, under the direction of Sultán Bahádur, to build the walls and the castle, which were completed in 1530, A.D., under the superintendence of Rúmí Khán, originally a Turkish Mamlúk.

The city seems to be in a decaying state, and the population therefore amounts to only one hundred and twenty thousand persons, one-sixth of the number of inhabitants sixty years ago. The government of the city is entirely under the English, and there are no less than twenty-four English officers here, inclusive of the court of Sadr' Adálat. There are two regiments of infantry and a strong party of Golandáz stationed here, I suppose for the purpose of keeping the neighbours in awe, which is quite unnecessary at this time. The expenses to Government seem to be too heavy, if compared with those of the time of the Nuwábs.

Being anxious to have an ocular view of the Guebre cemeteries, several of which I was informed existed near the city, I prepared one morning to proceed thither: but my friend, the Mu'azzin, told me it was foolish to run the risk, for a priest is always kept near as a sentry, and any person attempting to defile any of the places, by touching or looking into them, is sure to be murdered or very severely punished. This admonition of my friend, instead of being attended to, increased my eagerness. "Happen what may," said I, "I must have a look." Finding me determined upon the enterprise, my friend told me to wait till evening, when he would accompany me and give me his aid. We accordingly proceeded in the afternoon, and when about one mile out of the eastern gate of the city, we discerned several single towers, on the walls of which sat a number of ugly vultures, plumeless from the head to the breast. We halted under a tree, expecting in the dusk of the evening to avoid being observed by the sentry priest, as well as by the shepherds and passers by. The time having arrived, I left my friend under the tree, and advanced to the tower to satisfy my curiosity. My friend told me to be on the alert, that if he saw anybody approaching he would cough, which I should consider a signal to take to my heels as fast as I could to the direction of the tree. Thanking him for the kind advice, I went and reached my destination in a minute, and ascending the few steps into the doorway, and, being an expert climber, I scaled the wall, resting my big toe on the heavy padlock of the door; and thus assisted, I soon found myself on the top of the wall, whence I beheld the horrid scene. The human skeletons, some whole and some in pieces, mingled with rags of the shrouds, lay, some on the rampart, and others had found their way into the middle pit. The strong and offensive effluvia not allowing me to remain more than five minutes, I quickly began to descend; but unfortunately my hands slipt from the parapet, whilst my toes were engaged in searching for the support of the lock. I slid down on the portico, and my chest, rubbing against the side of the wall, was considerably excoriated. The noise of my fall, and the rattling of the lock, roused the Pársí warden from his small hut, about two hundred yards from me, and he came out in a furious manner, with a mouth pouring forth curses and bad names, and a hand armed with a long stick, at the same time calling for help, and crying that he was going to be murdered by robbers. This noise, and the cough of my friend being simultaneous, I fled to the tree, whence we found out that the poor keeper was an old man, toothless, weak, and half blind, or perhaps labouring under nyctalopia, for instead of advancing towards us, he took another direction, every now and then feeling the ground with his stick, and cursing as if his long tongue had been a compensation to him for the other powers he had lost. Nobody coming to his aid, we departed coolly; but, seeing the old man going towards the same gate we had come through, we passed through the next gate unmolested, and returned home. I soon cured my chest by washing it with litharge diluted with rose-water.

On the morning of the 29th of September I left the city of Súrat for Broach, on my way home, hiring three begárís, or porters, to carry my luggage. These I had to change at every village on the road. I paid them liberally. A penny or two for a draught of the fermented palm juice, of which they are very fond, rendered them entirely submissive; and, dividing the load between two, the third prepared my pipes every now and then, shampooed me at the resting-places, and held my umbrella to keep off the sun, which I felt very oppressive at this season, though the rains had just ended. Toddy, or palm-juice, is a general calamity for the low people of this district. Toddy shops are to be found in all the villages, and even the roads are not without them. At the distances of one or two miles you can always find a shop under the inviting shade of a large tree or shed, with a small flag waving over it; and the keeper, generally a Pársí, with a soft flattering tongue, entices you to drink, expressing, though less poetically, the idea of the English bard—

> "Drink of this cup! you'll find there's a spell in
> Its every drop against ills of mortality;
> Talk of the goblet that sparkled for Helen,
> Hers was a fiction, but this is reality!"

This diabolical drink is the cause of many evil deeds being done by the poor ignorant people of the district.

I reached Broach on the evening of the 30th of September. It being about thirty miles from Súrat, I was obliged to make a halt for the night at a station called Chaukí, nearly half way. Broach, though in the middle of a very fertile district, is itself an ugly dilapidated town, situated partly on a small hill, and partly on the skirt of the same, on the northern bank of the river Narbadda, which falls into the gulf of Cambay, about twenty-five miles from this. The houses are like those of Súrat, but the streets are narrow and more filthy. The population I was informed amounts to about thirty thousand inhabitants. It is under the English Government, who obtained it from Daulat Ráo Sindhiah in 1803, A.D. My stay of one day and two nights was not sufficient for me to acquire more information regarding the city and its inhabitants; so much, however, I can safely say from my personal observation, that the morality of the people does not deserve any encomium. Feeling desirous to proceed by water, if possible, I inquired if there was a means of going up the river as far as Dharampur, but was informed that several cataracts in the upper province were insurmountable obstacles to the navigation.

Before I leave Broach I must mention a natural curiosity, attributed to the miracle of the saint of this place, namely, Saiyid Ismaíl Sáhib, commonly called "Pír Chattar." I proceeded there in person to visit the shrine of this holy man, which is situated about two thousand paces out of the western gate of the city, upon a rising ground. The tomb is said to be upwards of three hundred years old. It is built of the ordinary form, in a small enclosure of about thirty-four feet by ten and a half. It is shaded by a khirní tree (*Mimusops kauki*) of evergreen foliage, which grows by the side of the eastern wall out of the enclosure. In the middle of the tomb is a reservoir about five feet four inches by one foot eight, and in depth about one foot two inches. In the midst of the water there rises, about one inch above it, a small island, or the inner tomb, of four feet by one. This miraculous reservoir is always full to the brim of very cold water, somewhat nitrous to the taste. Hundreds of visitors go to the shrine every Thursday, and each of them takes a tumbler full of the water to drink; but the water never diminishes, nor does it ever overflow when no water is taken from it. There were no less than fifty persons present when I paid my visit to the shrine, and all of us drank without making the slightest difference in the original quantity. The warden of the place, a good old man, very nearly one hundred years of age, on being examined, informed me that he recollected, when he was a boy, a Marátha chief coming there and putting the miracle of the saint to test by ordering his three elephants to drink from the reservoir; but, seeing the quantity of the water undiminished, he prostrated himself at the threshold, which he solemnly kissed, and ordered the enclosure and the tomb to be thoroughly repaired at his own expense.

From what I have heard and seen, my opinion of this holy water is that it must be the mouth of the vein of a spring opened at this place, but I cannot account for the quantity of water never increasing or decreasing.

In two days' easy travelling from Broach I reached Baroda, where I was obliged to stay for seven days, on account of the fast of Muharram. On my entering the city, I happened to meet His Highness Nuwáb Mír Amíru'd-dín Husain Khán on horseback, with his retinue. Having formerly had the honour of his acquaintance, he recognised me, and persuaded me to put up with him; but I, being inclined to take a lodging and live by myself uninterrupted for the time, begged His Highness to excuse me, thanking him for the offer. I told him that my whole family and myself were sensible of his late father's kind aid when in distress in my native city; and that, not being endowed with the means of making any suitable return, we were and should ever be thankful to him, and always raised our hands in prayer to God for his happiness and success in all his undertakings. But the true spirit of goodness and hospitality in the man would not permit him to leave me. He dismounted from his horse, and, taking me by the hand, he led me to his own noble house, and assigned a private and comfortable room for my sojourn. I passed a week, partly in going about the town, and partly in this noble-hearted nobleman's amiable society. I then requested his permission to proceed to my native country, which was kindly granted, with a handsome present both in dresses and money. This noble-minded Nuwáb left this transitory abode for the next at a premature age, in the year 1837, A.D., leaving one of his two brothers to succeed him in the dignity. He died, but his memory in many hearts shall remain respected and unextinguished.

Leaving Baroda on the 10th of October, I reached my native land in thirteen days, all safe, and had the satisfaction of seeing my uncle, my grandmother, and other members of the family all well.

Soon after my arrival, our young Prince Rámchandar Ráo making his preparations to proceed to Gwálior to be married to the daughter of Sindhiah, I could not but seize the opportunity of a break to my monotonous life at home. I purchased a small horse and accompanied the procession, in the hope of getting employment. After a few marches towards our destination, an English political officer named Mr. Robinson, destined to accompany the prince, overtook us, and was received by the Rájá with marks of respect and courtesy. He delivered a couple of letters in Persian to the Rájá and his Minister, Raghunáth Ráo Bápu; and, staying a little while with them, returned to his tent at a little distance from our camp. None of the Rájá's companions being well qualified in the Persian language, the contents of the letters remained undeciphered at the time; but, the Minister issuing inquiries if there could be found a person in the camp competent to decipher the papers, I was introduced as a Persian scholar to the Court by one of its staff-bearers. I then, making my obeisances to the Prince, and raising my hand to my forehead to the nobles about him, was desired to sit down, and the papers were put into my hand to be read out; this I performed with a masterly fluency, and astonished the assembly still more by *vivâ voce* translating the sense into the Maráthí, their own language. The minister, a very clever, bold, and sagacious-looking man, seemed to be delighted with this performance, and, on my taking leave, sent his clerk to me with a kind offer of employing me under him for a salary of fifteen rupees per mensem, dinner and breakfast with the courtiers, and the horse allowance. This being my very object, I at once accepted the offer.

The duty I had to perform under the Minister was not an onerous one. I was to attend the Court twice a day to pay my respects either to the Rájá, or the Minister, or both. I was obliged to read and write for them only three or four letters a month, and sometimes in the afternoon had to play a game or two at chess, in which I was obliged to be beaten. The Minister, I confess, was a better player than I, but every third or fourth game would have been mine if he had been just; but, alas! he was very unfair on this subject. Whenever I succeeded in taking his queen, or in obtaining another advantage over him, by sacrificing a piece or two of my own, he asked me to give him the queen or to allow him to take the move back; and, finding it beyond my rank to refuse or reject his request, I always granted it, and was vanquished in consequence, at which his rejoicings were great and my mortification greater. He was also clever enough to check every opportunity that might have tended to my rise in the opinion of the prince. At this conduct of his I could not help being disgusted.

After the wedding, with all its splendour and princely pomp, was over, all of us were first invited to the palace of His Highness the Sindhiah, feasted with the most delicious dinner, and gratified with excellent music and dances. His Highness being bridegroom, could not, according to Asiatic custom, appear to the guests in person, but all the nobles of his Court superintended our entertainment. Valuable dresses were then presented to every one according to his merit, and afterwards atar and rose-water, with betel-leaves covered with gold, as a sign of dismissal. Then all retired except the bridegroom, who entered the apartment assigned to him in the palace, for the enjoyment of sweet repose, etc.

A week after the above final entertainment, preparations for our return being made, we left the camp of Sindhiah two months after our arrival. Our small camp now became a large one, being dignified with an elephant, and horses with bejewelled trappings, and tumbrils carrying jewels and treasures, magnificent pavilions for the Seraglio, and domestic attendants of both sexes. A strong escort under an experienced Marátha officer attended us, and we proceeded on by continual marches towards home with the precious prize, and safely reached our destination in seventeen days.

Another event greatly added to my disgust at my situation under the Maráthas. The dresses, etc., given to the persons of rank on the night of the last entertainment were, immediately upon our return home, collected by the Minister's people and deposited in the Government treasury, for the purpose of taking a despicable advantage, highly unbecoming the character of those who assume the title of Sarkár, or the head of a State. These dresses, etc., were exchanged in the market for some of lower price, which were distributed amongst all, before leaving the camp of His Highness. As for myself, I was left unnoticed, in anxious expectation, until we had reached more than half way towards home. On the day of our halt at Bhilsa, a clerk came to me with a servant bearing a bundle, which, after seating himself by me, he opened, and taking out a turban and a pair of shawls, he delivered them over to me with the Minister's compliments. I found them far inferior to what I had received from the original donor, and besides missed a necklace of pearls, worth about two hundred rupees, which accompanied my dress. I asked the man if he knew any reason for the reservation of the first article of the three presented to me at the Court of Sindhiah. He replied in the negative, with a scornful smile at the conduct of the authorities, hinting in figurative language, to avoid being understood by his companion, that the calamity was a general one. Being obliged to submit to the treatment, I received the present, as he advised me, with an expression of feigned gratitude. Such messengers, bearers of a present from superiors, according to the usage of the country, expect a reward from the recipient before they leave him. I therefore dismissed the deputation more than usually pleased with me. I offered them the present itself, but they having declined to receive it, I gave them a handsome sum in money, more than their expectation, in order that their master might be informed of my generosity and independence. In short, in a very few days more, having reached home, I tendered my resignation from the service, and am proud to say neither the Minister's remonstrance against this measure, which he said was an imprudent one, nor his offer of an increase of salary, could dissuade me from my determination; and I again became free and independent for a short time.

I passed a few idle days at home after obtaining my dismissal from the service of the Maráthas, during which time Sir David Ochterlony visited our town to see the Rájá, perhaps on some political matter, under pretence of congratulating him on his marriage. On this occasion the old and renowned general paid a visit to the shrine of our ancestor, and gave us a handsome present in money. His meed to us exceeded that of Sir John Malcolm's, but his visit did not create that general pleasure in our hearts which Sir John's alluring and amiable conversation had done. I read several Persian and Arabic inscriptions upon the gates of this shrine and other ancient places to His Excellency, in which he found me surpass his two learned native Persian secretaries Karam Ahmad and Háfiz-u'l Husain; for, having the advantage of being a native of the place, I knew them almost by heart, whereas the secretaries were obliged to collect and spell the words before they could read the inscriptions, which were in a peculiar flourishing hand. In the course of reading one of the inscriptions with fluency, His Excellency checked me, and questioned me to show the spot of some particular words I read to him. I pointed out the exact place and number of the lines. This pleased him much, and, after the work was over, I was honoured with a suitable reward.

CHAPTER VII.

Bombay.—I disrobe a porter.—The mosque of Zacharias.—Delights of a passage boat.—Panwell.—Púnah.—Párbati.—Satárá.—Aurangzeb's siege, and witticism of Niámat Khán.—I marry and repent.—Monogamists *versus* Polygamists.—A Satí.—The Hindú religion originally pure.—I return to Surat.—Arabic studies.—The high priest of the Borahs.—Paradise tickets.—Ensign W. J. Eastwick—his fever. Dr. R——.—Azrail's assistant—Tankarir Bandar.—Ensign Eastwick appointed to Lord Clare's body-guard.—Baroda.—A'bú.

After having left Raghunáth Ráo Bápu, I remained at home for four months; and then, feeling myself tired with the monotony of home, in the early part of the year 1823 I again thought of taking English scholars as a first step to advancement in the world. To obtain this employment I required some English friend, and as I had none in my native province, I inquired after the 6th Regiment and my former scholar, whom I had left at Gogo; and, being informed of their being stationed at Satárá, I determined on proceeding thither. On consulting my map, I found the nearest way to be *viâ* Khandes; but the high mountains and thick forests, infested both by robbers and wild beasts, and the disturbed state of the country I had to pass through, discouraged me from adopting that route; so I decided on the circuitous way, *viâ* Baroda, Súrat, and Bombay. And again leaving home, I reached Súrat in twelve days, whence I embarked on board a native boat for Bombay, of which place I had read and heard much. A favourable wind carried us smoothly over the sea, and on the fourth day of our departure from Súrat we had the pleasure of seeing the island of the Presidency, surrounded first by the sea water, and then by lofty and handsome-looking hills, except on the western side, which overlooks the vast sea as far as your eyesight can extend. On entering the harbour I was astonished at the sight of a multitude of ships, some of them like floating castles. The first sight of the innumerable masts and riggings from one end of the harbour to the other would lead one to think that it was an extensive forest of vessels all round the town. Our small boat really lost its consequence in my mind, as its proportion to the other vessels was no more than that of a sparrow to a phœnix. The magnificent view of the castle, encircling handsome and lofty edifices, quite different from what I had ever seen yet, then attracted my attention, and the scene altogether was a charming one.

The appearance of Bombay Castle was quite new to me, being built of stone after the European style, the walls very strong and thick, though not high, with battlements flat and sloping outside. The broad and deep ditch, filled with water, and the strong gates with drawbridges, gave the place an air of impregnability.

In the castle are the Christian cathedral and the dockyard, The former is weekly visited by Christians of every class for their divine service every Sunday, that day being their Sabbath. In the latter are employed about one thousand persons of every caste in building and repairing ships, etc. Thus they obtain their livelihood, being well paid by Government. Nobody is pressed to work here without wages.

History informs us that this place, now rising to be an emporium of the East, was no more than a fishing town of little or no consequence in the district of Aurangábád. About the year 1499, A.D., after Vasco de Gama's arrival, the Portuguese, being struck with the beauty of the place, and the superior excellence of its safe harbour, resolved to obtain it; and it came into their hands in the year 1530, A.D., during the reign of Humáyún, without much difficulty, as the viceroy of Aurangábád did not consider the subject worth his notice. The proud and ambitious Portuguese then having built the formidable castle to the fishing town, it began to assume consequence; and the confused state of the country during that time of disturbance inducing the neighbouring population to take shelter under the new patrons, who seemed to be just, and far from a tyrannical sect. Upon this, inhabitants of the neighbouring districts flocked daily to this place of security, and it soon became a city, but a very unhealthy one, on account of the site being intersected with numerous small streams, filled and emptied by the flow and ebb of the tides, and the putrid damp proved very injurious. The Portuguese, however, retained it about one hundred and thirty-one years, till 1661, A.D., when it was ceded by them to the English Government, to King Charles the Second, as a part of Queen Catherine's dowry. Even at this time the town was so poor, that it was leased to the Honourable Company for one hundred rupees per annum.

On being landed at this capital, a porter, unknown to me, seized upon my small luggage and ran with it among the crowd. Poor man, he did this to secure employment with me, without any bad design; but I, not being accustomed to such persons, mistook his favour for an outrage, and ran after him to recover my bundle; and, after a good smart run, I succeeded in catching hold of the back part of his langotí, the only defensive and ornamental dress he had on his body, and I am sorry to say that it, being very old, gave way, and at the first pull the whole concern came off in my hand. The custom-house officers and others laughed very heartily at both of us, to our great annoyance; but the goodnatured porter, taking very little or no notice of the matter, sat down upon the ground and re-arranged his scanty dress in a minute, telling me at the same time it was not my fault, but the cursed cloth's weakness.

"I bought it," said he, "only two years ago, and it is now worn out; whereas my former dresses lasted for five years at least."

The luggage having been examined by the custom-house authorities, I entered the town with my good porter, and, to my great sorrow, on inquiry I found that there was no place in that city for travellers to put up at; that private lodgings were also not obtainable unless one month's rent were paid in advance, a thing beyond my means to afford. In this difficulty I asked my naked friend the porter's advice, and, at his suggestion, I put up in a mosque called Hájí Zacharias' Masjid. Here I was treated by the servants of the Hájí himself with respect and hospitality. I wished to have the pleasure of seeing the founder of this mosque, the Hájí, of whose benevolent character I had heard much whilst in Bombay; and on inquiry I was informed by his servant, who waited on me, that the Hájí often sat and talked with me after prayers. Indeed, I recollected a man having done so, but never taking him for that great man, I always slighted and despised him for his clownish manners and coarse dress and conversation, instead of acting politely towards him. I regretted much having been so rude to a man who treated me with hospitality, yet could not but impute part of the blame to his own rude dress and manners. It being, however, incumbent on me to apologise for the past, I repaired to his office, where I found him squatted down on an old cushion spread on the floor, with an old bolster pillow behind his back, whilst his servants and attendants, being smartly dressed, every one of them excelled his master in appearance. There were also English gentlemen, a captain and his second officer, belonging to one of his ships, standing there, hat in hand, perhaps for his orders. These were going to be given when I arrived. I was received with much civility, and seated next him. I begged pardon for having unintentionally slighted him in his former visits to me, which I assured him was owing to ignorance of his station. He replied bluntly that, being made of humble dust, his duty was to be humble. I then asked him to furnish me with a passport, as without such security from a person of consequence nobody could go out of Bombay at that time. Upon this he told me to take my oath that I was not imposing upon him in this matter; and on my having done so, he ordered his people to give me one, which being immediately written out, was signed by him and delivered over to me. I then, having offered my thanks to him, returned home to the mosque.

After about four days' stay at Bombay, I embarked on board a small native boat to Panwell, about twenty-one miles from Bombay: we started at five o'clock, P.M., and arrived at six o'clock the next morning. This short voyage may be considered a trifling one by inexperienced persons; but, by

Heaven! it was a severe ordeal for me to go through, and I warn my readers not to attempt it on any account in a native vessel of the ferry contractors. If they do, I am sure they will have to experience what I suffered. The vessel was crowded to its every inch with men, women, and children of all classes and descriptions, crammed together; its ballast I believe being composed of filthy mud and rotten fish, which diffused such an effluvia as to try the brain of a currier himself; besides, it being an unusually sultry night, though in the month of March, all the crew falling into a perspiration, imparted no pleasant smell. Their bodies thus being drained, a general cry for water was raised, which being brought to the lips, was not only found warm, but strongly impregnated with the smell of the ballast. A host of flies and bugs penetrating our dresses with impunity, engaged themselves in biting and sucking our blood. Their number was so great, that if one was killed the vacancy was immediately filled up by half a dozen others. The open part of the body was attacked with mosquitos and cockroaches; the former, buzzing about the head, inflicted an occasional sting, and the latter, in flying from one direction to another, came slap every now and then against the face and neck. To crown all, the boatmen wearied our lives out for a present, in addition to their freight, which they had already received in advance. One of them went round, holding an empty cup before every passenger, to receive the extortions, whilst another, standing upon a keg placed near the mainmast, preached as follows: "My friends, be charitable, that you may reach the shore in safety. You know your dangerous situation; there is but a small plank between you and death, and a slight blast of wind may destroy all of us in one moment. We exert ourselves in saving your life and property; do not therefore withhold a small donation from us. Be charitable and good, that God may soon release you from this difficulty." The poor credulous passengers, thus being imposed upon, subscribed something a second time to the villains, until the man, or rather the brute, held his cup before me, when I spoke to him sternly, thus: "I have paid my passage, and will make no contribution for those who never washed their boat, and have no idea of the comfort of others." Hearing this unfavourable reply, he turned to his comrade on the cask: "Look at the insanity of this young man," said he, "complaining about the boat being unwashed and himself uncomfortable; he does not see that the boat on the surface of the water is continually washed, and he is uncomfortable because he is not drowned." This unreasonable language of his kindled up the fire of my rage, and, getting up from my place, I bade him hold his tongue or he should see the consequence. This rendered the beggars mild, and then the unmanly man on the cask sang out, "Leave that gentleman alone, we have got other worthy, liberal, charitable, and good people to extend our humble hands to." My just words, I am glad to say, produced the desired effect; nobody, after having heard my speech, would pay anything to the rogues, but all of them joined with me in reproaching the rascals, whose fallacious logic thenceforth proved fruitless.

On landing at the town of Panwell, of the district of Konkan (Concan), early in the morning, I ran to the land like an imprisoned bird escaping from his cage. Here I took one day's rest under an umbrageous banian-tree, enjoying the free air of the Konkan combined with the fine sea breeze, and had all my clothes and self well washed and cleaned, after my four days' stay in the then filthy town of Bombay and one night's voyage on board the filthiest of boats. The next day I took my way to Púnah, about seventy-one miles distant. The road was excellent, mostly shaded by the forest trees as far as the pass, and being built and cut all the way in the mountainous parts by the English authorities, except the Ghát or Pass of Khandála, about thirty miles from Panwell. This pass is not a very high one, being about two thousand feet above the level of the sea; but the natural acclivities being left unadjusted by man's art, it was then quite impassable for wheeled carriages, and most difficult for quadrupeds to ascend with their loads. From Panwell, in three days' easy marches of about twenty-five miles a day, I reached the ex-capital of the Marátha power, namely, the city of Púnah, formerly in the province of Aurangábád, but latterly under the Maráthas. The late Peshwá's dominion in the Dakhan being invaded by the English in 1818, this became a British district. The appearance of the city is not unlike that of Ujjain, but the material difference between the two is, that Púnah is surrounded by hills. The castle of this place, which is called the palace, is quite unworthy of notice; it is more like a gaol, having only one entrance, and thick high walls angulated with four round towers. On entering the town by the northern side of it, we crossed the river Múta, which, at a little distance from this joins the river Múla, and the place of their junction is denominated Sangam, where the house of the British Resident stood in the time of the Peshwá. I halted here for two days to see the city, about the wealth and splendour of which I had heard a good deal. On personal examination, I was quite disappointed, and was informed by the inhabitants that the splendour had departed with its former master. "Those markets," said they with a melancholy tone, "where heaps of golden coins, strings of pearls, and caskets of precious ornaments, were exposed for sale, are now all deserted." The amount of the population of the city at this time is said to have been reduced from half a million to about one hundred and twelve thousand persons, on account of the banishment of the Peshwá and the consequent dispersion of his armies and emigration of the people.

It having occurred to me to ascend the Párbatí Hill to have a full view of the city at once, I employed a guide for the purpose and soon reached the summit. It commands a view of the whole city, with its environs and a beautiful landscape of the town, the English camp, and the suburbs, ornamented with nine lakhs of mango-trees planted by the Peshwá, called *nau lakha bágh*.

The next day I left Púnah for Satárá, the place of my destination, which, being about fifty-six miles distant, I reached in three days by easy marches on the 30th of March, 1823. Satárá, originally belonging to the province of Bijapur, is situated in a mountainous country, environed by lofty hills on three sides: or, I may observe, the town is lying under and within the south-western angle of hills running in the form of a syphon, the southern leg of which is the short one, and is walled and towered, partly scarped and partly built into a hill fort, the eminence being about two hundred and seventy-five yards high. The fortress was commanded from many places, particularly from the west.

The sight of the fortress reminded me of the anecdote of Aurangzeb's able secretary, named Niámat Khán, who, on the morning of the day when this fortress was stormed, was the first person to bring intelligence of its capture. On reaching the royal pavilion, he found His Majesty sitting at the door of his tent anxiously looking at the fortress and counting the prayers on his fingers, with his thumb at the root of his little finger: when the Minister performed his obeisance, the King asked him, "What news?"—"I have glad tidings, my Lord," observed Niámat Khán, and added, extempore, "the effect of your Majesty's prayers has become evident, as the fortress is subdued by the royal arms, the date of which achievement is shown by your Majesty's hand;" *i. e.*, the fingers of his hand, with the thumb under the root of the little finger, represented the figure of a unit four times repeated, and that was the year of the Hijra 1111, A.D. 1700.

The British cantonment and the Residency being about two miles east of the town, I proceeded there and had the pleasure of seeing my old friend of Tulsí Shám, Sikandar Khan, now Havaldár Major of the regiment, with whom I put up in the lines, and found in him a sincere, obliging, and hospitable friend.

The news of my arrival was soon on its wing through the camp, and there being no other competent teacher there at the time, I obtained six scholars,—a lucrative employment but hard work, the performance of which took up all my time during the day. At night, as long as I could keep myself awake, I studied English from the valuable works of Dr. J. B. Gilchrist. Thus I passed six years at this station, during which time many young officers having passed in the languages by my aid, I obtained some reputation and a good sum of money.

After a short stay with my good host, I did not like to press on his scanty means, which were hardly sufficient to maintain his own family, so I took a comfortable lodging in the town, where I passed my nights partly in my favourite study and partly in repose, the sweetness of which can only be felt by those who enjoy it after hard labour.

Thus I passed my time in quietness without being disturbed by anything excepting domestic affairs, such as the neglect of my servants in the performance of their duty and their treacherous conduct, attended with petty larceny in my house, where, on my absence during the day, they had uncontrolled authority. These domestic troubles often embittered my thoughts and disturbed my peace. To remedy such evils I felt the necessity of having a person to superintend my household and be a companion to me during some of my lonesome hours.

Thus, being compelled by circumstances, on the 23rd of September, 1824, I married a young lady whom I had known when in Kach, and whose destiny had brought her hither some time before my arrival. Man is naturally deluded by temptations, and in many cases he is not undeceived until he finds himself completely entangled in the net of trouble. In over-rating small evils we generally bring upon ourselves heavier ones. The dream of my happiness in the married state was but a short one, and I soon found myself more involved in domestic anxieties than before. When a bachelor, I thought for myself only, but now I had to think for another person too, whose fate had joined mine. The repletion of my purse likewise began to be changed for depletion; and to crown all these difficulties, to my great sorrow, I discovered my new companion to be of a very pettish and hypochondriacal temper, to which I had to submit in future.

Such inconveniences can be easily obviated by our law in divorcing a wife, not only for crimes, but even if she is disagreeable. But who can have the heart to part with his faithful companion without serious cause. This bad practice prevails only amongst the lower classes of the people. A man of high station in life may marry four wives at once or gradually, and may have as many handmaids as he can support; then, from amongst such a number, he is sure to find one who gives him every satisfaction, and the rest may be maintained without being repudiated, each knowing that she has only herself to thank for a rival in her lord's affections, as she ought to have made herself so dear to him that he could not have desired a change. Here I drop the grand subject of monogamy and polygamy, controverted between the doctors of Mohamedanism and

Christianity. There are many things to be said on both sides, but I will not enlarge my journal with these discussions. I side with my own law, though I have been a monogamist throughout all my life.

One morning, as I was sitting with Lieutenant E. M. Earle,* of the 24th Regiment N. I., who studied Persian with me (after having passed in Hindústání and Maráthí), we were informed that a satí (suttee) was going to be performed that forenoon at the village of Maholí, near the river side. The news startled my young friend as well as myself. We could not believe that such an outrage could be committed with impunity whilst a British Resident remained near the capital. We had hardly finished our conversation on the subject, when we descried the ominous procession, attended with native music passing from the town, along the high road close to the Resident's gate. Upon this, we ran to our horses and rode to the place of execution, which we reached in about half an hour in the heat of the sun. Another scholar of mine, by name Dr. M. F. Kaye, having heard of the sad news, presented himself on the spot immediately after us.

After waiting about a quarter of an hour under an umbrageous pípal-tree on the bank of the river, the procession arrived, and the Bráhman carriers placed the bier at the brink of the water, so as

* This very promising young man was drowned in the wreck of the "Lord Castlereagh," 13th of June, 1840.

to keep the feet of the corpse washed by that element. The face and hands of the dead being exposed to view, we found the deceased to have been a strong well-made Bráhman, about forty years of age.

Having examined the dead man, we proceeded to the young lady, who seated herself under another pípal-tree, at a little distance within sight of the corpse, ready to immolate herself on the pile under preparation near the dead body. She was surrounded by her relatives and others, about twenty persons in number. To these she kept on talking and foretelling many things, on being interrogated. She was handsome, about fifteen years of age, and her charming countenance showed no marks of fear or anguish. Lieutenant Earle, being an excellent Maráthí scholar, finding an opportunity, entered into conversation with her, and delivered a very eloquent speech, dissuading her most earnestly from this horrid suicide, which he said he viewed in the light of a wilful murder committed by the Bráhmans, whose evil advice, contrary to the pure Hindú law, enticed her to a death of torture in both worlds. To this her reply was but a short one. "You may say what you please, but I will go with my lord. It was written in the book of my fate to be his wife, so I must be his wife only, to the full extent of the meaning, and that of nobody else. I loved him only, and can never love any one else with that primary sincerity, so I must be his true companion wherever he goes. Take you no more trouble, sir, about the matter. Peace be with you."

Lieutenant Earle now, at the suggestion of Dr. Kaye and myself, begged her to listen to him for another moment, so she turned to him, and he further observed as follows: "My good lady, pray consider over the act once more; act not against your reason; you must be sure that we are your friends and not your enemies, that we would save you from the horrid death by all means at a slight signal of your consent, and would make an honourable provision for you during your life:" and, he added, "You should try the experiment of burning your little finger before committing your whole precious body to the flames." But, alas! her fanaticism had advanced too far beyond the reach of such wholesome advice; and, with a scornful smile, she told Mr. Earle that she was highly obliged to him for his kindness, of which she did not stand in need; that her word was one and unalterable. She then, boldly tearing up a slip of her handkerchief, dipped it into the oil of the burning lamp (usually placed before satís whether day or night), and, tying it round her little finger, she lighted it up with eagerness, and it burnt on like a candle for a little while, and then diffused the smell of burning flesh, during which the young beauty talked on to the audience, without a sigh or sob to indicate the pain; yet the marks of the blood's rush to the face, attended with a profuse perspiration on her brow, betrayed her feeling to our unbiassed and sorrowful mind. The fit of this enthusiastic frenzy is aided and maintained, I believe, by the effect of some narcotics, particularly of camphor, a large quantity of which is administered by the hard-hearted Bráhmans to the poor victims, which is swallowed up by them immediately after they have uttered their intention of self-destruction in the sudden impulse of grief at their bereavement. The effect soon spreads over the nervous system, stupefaction ensues, and the whole body is benumbed before it goes to the fire to be consumed. The pile now being ready, the corpse was washed and laid inside, and about half a pound of camphor in a bundle tied round the neck of the damsel; she got up with her usual alacrity, invoking her gods, and rushed to the fatal spot in the same way as a moth to the flame. She then walked round the pile seven times, and, having entered it, she placed the head of her dead husband in her lap, and herself holding a burning wick between the big and second toes of her left foot, she set fire to the combustibles interwoven with the logs of fire-wood. Upon her entering, the Bráhmans began to stop the entrance with heavy pieces of timber, when Dr. Kaye, being much excited at the scene, could not keep silence any more. Though he knew very little or nothing of the language, he called out with as much fierceness as he could command, "You scoundrels, this is not fair; *darwáza mat kholó:*" that is to say, "do not open the door," of course meaning the reverse. Such erroneous expressions of the good doctor, even at this tragical moment, produced a smile from most of the bystanders. Immediately the poor woman set fire to the pile, the Bráhmans and others surrounding it began shouting out the name of their god, Rámá, and ordered the kettle-drums, flageolets, and cymbals that accompanied the procession to be beaten and played, and rent the air with their cries, in order that no cry of distress might be heard from the victim: and, as soon as the flames issued from all sides, they cut the ropes of the four corners of the platform of the pile with their hatchets, so the enormous weight of the firewood, falling at once upon the delicate girl, crushed her in a moment. In short, in about fifteen minutes' time all the fuel became a heap of ashes, the music and the cries ceased, and the party of the executioners, being tired, seated themselves in calmness under the tree, in expectation of the embers being extinguished, that they might throw the ashes into the river and return home. We then hastened to our own places of rest, sad and dejected from what we had seen.

Religions, pure in their origin, in course of time beget superstitions, which give birth to such results as we have just described. The religion of the Hindús in its origin is pure and sublime, as will be clearly seen from the books of their Ved, or theological works, which were in existence about 1800 years before our era of the Hijra, or about 1100 years before Christ. They consider the only Supreme Being to be the self-existing ruler of the universe, styled Brahma. His first attributes are the following Trinity: Brahma the Creator, Vishnu the Preserver, and Siva the Destroyer. These attributes have each a peculiar image, as a medium required for the material being to think of the immaterial being, who is one creator of all the visible and invisible worlds. He is the Almighty, who rules and governs all his creation by a general providence, resulting from first determined and pre-established principles.

From so sublime a source of the genuine principles of their religion runs the pure stream of their law, which strictly prohibits all the crimes punishable by the laws of the present civilized world. Besides, suicide, infanticide, and sacrifice of all kinds, not only human, but of any kind of animal, are ranked amongst the heinous crimes. But superstition and fables, and the selfish character of their priests, have, in the lapse of ages, produced immorality and corruption to this degree, that the generality of the Hindús of this time are no more than infidels in the high opinion of their Vedantees or theologists.

During my stay at Satárá I had the honour of seeing a great man amongst the English, whose high renown had often come to my ears from people of his country and my own. This was the Hon. Mount

Stuart Elphinstone, Governor of Bombay, who paid his visit to the State for some political purposes just at the time when the celebration of the marriage of the Rájá's natural daughter to one of the sons of the Ghorpora of Púnah took place. On this occasion all the gentry of the city being entertained at the palace for a fortnight, I was one of them; and, being present at the conference, I greatly admired the amiable, cogent, and comprehensive conversation of the Governor with the Rájá. It appeared to me as if the great man was talking to a child, sometimes correcting his ideas, and sometimes tossing them up from one side to another to see if the young prince could re-arrange them well; but he was disappointed more than once in this respect. I recollect a remark of his in the same conference. The Rájá had expressed his desire to know the cause of His Excellency's talking to him in Hindústaní, and not in Maráthí, in which language, observed the prince, he was as well versed as himself. "Because," replied the statesman, "I speak Hindústání better than your Highness, and your Highness's Maráthí must naturally be better than mine."

Six years I passed at Satárá, during which time my lawful industry procured money for me sufficient to pass another period of six months without any employment. But, having lost many good friends, both English and native, by the 6th Regiment being ordered to another station, I found myself dull and lonesome at this place. Besides, the climate of the Dakhan and the insipid society of the Maráthas began to prove disagreeable to me, and I thought of leaving the place for another more civilized one by the first opportunity. During my anxiety about leaving Satárá I luckily had an offer from Lieutenant Webb of the Artillery, a very nice gentleman and an over-zealous Christian, who, having studied with me for some time, was ordered to be stationed at Súrat in charge of the garrison, etc. I readily accepted the offer, and proceeded forthwith to Súrat, which I reached with my family in April, 1828. My passage from Bombay to Súrat was a quick, rough, and dangerous one.

A vessel belonging to the same owner left the harbour at the same time, having on board about one hundred and forty Bohras, invited by their Mullá (or high priest) to celebrate the nuptials of his son. She was in sight of us for a few leagues, and then disappeared; and having at night encountered the severity of the storm, foundered about half way to Súrat, and all the unfortunate passengers, instead of enjoying the festival, met with a horrible watery grave. I fancy the Mullá at this time had a good long list of dead disciples to send to his brother Gabriel for accommodation in Paradise. The custom of this schismatic class of Mohamedans is to receive a certificate of the priest for every dead follower, addressed to the archangel, recommending a place in the blissful region suitable to the amount of the fees paid on such occasions, which document is carefully placed in the shroud of the deceased.

I recollect an anecdote of a friend of mine, Dr. C. D. Straker, the civil surgeon of this place for some years. This gentleman attended the Mullá during a bad illness. When it came to the month of Ramzan (the Mohamedan Lent) the doctor told his reverend patient not to observe fasts until his recovery, as that act of devotion at that juncture would prove injurious to his weak constitution. But the crafty priest, in order to show his religions zeal, observed that the omission of an indefeasible duty, strictly ordered in his sacred book, must be the cause of a severe punishment in the world to come.

To this Dr. Straker replied, with the characteristic frankness of an Englishman, "No, no, Mullá Sáhib, don't you fear about that: I will give you a certificate, which, being shown to your brother archangel, will surely procure absolution for this necessary transgression on your part." This remark of the pure-hearted Englishman produced a smile mingled with mortification from the priest, and the bystanders could not help turning their faces to laugh, especially two or three orthodox Mohamedan servants, who were obliged to leave the room to conceal their mirth.

At Súrat I found more scholars than I could attend, so I was better off than in the Dakhan.

By this time I may say my progress in English was not contemptible. I could read and write in that language well enough, and spoke it so well that some of my English friends often jestingly interrogated me whether both of my parents were natives of India, or one of them English, for my complexion and accent, said they, were different from the natives. In reply to such rude questions, I thanked them with a smile, and said their compliments were more than I deserved. In Súrat I was blessed with the society of men of science and literature; but my limited knowledge of the Arabic prevented my enjoyment of the same to its full extent. I therefore prepared myself to undertake the task of studying at any expense of time, money, and labour, that, next to the English, most difficult language.

I began the study accordingly with the perseverance of a true lover seeking a fair damsel, cheerfully undergoing all the difficulties inseparably belonging to the pursuit of such an object. Again I passed my days in earning my livelihood, and a great part of my nights in applying my mind to books, and I am happy to say that three years' hard labour produced to me the sweet fruit of success, and I obtained a good certificate of competency in the Mohamedan law from Shaikh Tájud-din, the chief law officer of the 'Adalat, and another from a famous physician, Mír Isa, in the theoretical part of medicine.

Amongst my scholars at Súrat, I had a young

ensign, by name W. J. Eastwick, of the 12th Regiment Bombay N. I., a very promising youth with an extraordinary memory. What he learnt once was always found indelible on the tablet of his pure mind. By my further stay with him I found that his endowments, qualities, and mental qualifications were superior to his age and station. He was amiable, mild, generous, and charitable in every sense of the word, and his liberality rendered me quite independent of taking another scholar. He passed with me in both the Hindústání and Persian languages in a short time, and made himself master of the elements of Arabic Grammar in a comparatively short period, learning them of me during my few mornings' rides with him. His invaluable society became so precious to me that I remained in his service almost all the time of his stay in India, excepting some intervals, during which higher emoluments tempted me to leave him for some time, but the attraction of his kindness again brought me soon to him.

In the month of May, 1829, being invited by Ensign John Ramsay, of the Bombay N.I., I proceeded to Sholapur, a distance of about four hundred and fifty miles from Súrat, which I travelled in fourteen days *viâ* Bombay and Púnah, in the hot season of the year. My passage to Bombay was a pleasant one, and thence I hired a small boat to Panwell for myself and servants, avoiding the ferry-contractors' boats by all means, as experience had given me a good lesson in the year 1823 to do so. The desolated town of Sholapur, situated in a burning, treeless place, does not deserve any commendation here. It is surrounded by a strong wall, to the south-west of which is an oblong capacious fort, built of stones, flanked by several large towers, and encircled by a deep ditch communicating with a large tank southward of the fort. The inhabitants, chiefly Márathas, amount to about twenty-two thousand persons.

Although the Dakhan is hot, Sholapur, I think, is pre-eminently so, on account of its situation, where hot winds have nothing else to act upon except the poor inhabitants. On my arrival, I proceeded to the cantonment at a little distance from the town, where, at the house of my noble host, I met with a very kind reception, and remained there for about seven months, during which time that worthy and magnanimous young man, having rendered himself competent in the Hindústání language, I returned to Súrat well rewarded, and was again received with open arms by my patron, Mr. Eastwick, in whose service I continued.

In the beginning of September, 1831, to my great sorrow, Mr. Eastwick had a very severe attack of fever, for the first time, I think, since his arrival in India. The hot and cold fits alternately succeeded each other for five days, after which time he became insensible, sometimes for fifteen or twenty minutes.

His life was despaired of by his English friends. I attended on him night and day, and, according to my little knowledge of medicine, I saw no danger, although the attacks were so severe as to deprive him of his strength entirely. So weak became he that he could not get up in his bed unaided. During some hours, whilst free from fever, I gave him doses of lemon sherbet, which afforded him refreshment for a time. I encouraged him whenever I found him dejected, and impressed upon his mind the necessity of a change as soon as possible. My counsel, I am glad to observe, had its timely effect, and he proceeded to Bombay, leaving his horses and effects in my charge. Had he remained two or three days longer, such a delay would surely have cost him his life, for I had found the medical gentleman, Dr. ——, under whose charge he was, to be one of the deputies of the angel of death. His prescriptions, when taken to the native apothecary (a friend of mine), were sometimes laughed at, and sometimes received with all the curses at his command. At the sight of them he generally said, "I believe master is mad, and if I obeyed him I should not only be madder, but an executioner and shedder of innocent blood." On one instance, as I took the prescription myself to him for my benefactor under suffering, he took me aside and read the paper to me in English (as they are usually in Latin), pointing out one of the ingredients—laudanum—fifty drops instead of five! Had this dose been inadvertently given to the patient, and taken by him, it would surely have produced a fatal effect, and he would have required no more anodyne, as it was termed by the doctor, for ever. I brought the ominous bottle, which only contained five drops of the venomous tincture; but even that I emptied on the floor, having obtained the consent of the invalid to my doing so, and I gave him a dose of sherbet instead.

Poor Dr. —— drank so hard that he was always "half seas over." For four nights he remained in the house along with us to look after the patient, but he overlooked him all the time. He sat up all the night at a table with a burning candle, a bottle of brandy, and a cigar-case before him; and he drank no less than a bottle a night, with glasses of which I had the honour of furnishing him at intervals with my own hands, as he requested me successively. As for the number of cigars, I am unable to give a correct account of them; but the table in the morning was covered with ashes.

On the fifth night, I am glad to say, my young patient was far on the sea on his way to Bombay, out of the reach of the doctor, and I, in my own house, no more furnisher of the forbidden liquor to a Christian drunkard. Not having heard from the young man for some time, I wrote to him, inquiring about his health, and receiving no reply for ten days, I felt anxious, and began to think of proceeding to

Bombay in person. On the 29th of October, however, I had the pleasure to receive an autographical letter from him, in which, after announcing his recovery, he directed me to go forthwith to Tankária with his horses and baggage, where he was proceeding in command of the escort of Lord Clare, then *en route* to Ajmír. The orders were duly executed, and, meeting at Tankária Bandar, we proceeded in the retinue of his lordship.

In five short and easy marches we found ourselves at Baroda, where we remained encamped a few days. His lordship was busy in paying and receiving visits to and from the Gaikwár. At the time of our departure, his lordship and all the gentry of his camp were, by His Highness, presented with costly gifts. My share was a golden necklace, a turban, and a shawl, and that of my employer consisted of more valuable articles; but we, as well as others, were soon deprived of them by his lordship, I believe for the Government. On the evening of the announcement of our march for the next morning, I returned the couch kindly sent to me by a friend, with my thanks, and made my bed on the ground, placing my new desk of Morocco leather at the head to serve as a pillow, and went to bed. In the morning, when roused by the bugle, I found my bed strewed with damp dust, my skin excoriated in some parts, and my back irritated in others. I called my servant, who was engaged in saddling my horse. "Mahdilli," said I angrily, "you have been throwing dust all over my bed and self, in shaking the trappings of the horse near my bed in the tent."—"No, sir, I have done no such thing," was his reply. When I took up my cloak it fell to pieces in my hand; the blanket was in the same state, and the bottom of my desk, with some valuable papers, were destroyed. "What misfortune is this?" cried I to Mahdilli, who immediately brought a burning stick to examine the cause, and coolly observed, "It is the white ants, sir, and no misfortune, but a piece of bad luck, sir." Poor man! in all mishaps, I always found him attaching blame to destiny, and never to his own or my imprudence.

By slow marches from Baroda, *viâ* Ahmadábád, we reached Dísa, a large cantonment established to keep the predatory robbers of the neighbouring wastes and mountains in check. From this we proceeded north-east to Abú, at the foot of which grand mountain we halted for three days, his lordship being inclined to ascend the high region and explore the antiquities of the place. So the next day, early in the morning, a select party of the gentry, headed by his lordship, began to ascend, along with whom I had the honour to go. Although I was left far behind by most, yet during my ascent I overtook his lordship, in company with one of his aides-de-camp, about half-way to the top, both of whom seemed much fatigued, though they had their swing chairs carried along with them, which they mounted occasionally, and I could not afford one. Nevertheless, the aide-de-camp, probably envying my agility, asked me to lend my fine strong walking-stick to his lordship. Seeing that it would be very impolite to refuse, I granted his request with promptness, and his lordship, having received the staff from my hand, thanked me for the loan (it should be termed a gift, as it was never returned), and seemed delighted to avail himself of the aid.

I remained with his lordship and suite as far as the Dailvára temples, and then, leaving them to themselves, I wandered about by myself for a little while. Upon the approach of evening—finding myself unprovided against hunger and cold, and disinclined to trouble my fellow travellers, as they had only brought sufficient provisions for themselves, and, above all, reluctant to eat of the bread of charity from the staunch pagans of the place—I commenced my return to the camp forthwith. Unfortunately, being overtaken by a heavy shower of rain during my descent, I got wet through and through, and reached home about nine o'clock, P.M., regularly exhausted. The effect of this was a severe attack of fever, but I soon got rid of it by medical aid and the careful attention of my good master.

This Abú is about twenty miles east of the town of Sírohí, belonging to Ráo Sewsingjí, and is an ancient place of worship of the Hindús, especially of the Jain sect. Its height is about one mile above the level of the sea. There are twelve known paths (by the natives called Pag) for the ascent of this lofty mountain, of which that by Annádra, being considered safest, is mostly frequented by travellers and pilgrims. The village of Annádra is about twenty miles from Sírolií, and three from the foot of the mountain, and thence the ascent to a tank on the summit, called Nakhí Taláa, is four miles and a half. The tank, according to the Hindú legend, having been dug out with the nails of their gods, is termed Nakhí (*nakha*, "nail"). Anchorites and austere devotees inhabit the valleys and caves of the mountain about this tank, but they are very rarely visible. In the month of August, when the sun is in the sign Virgo, bathing in this tank being considered by the Hindús a purgative of all sin, a great number of them, from far and near, then assemble there for the purpose.

Two of the twelve paths are considered most difficult. These are by the Kácholí and Nítorí villages. In the first, the traveller, in many places, whilst using his hands and feet like a quadruped upon narrow steps, if he looks upward, finds the proud precipice touching the summit of the sky, and, if downwards, beholds the immeasurable depth, bottomed with nothing but darkness. A false step not only puts a period to the career of his travel, but to that of his life too.

The ascent and descent of the second path is equally difficult; besides, it has a very thick forest, which being infested by wild beasts, is more unsafe in consequence. One of the valleys of this path being considered impregnable, the former princes of Sírohí have built a fortress there, for their family and selves to retire to in times of danger.

On the mountain are thirteen villages, three of which are in ruin, and, of the remaining ten, Dailwára and Achalgarh are said to be the largest, and contain about seven hundred inhabitants.

The Hindú temples, both Jain and of the modern Siva sect, are numerous. Some of these sacred edifices are very handsome and elegant in design. The marble of the ceilings and floors is pure, and that of the walls is so brightly polished that one can see his countenance in it. I particularly admired the five Jain temples, situated at the village of Dailwára, erected to Nemnáth and Rákhab-deo, etc., the deified Jain saints. The ornamental work engraved upon the pillars, the ceilings adorned with the lotus and jasmine flowers in bas-relief, are nature itself. In the rear of one of these temples there are ten elephants, and, at the entrance of another, the same number and one horse, all formed of pure marble, each about the size of a bullock, fixed in order on the floor. The labour and expense in procuring and conveying these large masses of stone to the summit of the mountain must have been very considerable.

The founder of these fine temples is said to have been a banker, who, having no heir, applied the whole of his fortune in building and making these places and objects of worship in A.D. 1243.

One moiety of the revenues of this mountain used formerly to be taken by the Rájás of Sírohí and some petty chiefs, and the other applied to religious purposes, such as the annual repairs of the temples, and provisions for the poor pilgrims, etc. But now Ráo Sewsingjí of Sírohí, after his ablution in the Ganges, has ordered the whole to be expended in charities. Our camp left the foot of this mountain the 2nd of January, 1832, and by slow marches we reached Ajmír in another fortnight, about two hundred and twenty-nine miles from Súrat.

CHAPTER VIII.

Udepur—Pálí—Pokharjí—Ajmír—I return to Súrat—I enter the service of the Nuwáb—The intrigues of a petty Court—My congé.

THE country beyond A'bú is very sandy, with the exception of parts, where spurs of the Aravellí mountain render it rugged and stony. This very unfertile district, called Mewár, appears a vast wilderness, except three towns of some consequence, through which we had to pass, Udepur, Pálí, and Pokharjí.

The first is the seat of the Sissodiya Rájputs, in Mewár, whose tribe is considered purer, and their rank higher, than other Rájputs of India. Their princes are called Ránás, and at their inauguration a spot of human blood is put upon their forehead. How it is procured on such occasions is a secret; but I believe a prisoner is generally killed to serve the purpose. The city is handsome, and situated on an eminence. The western side is adorned with a large lake, having an island in the middle, upon which two palaces are built, where the luxurious princes pass the hot season in the enjoyment of pleasures of all kinds.

Pálí is a mart on the borders of the desert. I

bought some European articles there cheaper than in Bombay. The inhabitants are wealthy in general, and there are above eleven thousand houses.

The third is Pokharjí, originally Pushkára, so called from a spacious deep tank, three sides of which are built up with stones, and have flights of steps down to the water at irregular distances. The shores are adorned with temples. The town is not large, but the view of it from the eastern side is most enchanting. The 17th of January was the day of our arrival. The evening was cool and calm, and the azure sky seemed in the twilight to shine with seven varied hues when I paid my visit to this romantic tank. Alone, and standing at a flight of steps, I mused for a while, and was highly delighted with the beauty of the place. The sheet of water lay like a mirror, reflecting the lofty edifices which began to be lighted up. By degrees, as it grew darker, a multitude of lamps glittered round the lake, and were multiplied in the reflecting waters. I then returned to my tent, well satisfied, and amply repaid for the trouble I had taken.

The next day, on the morning of the 18th, we reached Ajmír, the capital of Rájputáná, and pitched our tents in front of the Governor-General's camp, at a little distance from the city. The two great men secretly consulted on some grand political subject, and the chiefs of the neighbouring principalities having been invited, paid their homage to the ruler vested with supreme power over India. We stayed at Ajmír about six weeks, and then returned by Nasírábád and Lunawára to Baroda, leaving Mount A'bù on the right, and passing through a very thick forest and desolate country.

I must not leave Ajmír without giving a description of it. This ancient city, six miles south of Pushkára, stands at the foot of a mountain crowned by the fortress of Táragarh. The houses are of masonry, magnificently built, and the inhabitants are wealthy. Their number does not exceed thirty thousand. After the cession of the city to the British Government by Sindhiah, a civil commissioner, Mr. Wilder, was put in charge, and, by good management, it soon became a rival of Jaipur. A quarter of the city bears the name of Wilder's bazaar, the architectural uniformity and beauty of which is unequalled in the cities in these parts.

Saiyid Husain Mashadí and Khájah Muínu'd-dín Chishtí, the two most celebrated Mohamedan saints in India, have their eternal repose here. The shrine of the former is on the top of the Táragarh hill, and that of the latter at the bottom of it, adjoining the city. The Saiyid, endowed with both spiritual and temporal powers, was governor of the place for Kutbu'd-dín Ibak, them Emperor of Delhi, and it was during his government that the Khájah arrived, and made the place the end of his long journeys, in which, until his arrival here, he passed all his time. Being an accomplished archer, he was in the habit of passing many days without any companion in the wilderness of Persia and Turkistán, living upon the game killed by his bow, and employing his time in contemplation undisturbed by the noisy world. He was born at Sijistán, 527 A.H., and departed this life at the age of one hundred and eight. His intimacy with the Governor terminated in a relationship with him, though himself a Sunní, and the Saiyid a Shíah. During his sojourn at Ajmír he visited Delhi twice. On his second and last trip Saiyid Wajbu'd-dín, the uncle of the Governor of Ajmír, who resided at Delhi, was warned in a dream by his sacred ancestor to give his only daughter in marriage to nobody but the saint of the time, Khájah Muínu'd-dín, who, having heard of this, observed that, though the time of his stay in the world was nigh over, yet the sacred offer should not be refused. So the marriage took place, after which he lived for seven years, and had several children by his wife.

The large and spacious mosque near his tomb was built by the Emperor Jahángír, 1027 A.H. The shrine is held in great reverence by all Muslims. The famous Akbar paid his visit more than once to the tomb from Agra, a distance of two hundred and thirty-two miles. He walked all the way on foot out of respect, and barefooted when in sight of the sacred place. Many Hindús, whose superstitious minds can be easily persuaded to any belief, pay the same respect to the tomb as true believers. Máhádají Sindhiah, and Yeswant Ráo Holkar, annually sent an offering of money. Daulat Ráo Sindhiah, besides the usual gifts, had all the edifices thoroughly repaired. Thousands of pilgrims annually come to pay their respects to the tomb. The prayers of some of the supplicants being granted through the medium of the shrine, and their hearts' desire being fulfilled either by chance or destiny, the effects are attributed to the miraculous aid of the saint. In such respects mankind are like a herd of sheep, one blindly follows another. The inside of the mausoleum is both magnificent and solemn: the floor is paved with pure marble, the walls nicely latticed, the ceiling beautifully white and smooth. In the centre stands the tomb, covered with very valuable brocade. An oblong square palisade of silver grating is fixed about it, leaving a space of about three feet all round. At the head of the tomb is placed a large silver censer, from which the smoke of the burning incense diffuses its fragrance all over the place. A somewhat higher than usual fee to the warden in attendance procures admittance into the palisade, where the visitor touches the tomb with his right hand, which he kisses with solemnity and retires.

In the month of March, 1833, I returned to Súrat, and passed some time with my family and friends.

This year, my income being small, I began to

practice medicine, in which, I thank heaven, I soon obtained a good name beyond my merits, having administered medicine to the poor gratis, charging those only who could afford to pay. I took care not to take a difficult case in hand, but referred such to the Government Hospital. For fifteen months I was a doctor, during which time six hundred and sixty-four patients passed under my care, from which number six hundred and sixty-one recovered and three died, two of fever and one of cholera.

In November I was blessed with a son, whom I named Kudratullah. His birth afforded me great happiness, but it was overweighed by the embarrassment of my circumstances at this time. Burdened with the heavy charges of a nurse and the expense of alms and presents requisite on such occasions, I was under the necessity of bidding adieu to my profession as a physician; and, finding some scholars desirous of instruction, I resumed the office of a tutor. Having an offer of employment from Lieutenant H. Boye, at Ahmadábád, I proceeded thither. The young man, being gifted with a clear head and high talents, made himself perfect master of the Urdú language in a short time, and proceeded to the Presidency, taking me along with him. He passed an excellent examination before the committee, and rewarded me beyond my expectation; so I returned home once more with a sum of money sufficient for about one year's expenditure.

In June I returned to Súrat, and remained without employment for about three weeks, when His Highness Mír Afzalu'd-dín Khán, the Nuwáb of Súrat, requested me to enter into his service as secretary. I readily accepted the offer, and was invited to breakfast at the palace, when His Highness declared that I was to be his companion for ever, and that for the present he had been pleased to fix certain allowances for me, the memorandum of which, bearing His Excellency's signature, would be presented to me. He bade me not doubt of promotion when he was extricated from his present difficulties and had vanquished his enemy, the Guebre (meaning the native agent of the British Government). At the same time he presented me with a very valuable pair of shawls and the memorandum. Upon this, I rose from my seat, and thanked him with a low bow.

On reaching home I found a host of mace-bearers, waiting servants, and musicians of His Highness at my door, to congratulate me and to receive some presents in return. I dismissed them, satisfied with my liberality in the glee of the moment. When at leisure, I referred to the memorandum, which ran thus:—

"*Memorandum of the Monthly Allowances of the Munshí Lutfullah Khán Sáhib, from the Sarkár of His Highness Kamru'd-daulah, Hashmat Jang, Bahádur, Nuwáb of Súrat.*

"Rupees, fifty-one in ready cash; Free Table; Dry Provisions for the Family; one Horse, with a Groom and two Peons always in attendance upon him; two Suits of Clothes annually."

I found the stipend quite sufficient for a gentleman of India blessed with contentment, and was satisfied with it, having the promise of promotion in view. I was punctual and regular in my daily attendance upon His Highness, whom I found quite pleased with me, and he loaded me with presents of every kind every now and then.

His Highness was a gentlemanly old man, about fifty-three, only five feet seven, but portly and dignified. His complexion was brownish, and his manners and deportment very stately and pleasing. A Saiyid by caste, his grandfather was an inhabitant of Burhánpur, and of the sacred order, who came to Súrat as an adventurer in 1732. He managed to get himself married in the family of Safdar Khán, governor of the city at that time, and having purchased popularity and influence, himself succeeded to the government. His descendants ruled until the 13th of May, 1800, when the father of the Nuwáb, my master, was obliged to surrender the city and the territory to his patrons, the English, for an annual pension of 15,000*l.* Besides, he was kindly allowed by them to retain certain small privileges and the empty title of Nuwáb. After the death of this Nuwáb, in 1821, his son, my master, was placed by the authorities on the throne, and allowed by them to enjoy the stipend and immunities as before, without any change in his shadowy title and dignity. To this phantom of power it was my destiny now to swear fealty. I was informed by the Minister of His Highness that the native agent, about two months ago, had behaved very disrespectfully towards the Nuwáb in ordering one of his servants to be beaten, bound, and taken publicly, under a police-guard, to his Court, merely because he was found drunk. His Highness at the time, being in the house of his Minister, descried his servant in this disgraceful plight, and ordered the guard to be brought before him with their prisoner, whom he bade them release. This being done, in the fury of the moment he kicked out the guard, loading them with curses and imprecations. The native agent, who could not bear his magisterial authority thus degraded, was now working mischief by bearing tales to Mr. Lumsden, the agent, judge, and magistrate, all in one.

I had now to reply to eleven of the agent's unanswered epistles. His Highness took three days to read through the drafts, and then condescended to say he approved very highly of the language, style, and spirit of the papers I had drawn, that his Hindú clerks could not write Persian correctly, and sometimes it was difficult for them to understand the drift of the subject.

The cloud of dissension between the Government agent and His Highness being, however, removed by a compromise, the native agent sought to regain favour, and soon obtained it. The Nuwáb again began to send, almost every evening, his confidential officer to the nocturnal Court of the native agent, and sometimes I myself was desired to go to him to take down his answers.

For five months and a half I remained in favour; and then I found that some consultation was going on with the native agent, apart and secret from me, the result of which soon manifested itself. By the close association of nearly six months, I found that the poor old Nuwáb was a mere tool in the hand of others; he had no intellectual power to judge for himself, he was fond of low society, and addicted to intoxicating drugs and liquors. Now he was induced, I strongly believe, by his base and malignant Minister (a man—vulgar, illiterate, and perfect in depravity, who at first was a menial servant to Captain Rankin, the fort adjutant), at the counsel, or rather instigation, of the native agent, to plunder and sequester the property of the ex-Minister. The native agent lent his aid in the ruin of his bitter enemy, the ex-Minister, on condition that His Highness should dismiss certain persons from the service and fill up their places by those in whom he had implicit confidence. These were the secret consultations, and they took effect very soon by the dismissal of the Díwán Hardirám Sáhibrám, a very respectable man, who was suddenly surrounded by the guard in his office, and all the boxes containing cash and records, etc., in his charge being instantly sealed, he was told that he was dismissed from the service because he had secret communication with the ex-Minister. Poor Hardirám boldly replied that he had no secret communication with the Minister, but a secret feud with the native agent, and that, from the date of the compromise, he expected to receive the treatment he now experienced. "God is great, I am innocent, truth at last will certainly shine forth, and guilt will have its due recompense," said he, and so delivered over the keys and departed.

The next day the Minister and I were deputed to go to Atmarám and offer to him on the part of His Highness, the situation of Díwán.

Atmarám is the son of Kirparám, who negociated the treaty of 1800, on the part of the Nuwáb's late father, with Mr. Jonathan Duncan, and managed to obtain a perpetual pension of three hundred rupees per mensem for himself and his descendants, from the British authorities in return for his services. Kirparám's family, ever since the treaty, were held in odium by the late and the present Nuwáb, who found out afterwards that he had acted treacherously in that business of importance, and had sacrificed his master's power and dominion for his own benefit. His Highness, therefore, had turned him out of the service. After the death of Kirparám, his son Atmarám, a man well educated both in Sanskrit and Persian, became a hanger-on of the native agent for years, in the hope of getting an appointment suitable to his station in life. Besides his pension of three hundred rupees a month, he expended large sums of money in support of his interests, and got in debt to the amount of more than thirty thousand rupees. The native agent's support at last procured him the situation of Díwán, the salary of which was a small one of only fifty rupees per month; but the great advantage was that, having entered the Nuwáb's service, he had extricated himself from the civil jurisdiction, and no creditor, thenceforward, could sue him under the Regulations.

With Atmarám, another crafty Hindú named Matírám was appointed as accountant. This being done the next thing was to get the ex-Minister to put himself in the Nuwáb's power, and a message was sent to him requesting his attendance.

The man, although vulgar and illiterate, having been raised from the grade of a bread-seller to the rank of Minister, yet, by instinctive sagacity, well knew the object of His Highness, who was entirely under the influence of his malignant successor and the native agent. He, therefore, on receipt of the message, repaired to Mr. Lumsden and told him that he was then a British subject; and, being sent for by the Nuwáb, his former master, under pretence of examining accounts, his heart misgave him, and he suspected a snare being laid for him by the people about the Nuwáb, who was a mere tool in their hands. Mr. Lumsden referred him to the native agent, telling him that he had a letter from His Highness on that head, that he was sure the Nuwáb could do him no harm, and that he would desire the native agent to make every proper arrangement about it. Great as were the ex-Minister's suspicions, he could not mistrust the word of the British representative, so being obliged to satisfy himself with what had taken place, he made his bow and departed.

The next evening he went to the native agent's private Court, where, having asked to be heard alone, all present were requested to leave, when the ex-Minister, seeing no alternative, except submission, placed his turban upon the feet of the man in power, about whom a few months ago he cared but very little. He then said, "I have served my master faithfully for fifteen years, and have extricated him out of the difficulties of debt. I have conducted his affairs to his satisfaction, as more than once has been noticed to the British authorities in His Highness's official correspondence. My fidelity and loyalty obtained for me all my wealth and property; but, becoming the object of envy to all my master's court, they conspired against me and were bent on my ruin. I fear not the examination of the accounts, upon almost all of which I was prudent enough to obtain the Nuwáb's signature. I therefore most submissively beg your pardon for what occurred between me, yourself, and your late brother, and I take my oath to make reparation;" and, saying this, he knelt down to him. The native agent heard all this attentively, and, taking his guest by the hand, seated him by himself. He gave him all the comfort a politician's tongue could afford, and told him that he had not the least idea of what had occurred between him and his brother, and that he was liberal enough to have forgotten entirely if there happened anything in former times.

Next evening, the present Minister and myself were ordered to attend at the native agent's for his counsel. On our arrival there, all persons present were dismissed, and we alone remained in the private assembly. He then addressed me in his broken English, saying, "The Nuwáb was an ungrateful man; many a kindness had he done him, and many a fault covered for him, in vain. He applauds," said he, "the acts of such low, mean, and vile people as the horrid brute with golden necklace next to you" (alluding to the Minister my companion, who knew not a word of English). I replied to him in the same language, telling him that I, being a new servant, knew very little of the character of His Highness, but that I believed good acts would surely bring a good return at last. He then addressed himself very politely to the Minister in Hindústání, "You may tell the Nuwáb, with my best respects, that his adversary, having at last submitted himself, I prevailed upon him to make himself present at the palace. You may send for him and do as you like, but take care do not be harsh in the commencement." Turning then towards me, he observed that the question was a simple one; we were only to examine the accounts of His Highness with the man, asking him to give a satisfactory explanation of all the disbursements made through him, and we should soon find him commit himself. After this we had some conversation with him upon different topics, and then, taking leave, returned to the palace and explained to His Highness the result of our mission.

During the time this was going on, I met with a most severe calamity; that is, my poor son departed this life at the age of two years and three months. Poor boy, he suffered his fever and cough with the fortitude of a man; he took his doses of physic bravely, but without avail. The lance of grief pierced my heart through and through, but the loss was irreparable, and there was no remedy except patience, patience, and nothing but patience, under the decrees of heaven.

After this misfortune, I was left alone for ten days, and then was ordered to take two clerks and books of accounts to a small garden near the palace, where it was appointed for the ex-Minister to undergo his examination. I was to be strict, but not harsh, and to try my best to implicate the man somehow or other. Provided with such instructions, I proceeded with my companions to the place where we found the man waiting for us. I examined him in the best way I could for ten days, but he exonerated himself of all the charges, showing the signature of His Highness to the different items. The Minister himself sometimes superintended the examination in person. We compared the books of merchants, to whom the payments were made, with our accounts, but found them correspond. I told my friend the Minister, in private, that the man was innocent in my opinion in these accounts, and he must look for another stratagem to criminate the object of his animosity. "Could you not alter some of the items?" remarked he. To this my reply was, that my conscience was more precious to me than His Highness's service, if I was to commit such acts of atrocity. "Atrocity, d——d nonsense," rejoined he; "would you not be loyal to your liege lord in doing anything and everything for him?" "Expect me not," returned I, "to do anything against conscience." Some unpleasant words passed between us on this occasion, and from this time His Highness began to appear displeased and sullen towards me, though I affected not to observe it. In the meantime I went on with my duty of examining the man; but, to my great astonishment, I found Mutírám one of my subordinates, trying to overrule me, and acting the part of a prosecutor very authoritatively and harshly, instead of acting under me in the proceedings as he had hitherto done. He disputed the points wrongfully, and quarrelled with the man in very unbecoming language. He said he cared not about His Highness's signatures, which he believed to be either forged or taken whilst His Highness was sleepy or intoxicated. This line of conduct in my subordinate was highly extolled by the Nuwáb and the Minister, and then I knew I was required to play a game beyond my capability.

I then mentioned to the Minister that it was quite unnecessary for me to attend the prosecution any farther, since Mutírám acted his part in the business very ably and satisfactorily; that I was not unconscious of the treatment I had experienced from His Highness and himself for a few days; and that I would resign the service next week if it was continued. This he heard from me very quietly, without uttering a word, but I was informed he brought it to the notice of His Highness immediately, by whom he was ordered to consult the native agent about it the same evening. The time of warning given by me having expired without any amendment in the conduct of my master and superior towards me, I sent in my resignation, after serving His Highness for seven months and ten days; and proceeded in person to the British agent, to whom I stated my case, and told him that, having sent in my resignation to the Nuwáb, I had become a British subject again. Mr. Lumsden remarked that it was wrong in me to leave His Highness' service so abruptly, and that the poor old man, surrounded as he was by all sorts of rogues and rascals, would surely be ruined by them. I replied that I could not help it, and that I would not endanger myself and family for the benefit of others. Saying this, I took my departure from the agent's presence, and then paid my visit to the native agent down-stairs, who warmly shook hands with me, and observed that he knew the object of my having seen the agent, and that I had done well in having resigned the Nuwáb's service. "The old man," said he, "is a patronizer of mean upstarts, who will not allow any good man to remain in his service." From such and other phrases I perceived that he wanted me to impeach His Highness; but my reply to all was short and sweet,—that service and life were precarious, that nobody has read the line of his fate, and that I knew not whether I had acted right or wrong in resigning. Saying this, I took my leave and returned home.

After my resignation, His Highness sent messages dissuading me from giving up the service. He would not recal the peons, detached to do duty at my house, for some time; but, finding at last that my word was one and unalterable, he sent my pay that was in arrears, and called away his peons. In the meantime I resumed my old profession of a tutor to English officers, and was better off than with the Nuwáb.

CHAPTER IX.

I am appointed to an office under the Political Agent in Káttiawár —The Nágar Bráhmans—I resign office in order to accompany Captain Eastwick, assistant to Colonel Pottinger, Resident in Sindh—Mr. Erskine presents me with a certificate and a Kashmír shawl—I find three unexpected companions—Sara, the fair Maimuní—I leave Rájkót—The Jám of Nowanagar—Dharol—The merry Governor of Juria Bandar—Pleasant sailing—Frisky monsters of the Deep—Speculations of the Sindhís as to our purpose in coming to their country—I act priest at the I'du'l fitr—March to Tatta—Description of Tatta.

In the month of February I resigned the service of the Nuwáb, and had hardly passed eighteen days with my scholars, when I received an invitation from Mr. J. Erskine, the Political Agent at Káttiawár, through Mr. Vibart, the principal collector of the Súrat-Zila. I arrived at Rájkót on the 1st of March. After a short stay at Rájkót, I was appointed superintendent in the neighbouring district of Bábriawár, on a salary of one hundred rupees a month. I, however, never entered upon my duties, being detained to investigate charges of corruption against some native officers of the Political Agent's establishment. The accused parties were Nágar Bráhmans, and they defended themselves with so much ingenuity, as to turn the tables on their accusers. I was detained, in common with the rest, and was soon glad to avail myself of any opportunity to quit Káttiawár.

In the early part of this year I was delighted to hear of my beloved master, Captain Eastwick's, return from England. His regiment chanced to be stationed here, and he soon arrived to join it, and again I had the pleasure of shaking hands with him, and found his heart as warm as ever.

After a few weeks' stay with his regiment, he was placed at the disposal of the Governor-General of India, and proceeded to Sindh, where he was appointed Assistant-Resident, under Colonel, now Sir H. Pottinger, a real man, wise as Solomon and enterprising as Alexander.

Resolving to accompany my former master, I tendered my resignation to Mr. Erskine, and received the following certificate:—

"*Rájkót Political Agent's Office, Káttiawár,*

"*July 1st*, 1838.

"This is to certify, that Munshí Lutfullah Khán has been known to me for years, that from the beginning of the year 1836 he has been employed by me in various capacities in the service of the H. E. I. Company, principally as a translator of Oriental documents.

"He is master of the Persian, Hindústání, Maráthí, and Gujaráthí languages, besides having a knowledge of the idiom, structure, and details of the English language that very few Orientals have attained to. As an instructor in the above-mentioned languages he is invaluable. His intimate acquaintance with the Européan character, and his contempt for the follies and depravities of the natives of India, render him a most valuable servant to the British Government.

"I believe him to be a man of integrity, veracity, and ability, to such a degree, that I have never elsewhere met with his equal among those of pure Asiatic descent.

"I have given this paper to Munshí Lutfullah as a sincere testimonial to his excellent character and superior attainments, of which I have been a witness.

(Signed) "JAMES ERSKINE,
"P. A., Káttiawár."

On Friday, the 23rd November, I repaired to the Political Agent's Office to take leave. All my office friends felt deeply for my loss, and we exchanged tears of parting with one another: they were so obliging as to raise a subscription, and presented me with a valuable dress of honour. Mr. Erskine, likewise, made me a present of a valuable Kashmír shawl, and poor Dr. Graham, since dead, gave me a small chest of medicine. So, loaded with presents and good wishes from my friends and master, I returned home, with a heart partly beating with pleasure at having a wide field before me, and partly dejected at separation from friends, in whose society I had remained nearly three years.

On my return home I found Parshotam Takkarsí, the head of the firm of that name at Rájkót, waiting for me. On inquiring the cause, he observed that he and his family, consisting of sixty-five in number, were all under obligations for my having been the cause of the restitution of their property, ten thousand rupees, carried off by a gang of robbers, who had wounded and killed three members of the family; that they felt very sorry at my departure, and would not allow me to depart without my accepting a present from the firm; saying this, he poured two hundred rupees out of a bag and begged my acceptance of the sum. I thanked him for his too good opinion of me, which I told him was more acceptable to me than the coins: so saying, I dismissed him. Thinking I had considered the present too small, he returned to me again in about half an hour with a gold necklace, worth about five hundred rupees, which he begged me very strongly to accept. I did not like to hurt his feelings, so I took the necklace and put it on before him. I asked him if he was satisfied to see me in possession of his kind present. He was greatly so, replied he, and then got up to depart, upon which I took the necklace off and put it on his neck, adjuring him in the strongest terms to accept it from me. The old man, then in tears, said he was very sorry to meet with such a disappointment; but I told him I would accept some sweatmeats from him for his satisfaction, and would always think of him on my way up to Sindh.

In the evening three other visitors did me the honour of calling upon me, an old lady and two daughters. The oldest had passed the time of her charms, but the youngest, at the age of about eighteen, by name Sara, was a consummate beauty. Although her complexion was sallow, her form and features were exquisitely handsome, shaped with the chisel of the Goddess of Beauty herself. But they were all three in a most wretched condition. They begged to be allowed to travel with the carts of my baggage as far as Juria, and I not only granted their request, but ordered my servants to take their small bundles of clothes, etc., on my carts. They then thanked me for the kindness, and the old dame began her narrative as follows:—

"We are Mohamedan culivators, clan of Maimun, inhabitants of Bhúj; my husband was a man of wealth and consequence amongst the farmers of the province. The fruit of our union was these two daughters only, and no son. It pleased Almighty God to take away my good husband, the father of these orphans, when my youngest girl was about two years old. After his death the Government confiscated all our property, under the pretence of his having been in debt to it for the lease of the village to him for some years past. Some months after my husband's departure from this world, my son-in-law, too, followed him; and thus we remained helpless, without any asylum, for some years, pressed hard under the cruel foot of indigence, labouring in the fields of others for our livelihood. My eldest girl, unfortunately having been seduced by an English gentleman, Mr. ——, absconded, and left us in a miserable condition, worse than before. We never heard of her until lately, when she wrote to me from this. The gentleman, her sweetheart, died of cholera on a sudden, and left nothing for her to subsist upon. She had, however, about three or four hundred rupees worth of jewels, a part of which we have already sold for our maintenance: and, not to conceal it from you, we have still something left, which we intend to apply in agricultural speculation on our return home. The fate of the young Sara is worse than that of the other. I gave her in marriage to a young gardener of Drángdra. She lived with her husband for about two years, when the career of his life was cut short, after which she remained under the care of her late husband's sister, by whom she was considered an unlucky woman, as her husband died so shortly after the marriage. She was tyrannized over and maltreated to a great degree, and at last secretly sold by her remorseless sister-in-law to an old gardener of Limrí for twenty-five rupees. I heard of her misfortunes, and, coming to this place where slavery is said to be discountenanced, I sent her a message to effect her escape and come over to me. It is now about six weeks since she arrived. The gardener, her unlawful master, with a couple of peons, have also come here, and they are watching an opportunity to seize upon the girl and take her to Limrí. We heard of your going to Juria Bandar, and now wait upon you to seek your protection as far as that place, whence by the first opportunity we shall go to our native land, where we shall pray for your long life and prosperity."

I listened to her tale with compassion, and told her that she and her daughters should consider themselves safe under my protection, being that of a British subject; that they should not only be conveyed to Juria (where they could not be safe from the intrigues of the native States), but landed on the coast of their native land, free of expense.

Poor creatures, they thanked me heartily for the kindness I showed, and started very early next morning with my baggage.

On the 24th of November, 1838, I left Rájkót, and arrived at Pardhárí, eleven miles distant, about nine A. M. I met with a hospitable reception from the agent of the Zamíndár. Pardhárí, though small, is the principal town of twelve villages belonging to H.H. the Jám of Nowanagar, who is graciously pleased to continue the farm of it to the son of Fakír Mohamed, his late favourite Jamadár, still in his minority.

H. H. the Jám, though illiterate, is a high-minded Prince. His name—Ranmallijí, "hero of the field of battle," coincides with his character. During my stay with the Political Agent, I had the honour of conferring with him several times on the part of the British Government, on the subjects of boundary disputes and infanticide. On all occasions I was pleased with his manly conduct and sensible conversation. Though a Járejá chief, he has preserved a daughter.

On the 25th, I left Pardhárí at sunrise, and reached Dharol, the principal village, belonging to Járejá Bhúpatsingjí at ten A. M. I was received with great kindness and hospitality. The chief himself did me the honour of visiting me at my quarters out of town, in company with his son, a promising lad of about fourteen, his daughter, a very pretty young girl of six, and his guest, the chief of Amran, attended with a numerous retinue. He stayed with me for three hours engaged in conversation about the impending war with Russia. He seemed to take an especial interest in my account of the Russian Empire. I satisfied his curiosity, to the best of my knowledge, regarding the customs, manners, and habits of Russians.

On the morning of the 26th, I left Dharol. It was an unusually misty morning. We reached Juria, a very populous and large town, at half-past eight A. M. Here I was received with greater hospitality than I ever experienced in Káttiawár. The governor of the place, by name Ahmad Khawáss, had the politeness to send his people to receive me. They conducted me to a very nice place, where I put up and made myself as comfortable as at home. A very good breakfast for myself, and for all the people with me, had been prepared before our arrival. All of us jointly thanked our host for his goodness. Although his title is "Khawáss" (which in Káttiwár means "slave"), yet I found him excel many masters, princes of the country.

On the 27th, I was obliged to make a halt, as I had several letters to write to my family and friends, and this was the last stage whence I could communicate without fear of the letters being lost. I sent away the Gaikwár contingent horsemen who were ordered to escort me as far as this place. I then went to the harbour, which is two miles from the town, to select a boat for my voyage to Sindh. The governor accompanied me. I found the harbour a poor one. The number of the small vessels not exceeding the tonnage of 100 khandies (or 25 tons) was but 26. I took one of 60 khandies, or 15 tons.

Dined with the governor at six P. M. My jolly old host commenced drinking, or rather sipping, raw brandy, an hour before the dinner was brought. He insisted upon my joining him, but I could not grant his request. The old man was merry by dinner-time. In short we passed the evening very pleasantly. After the dinner was over he showed me two magnificent palaces belonging to his government. The edifices, though not well furnished, are of an excellent design.

At my departure, he bestowed on me, on the part of his master, a dress of honour, consisting of a very handsome scarf and a turban, both worth about 100 rupees. I tried my best to decline the honour, but he insisted strongly on my accepting them, telling me that, five days previous to my arrival here, he had received strict orders from his master upon the subject, and His Highness would certainly be displeased with him if they were not accepted. In short,

I was so much pressed by the good old man that I consented to receive the things. Seeing that he was very fond of, and in want of, tea, I gave him one half of the quantity I had along with me, and a native saddle which he seemed to admire much, and of which I had no use for the present, having disposed of my horse.

On the 28th, at eleven A. M., I left the town of Juria for the harbour. The governor accompanied me to see myself and the baggage, etc., safe on board. I saw a European priest, just landed from Bhúj, and exchanged a few words with him respecting his journey to Rájkót, etc. They say it is unlucky for a traveller to see a priest at the time of starting on his way, and it proved to be so in my case; for, whilst engaged in conversation with him, the tide that would have carried my vessel out of the harbour ebbed, and we were obliged to remain at the mouth of the creek until nine P. M., to our great annoyance. Not wishing however, to keep my new friend, the old governor, exposed in the sun, we parted, mutually expressing our best wishes for each other. I went on board at one P. M., and bade adieu to the Peninsula—the land of ignorance, opium-eating, and infanticide, and its one million six hundred thousand inhabitants and two hundred and forty-four chiefs—in the words of the good ploughman of Scotland,

"Farewell my friends, and farewell my foes;
My peace with these and my love with those."

We weighed anchor on the night of the 29th at nine P.M. It being calm, the night and day passed well. The pure atmosphere, the cold breeze, and the gentle exercise of sailing, produced in me a healthful exhilaration. I felt my appetite insatiable, and we had no meat on board, it not being procurable at Juria, where the governor alone killed sheep, and that secretly, not to offend the prejudices of his Hindú Jain subjects, who are generally the richest people.

Early in the morning of the 30th, when I opened my eyes, I found myself at the port of Mandaví. The scene of nineteen years ago presented itself to my mind. The memory of my reverie when I stood there gazing at the ocean for the first time, and my being startled by the bite of the dog, etc., came back, and it seemed as if all had taken place but yesterday. My Tindal Jum'a, of the clan of Miánas or pirates, coming up to me, put himself in a complimentary attitude very unnatural to him. "Well, Jum'a," said I, "what is the news?" Poor rough creature of the sea! summing up all the words of politeness he knew, which did not exceed five, he said, in his growling voice, that he would make a stay of one day there to try his luck in taking charge of some cargo for Sindh. He bade me go ashore and order my servants to buy provisions for five days, as he did not like to see me starving without meat.

I thanked the good man for his kindness, and complied with his request, telling him that he might take my servant with him for the provisions, and put the three ladies on shore at the same time; as for myself, I told him a sore foot prevented my going on land, so I remained on board engaged with my book, whilst my friends proceeded to the town.

At midnight, on the 1st of December, we sailed with a fleet of vessels carrying an English regiment. By the grace of the Almighty God, on the 3rd we passed the "Ghorí Kíchar," an island of sand. A couple of monstrous sharks, each of them in size somewhat bigger than an elephant, came near our vessel; they seemed to play with each other, sometimes one lying flat and the other mounting it, and, at others, one running after the other, passing under our vessel and going round it, in which act they often gave a shake to our boat, which distressed us and roused the spirit of our Tindal. He said to me, "It is true these brutes are sometimes dangerous to the vessels; but have no fear, they are as cowardly as huge; I will soon remedy the evil." Saying this, he came to the side of the boat and, finding them floating along with us, began his remonstrances as if they understood his language: "You are kings of the sea, leave pursuing us, in the name of God and of the prophet Solomon. We are poor people, our vessel does not contain more than ten men; go, therefore, to the other vessels, they are filled with fat soldiers of the Honourable Company." Old

Jum'a's words, instead of producing a good effect, made the animals more frisky and furious. They spouted* up water from their immense nostrils into our ship, in addition to the former annoyances, and played at "hide and seek" round the boat with new vigour, from seven till about a quarter past eight o'clock, A.M. Our good Tindal then, having lost all patience, took up one of his ballast stones, very sharp on one side, pronounced the name of God, and flung it with all his might against the bigger monster's head, inflicting a good blow not unlike that of a hatchet. After the receipt of this compliment, the animal went down at once with his companion, without making its appearance again, and all of us jointly returned our thanks to the kind Providence for this narrow escape. I regretted much not having brought my gun with me.

"Ghorí Kíchar" is now a large sand bank, which, twenty years ago, was the site of Ghorí Bandar, now all sunk below the wave.

On our approach to the aforesaid sand bank, Jum'a desired me to taste the water of the sea, which I did, and to my surprise found it on one side of the ship quite fresh and sweet, and on the other very salt. On inquiring the reason, I was told that the strong current of the Indus ran so far uninfluenced by the sea. We moored about nine o'clock P.M. ten miles off Vikkar Bar.

* From this it is evident that the Author's sharks were grampuses.

4th. It being dead calm, the whole day was spent in reaching the bar. Here we found twelve British men-of-war, two steamers, and about one hundred *battelahs* at anchor, all of them bearing the British flag and containing soldiers and supplies. My friend the old Tindal passed close by a vessel newly wrecked upon a sand bank. I told him the wreck warned us not to come too near, unless we would share her fate; but the old pirate replied, that the Tindal of the boat must either have been blind or had some sinister motive to wreck the vessel, for all the banks here were known to every boy of the coast. Moored at the bar for the night.

On the 5th we entered the mouth of the Indus, and on the 6th we arrived within seven miles of Vikkar. There being a small village on the left bank, I went ashore to see it. Visited the head man of the village. Conversed with him through the old Tindal, whose mother tongue was Sindhí. The old chief's replies to our queries were so loud that at first I thought he either took us to be deaf, or was offended at our intrusion. On asking the reason, Jum'a told me that nothing was wrong, but that such was the custom of the country. These people seemed miserable beings, living in such huts as the villagers of India have for their cattle, without any partition. All members of the family—husband, wife, son, daughter-in-law, etc.—sleep in the same stall, upon one bed, the materials of which are no more than a mat spread over a little grass. Their food is a very coarse bread of rice, with fish, fresh or dry. They are very fond of tobacco and onions, for which articles the head man begged. I inquired about the system of taxation in his country, and he informed me that taxes were mostly taken in kind. The agriculture in general is confined to rice, which is produced in abundance. The cultivator gets one-fifth of the produce, the remainder being divided into two halves, one of which goes to the Government, and the other to the landholder.

On the 7th I landed at the camp at Vikkar, and was most hospitably received by my master and friend, Captain Eastwick.

The 8th I passed in exploring the village of Vikkar. It consisted of about two dozen miserable huts. Colonel H. Pottinger arrived in the evening from Hydrábád.

On the 9th we removed our tents from the military camp, and pitched them near the Resident's. From this date I regularly commenced the performance of my duty. I had the pleasure of seeing Sikandar Khán, my old friend of Tulsí Shám, now Súbahdár Major, the highest rank that a native soldier attains to. He now belonged to the Sappers and Miners. He introduced to me a friend of his, Mírza Ali Akbar, Captain S. Powell's Persian teacher. The young Mughal appeared to be a promising lad.

I began Sindhí grammar, which I found to be easy

work. A man acquainted with the rudiments of the Asiatic languages could learn Sindhí with little trouble.

On the 14th, after the usual work in the office, I was engaged in an onerous task of counting and taking down the numbers of Government treasure boxes, one hundred and seventy-eight in number, arrived from Bombay. A horrible case of suicide occurred in the evening. An officer of Dragoons shot himself; cause unknown.

On the 15th I had the honour of being introduced to the Resident, Colonel Pottinger. At the first sight his abilities and resolute character were apparent.

I now began to mix with the Sindhís and learnt the idiom of the language by conversing with them. Idleness is the main feature in the Sindhí character. The Tindals of the river sat almost all day at the door of my tent, engaged in confabulation and disputes. The general theme of their discourse was Government affairs. One party remarked that the country was lost—the English would take it very soon. "The Tálpúrs themselves, especially Mír Súbdár," said they, "are to blame for being too friendly with the omnivorous English: they have taken all India; in the same way they will soon take this country." Another responded, "You are mistaken, my friends. Let the Tálpúrs of Hydrábád make themselves Christians; but fear not, as long as we have Shír Mohamed of Mírpúr on our side.

His late Highness Mír Karam Ali's widow has furnished, and will always furnish him with funds sufficient to carry on a perpetual war with all the Feringees in the world; and, if God pleases, we can be masters of all the gold and implements of war that they are labouring to bring into our country. Know ye not the verse of our Holy Book, "One true believer is sufficient to defeat ten infidels?" A third white-bearded Sindhí, with a profound sigh, observed, "Ah! my friends, your dream is somewhat too extravagant; you have never seen the tri-coloured, viz., the white, brown, and dark devils, fighting jointly on a field of battle. Whilst in the service of H. H., the Peshwá, I was an eye-witness of their hard fights in the Dakhan. Here is an unquestionable proof:" saying this, he tucked up his sleeve and showed a scar, which demonstrated a clear transit of a bullet through his left arm. He concluded by saying, "A man may over-match another, or perhaps two or three, if the contest is to be decided by the sword, but these cowardly Satans have no sword, and if they have any it is as blunt as your walking-stick. They will kill you with their rascally shots whilst you are a mile or so off from them, and then what is the remedy?" Such discussions by the side of my tent walls often amused me much; and sometimes, rising from my seat, I intruded upon them, and preached to them in my broken Sindhí, that the English would not take their miserable country, poducing only fish and rice, even if it were forced upon them; that they had sufficient golden territories to govern and manage, and that they were staunch friends of the Amírs; that their forces were now passing through the country for the purpose of protecting their possessions in India, as well as the Amírs' territory, from foreign aggression. To this they would reply with a chorus of laughter, "What you say, sir, may be true, but we are rude people; we cannot comprehend high politics of government. Ha! ha! ha!"

Being desired by my employer, I made acquaintance with a Sindhí Hindú merchant, Naomal, of Karáchí, who made himself very useful to the British authorities in Sindh. He visited me every now and then, and tried his best to supply the wants of our army. He was a wealthy man, had a large family, consisting of a father, six brothers, and a number of women and children. He was also a man of consequence and influence in Lower Sindh.

On the 19th December happened the I'dul'l fitr, it being the first of the month Shauwál. This is a joyous festival in the Mohamedan world, as it concludes our Lent. But there being no Mohamedan priest with the army, I was obliged, at the request of some friends, to act as one; and, although out of practice for many years, I led the prayers and delivered the sermon to the congregation, composed of the Mohamedan horsemen and footmen, etc., of the Company, and received the usual fee in a turban and scarf, which cost about forty rupees, subscribed by the commissioned officers.

In these days we had often false alarms of Shír Mohamed's giving us a night attack. On the night of the 20th all the men were kept on the alert, and officers patrolled all the night by turns. I noticed that the cocks in this province seemed superfluously religious, as, in addition to their morning and afternoon calls, they took two hours of the night more for crowing, *i. e.*, they began the surplus duties at eight and ended at ten, P.M. This untimely crowing is considered an ill omen in India and Persia, and such over-officiousness of the bird would cost him his life there, but the Sindhís are indifferent about it.

Visited the village of Ghorabárí, about one mile off. It is considered a large village because it consists of one hundred miserable huts. The river in this part of the province, at this cold season, is about a fathom and a half deep. Its width too, in general, is not more than two hundred and fifty yards. The water is muddy, mixed with sand, according to the character of the soil here.

On the 23rd, we were glad to hear of orders for marching next day towards Tatta, and sent off all our baggage with that of the army. In the morning, striking our small tent, as we were going to mount our horses, my master was ordered by the Resident to stay where he was until some arrangement for more camels of burden was made, as the demand for them was on the increase. The 24th passed in making arrangements about the camels, but something remained to be done on the next morning. I slept in the same tent with Captain Eastwick. The cold was intense; I had never felt so cold in India. We had to content ourselves with very unpleasant lonesomeness. The day before, we were in the midst of an army of ten thousand men, and now we had with us but two peons and two Sindhí grooms. We pitied our four attendants who were shivering with cold, and asked them to sleep with us in the tent, but they on no account would overstep the bounds of respect, and slept close to the tent walls. After the day's work we had neither servant nor provision to satisfy the cravings of hunger. Luckily, I had obtained some dates and half a cake of the coarse Sindhí rice bread for a few pice. Upon these articles we made our dinner. To my master it proved a most palatcable meal, and to me better than dainties I afterwards tasted in Mivart's Hotel, London. He said his grace like a good Christian, and I returned my thanks to Him who overlooks our faults and supplies our wants more than we deserve. I made a trial of my good companion at this time, making the following remark: "We must not thank Heaven for bad meals, for if we do, it will never furnish us with better." At this he smiled, and observed, "Let the badness of what we have dined upon be proved first, and then we shall argue on further." Thus we beguiled our time in conversation until he was fast asleep; and then I, having enjoyed my cheroot, went to my bed.

The 25th of December, the birthday of the prophet Jesus Christ, is a holiday of rejoicing to all the Christian world. Early on the morning of this day we were roused from our sleep by two officers, Mr. Jenkins and Captain Ward, just arrived from Mandaví. They asked Captain Eastwick to guide them on to overtake the army; but the remaining part of the compact with the owners of the camels requiring his stay a few hours more, he ordered me to go on with these officers, himself remaining alone to conclude the affair.

We galloped on to Somria, a miserable hamlet of thirty huts, about twelve miles distant, where we overtook the army. Captain Eastwick likewise arrived in the afternoon, successful. Our next march with the army was a long one of twenty miles, to Karampur, consisting of about fifty huts, situated on this side of a branch of the Indus. On the other side is the village of Ghulám Ká Got, of the same size.

On the 27th we halted, and the 28th brought us to the ancient city of Tatta. Having marched early in the morning, we reached the halting place at Makallí, about two miles from the town, at nine o'clock A.M. Our road this morning was partly sandy and partly stony and uneven. • It passed through the ruins of Kalánkot, about two miles from this. The fortifications of this remarkable place appeared to be very old and strong. The materials are mortar and baked bricks, which, at this remote period of time, seem quite new, and as strong as stone. In these heaps of ruins certain signs of antiquity, such as old coins, etc., are sometimes found by the inhabitants, and sold for a good price.

On the 30th it was cloudy, tempestuous, and bitterly cold; so much so that, in the morning when I got up to perform my ablutions, I found the water congealed in the vessel, so was obliged to purify myself with the dust. This being Sunday, I had no office work, and therefore repaired to see the city.

The town of Tatta has no city walls, and great part of it is in ruins. The inhabited houses are about ten thousand. The markets are narrow and the streets filthy. Most of the inhabitants are weavers. Long silken scarfs (called lungís) and blankets are manufactured here better than in Upper Sindh. The fair sex of this town, and indeed of all Sindh, are in general very plain, and very clumsily dressed. Mills for grinding grain and expressing oil, are worked by camels. There are upwards of four hundred mosques in the city, but almost all of them are going to decay.

Visited the Grand Mosque (Jamá Masjid), begun by Sháh Jahán, in 1057 A.H. (A.C. 1647), and finished by Aurangzeb in 1072 A.H. (1661 A.C.), as I found by the inscriptions. The edifice is a magnificent one, about two hundred yards long by one hundred broad, built with baked bricks and mortar. The inner plaster is glazed in white and blue colours. The whole site is roofed with one hundred domes, every one of them painted in a different style from another. The inscriptions carved round the great arch of stone, and those upon the two date stones, are excellently done in large letters. In short, the whole scene presents a picture of beauty and solemnity to the spectator.

The bricks and earthenware of this city are very strong and durable, I believe owing to the peculiarity of the soil, which is a composition of white clay and sand. The houses in general are single storied and built of mud and flimsy timber, flat-roofed, clay only being spread over the upper frame; and partitions plastered with mud are the walls. There are a few houses of double stories, built of bricks, belonging only to very rich individuals. Happening to meet a very handsome Arab, by name Saiyid Mohamed, of the sacred city of Madína, in the market-place, I made his acquaintance, and visited the great priest of the city, Makhdúm Shaikh Abdullah along with him. Both of these men had great influence in the city, the former on account of his birth, and the latter for his station in life. Passed two hours with these gentlemen in conversation. Saiyid Mohamed travelled through Baghdád and Persia for the last three years, leaving his *khums* to accumulate, this being one-fifth of the property of all the heterodox community of the Shiah sect, paid to him as a religious fee. He has thus enriched himself like a Jew. He speaks Persian fairly enough for an Arab, for Arabs are naturally bad linguists. But my host is a man of learning and good breeding. He has a large and beautiful library containing many standard works both in Arabic and Persian.

On the 1st January, 1839, a mission, consisting of four or five officers of rank of the court of Hydrábád, having arrived in the camp, was received in the Resident's tent by Sir John Keane and Colonel Pottinger. The amity and friendship between the two Governments first being talked of, some differences and discontents of their Highnesses, the Amírs, exuded from the discourse of the Ambassadors. The meeting was then adjourned, on their full consent to afford us all the aid in their power for the progress of the army.

On the 4th I obtained leave to explore the Hill of Makallí near the camp. I proceeded early in the morning and amused myself till four o'clock P.M.

This celebrated hill is situated at the distance of about one mile from Tatta. The range runs from west of the town to north, being eight miles long and under one mile broad. Its average height is fifty-five feet. The name is said to be derived from that of a fisherwoman who had her shop there in days of yore. This small hill contains about five hundred domed, and innumerable unroofed, tombs. It is a well-populated city of silence. I had time enough to see only fourteen edifices, as follows:

1. Idgáh, a splendid mosque, where all true believers gather together twice a year, and perform the divine service of the two holy days. The mosque was built by Yúsuf Khán, governor of Sindh. Its inscription is in beautiful large Naskhtalík characters, as follows: —

"Yúsuf Khán, the powerful lord, erected this place of worship as high as his fortune. The year of its finishing is found by Cherubim—the temple of Makkah for the virtuous, 1043 A.H., 1633 A.C.

1. The tombs of the two Vazírs—Mírza Jáná and Mírza Ghází. Date, 1095 A.H., 1683 A.C.

3. A grand mosque, built by Tughral. 1090 A.H., 1679 A.C.

4. Tombs of Mírza Isa and Mírza Ináyatullah, two governors of the place. Magnificent edifices of yellow marble, beautifully carved, with flowers in bas-relief, and surpassing all the buildings of the place. The inscription gives the year of 1058 A.H., 1648 A.C.

5. The tomb of a Minister. 1048 A.H., 1638 A.C.

6. The tomb of a Nuwáb. 966 A.H., 1558 A.C.

7. The tomb of Pír Asad, the Kází, 9 feet long. Era illegible.

8. The tomb of Saiyid Abdullah, son of Saiyid Abdul Kádir Gilaní, the great saint of Baghdád.

9, The tomb of Mírak Mohamed. 1059 A.H. 1649 A.C.

10. The tomb of Shaikh Zia. 1129 A.H., 1619 A.C.

11. The tomb of a King, name illegible. 1109 A.H., 1697 A.C.

12. The tombs of Jám Ninda and Tamáchí, the governors of the Summa tribe, of yellow marble. The building contains three tombs. 925 A.H., 1519 A.C.

13. The tomb of Bábá Isa Langotiband. 920 A.H., 1514 A.C.

14. The tomb of Saiyid Ali Shírází the Saint of the Jokhia Sindhí tribe. 1190 A.H., 1776 A.C.

Amongst my official duties I had the special honour to translate the draft treaty of the thirteen articles now about to be enforced upon the Amírs of Sindh. This task I performed in ten hours, sitting up all night. In the morning the work was taken to the Resident, who held the English draft (in his own handwriting, very difficult to read), in his hand, and ordered me to read the translation. This was found to be correct, and met with the Resident's approbation. Captain Eastwick gave me a present of five hundred rupees out of his own pocket as a mark of his approbation of my services, and the Resident promised me a higher reward.

On the 5th, at five o'clock, P.M., our guard killed a Bilúch who was taken prisoner for selling liquor in the camp, and was consequently ordered to be flogged.

Poor devil, he committed the crime without knowing the retribution. After he was taken to the quarter-guard, he began to wield his sword and shield (of which he ought to have been dispossessed) and inflicted three cuts upon the sentry, who parried, in the best manner he could, with his firelock, the butt end of which was cut in two. The prisoner then attempted to escape, and had got about five hundred yards from the guard, with the naked sword and the shield in his hands, when, passing between the tents of Sir John Keane and Colonel Macdonald, three muskets were fired at him: the ball of one of them, passing through his side, brought him down dead upon the spot, and thus he escaped the flogging.

Rumours of our camp being surprised at night were again prevalent. Several camp followers had been plundered near Lakpat, by a party of twenty-five armed Sindhís.

On the 16th Captain Eastwick was ordered to Hydrábád, so we prepared ourselves to start, and the next morning we proceeded to the ferry, about two miles off, whence we embarked on board the Snake, a small steamer. Here Captain J. Outram joined us. It was a very cold morning, it having rained much all last night. We sailed up about twenty miles during the day, and moored near a village. Passed several Shikárgáhs, or hunting seats of the Amírs. These are large tracts of forest land by the river side, fenced all round, containing all sorts of game.

After steaming and sailing for four days, we reached the port of Hydrábád on the morning of the 20th. The view of the hills and the country, on both sides of the river, is excellent all along. Flocks of large birds, with rosy hued plumes, were seen every now and then floating on the water. On the morning of the 18th we saw a large alligator fast asleep on the right bank, within musket shot, and Captain Outram saluted him with a bullet, which rebounded from his scaly back. But the compliment had only the effect of startling the monster from his sleep and sending him to the water.

A young nobleman, Dost Alí Khán, the son of Khairullah Khán, a near relative of the Amírs, came on their part to receive us. After the exchange of long complimentary sentences he departed, and we located ourselves at the Residency. Munshí Jeth Anand, the native agent of this place, was deputed to the Court, to know when it would suit their Highnesses to receive the British representative and his companions. He brought answer on the 21st, that the Amírs could not see the British officers that day, as they were undergoing the bi-weekly operation of depilation.

On the 22nd, however, Mír Súbdar Khán was foremost to send his confidential agent, by name Badru'd-dín, to Captain Eastwick, with a secret message that he had from the first devoted himself to the British cause, and would ever be found most sincere in it; that he must not be held responsible for the acts of his cousins; and that he felt anxious to receive an assurance of the same nature on the present occasion from Captain Eastwick, before seeing him. Upon this I was forthwith deputed to accompany Badru'd-dín as a bearer of renewed assurances to His Highness.

After going somewhat more than three miles, we came in sight of the citadel of Hydrábád, of which I had heard so much. The near sight of it disappointed me. It is no more than a pentagonal fortification, built of baked bricks and mortar, irregularly bastioned, without any ditch, containing the families of the Amírs and their relations and dependents. In passing through the town we saw several parties of Bilúchís sitting in groups with their pipes, and the extract of hemp under preparation before them. They scowled upon me, and some reviled me in their language. "What do you say to this," said I to my friend Badru'd-dín, "Is this the way of treating foreigners in your country?" "Do you not know," replied he, "a jar exudes whatever it contains. These are vile soldiers from the country. They don't like Feringees, and taking you to be one of them, they are eating this dirt; turn, therefore, a deaf ear to these things in the same way as the Resident himself does sometimes." Considering it expedient to follow my friend's advice, I did so, and entered Mír Súbdár's palace, and was duly presented to him. He was sitting upon a bedstead with his son Fath-Alí, a handsome boy of about ten, attended by a secretary and slave, in a large spacious room without any furniture. After I had ejaculated my salutation in the Mohamedan style, His Highness stretched forth his hand, which I touched with my right, and was going to take my seat upon the floor like the others, but was particularly desired to take a chair that was brought for the purpose. After compliments, I delivered my message, which His Highness heard with attention, and was satisfied. After this, some conversation upon the subject of the manners and customs of Europeans took place, and then I took my departure. A couple of Sindhí horsemen were ordered to escort me to the Residency, and to protect me from the insults of the wild Bilúchís. When I had got half-way to our camp, another pair of horsemen galloped up, begging me to return for a moment as the Amír wanted to speak to me. I returned and had to repeat my message, some words of which Mír Súbdár had not fully comprehended.

Having done this I took my departure and began to return to camp with my Sindhí attendants, when I saw my master in company with Captains Outram and Leckie, proceeding to the Court of the three Amírs. My presence also being requisite, I was desired to go along with the British representative. This was a day of hard work and starvation for me; I took only a piece of bread and a cup of tea when I left home in the morning, and the day was coning fast to an end, without any end to my business.

On arrival at the Darbár, we found the crowd of armed Bilúchís and attendants so thick that I thought it was impossible to pass. Road, however, was made for the admission of the European gentry. As for myself, I remained behind and could not possibly penetrate through the concourse. Captain Eastwick, fortunately thinking of me, when with the Amírs, turned his head a little and observed, "Here, Lutfullah, take care of these papers." No sooner was this pronounced, than the attendants, breaking through the mob, took me upon their hands, and in a minute conveyed me sliding over the heads of the multitude to my master, at whose elbow I seated myself and took down notes of the conference.

The three Amírs, Núr Mohamed, Nasír Khan, and Mír Mohamed, and a young man, Mír Sháhdád, sat on a large four-legged square plank, covered with a simple Persian carpet, called the throne, with their swords and shields placed before them. The British representative and his companions sat on the chairs placed for them, but were obliged to take off their shoes before entering the Darbár. The rest of the people sat on the floor, which was well carpeted. There was no order here such as is observed in Indian Courts. The armed Bilúchís and Sindhís sat as they pleased, wherever they could find a place for themselves, talking as loud as possible with each other, and scowling upon us every now and then, as if we were their murderers.

Núr Mohamed seemed to be a man of high talent and exalted views, brave and handsome, middle-aged and middle-sized. One deep and perpendicular wrinkle between his eyebrows indicated that he was a man of passion and cogitation. He was the only person to be addressed in the conference about the State affairs, as Nasír and Mír Mohamed seldom gave any replies, and, if they did so, then only through him. I highly admired his brave countenance, and his conversation, full of truth, spirit, and valour.

Nasír was handsome, but very corpulent. Affability, mildness, and generosity, seemed to be prominent in his disposition.

Mír Mohamed was a well-made, soldier-like man, with handsome features, but hare-lipped. It seemed that the hand of Nature, in finishing his face, accidentally dropt its chisel between his lips and left the blemish unrectified. He sat to the left of Núr Mohamed at the edge of the throne, leaning his left hand against his shield, and resting his right upon the hilt of his sword.

Such were the Presidents of this semi-civilized Darbár. After the overflow of compliments had subsided, Captain Eastwick seized the opportunity to administer the black dose of his mission to his hosts.

He took the papers from my hand containing the draft of the treaty lately translated by myself, and read it to their Highnesses with a clear Persian accent. The Amírs listened composedly, though marks of displeasure could be traced on the face of Mír Núr Mohamed. He changed colour, becoming now red, now pale as a ghost. When the reading was over, the Bilúchís showed great excitement. At this time a slight signal from their Highnesses would have been sufficient to terminate the lives of all our party under the swords of the barbarian and remorseless Bilúchís, many of whom stood at our head with naked scimitars, in the same way as executioners do at the moment of the performance of their horrid duty. Mír Núr Mohamed first observed, in Bilúchí, to his two colleagues, "Cursed be he who puts reliance upon the promises of the Feringees;" and then, addressing himself seriously to the British representative, he spoke thus in Persian: "Your treaties, I believe, are changeable at your pleasure and convenience; is this the way to treat your friends and benefactors? You asked our permission to allow your armies a free passage through our territories. We granted it without hesitation, depending upon your friendship under your honourable promises. Had we known that, after the entrance of your army into our lands, you would threaten our safety, and enforce another treaty upon us, demanding an annual tribute of three hundred thousand rupees, and a ready payment of two million one hundred thousand rupees for the immediate expenses of the army, we would, in such case, have adopted measures for the security of our country and persons. You know we are Bilúchís, and no traders to be frightened easily. We do not govern the country alone, but the interest of the whole of our clan is involved in the government."

Captain Eastwick heard all this with calmness, and gave brief replies in Persian and Arabic proverbs, such as, "Our Government has no intention of putting your Highnesses under any inconvenience, but necessity has no law;" "Friends must aid friends in emergencies;" "The present campaign is not only for the security of India, but the safety of your Highness's territories likewise depends upon it," etc. Mír Núr Mohamed smiled, and spoke to his cousins in Bilúchí, which we could not understand; and then, with a sigh, he said to Captain Eastwick, "I wish I could comprehend the meaning of the word 'friend' which you use. We cannot give a decisive reply to your present demands at once. The matter requires consultation with those whose interests we cannot sacrifice for ourselves, and who are not altogether under our control."

We left the Court at sunset. There was no sprinkling of atr and rose water, etc., at dismissal, as usual in Indian Darbárs. We reached home at half-past six o'clock P.M., tired with the business of the day.

On the 23rd we remained, expecting a reply from their Highnesses, but affairs seemed to take a bad turn. The native agent sent a secret message requesting us to be on our guard; and his warning was perhaps not void of reason, for we saw a party of about two hundred armed Bilúchís sitting unaccountably in a dale within five hundred yards of us. One or two of them more than once reconnoitred our small party; but, finding us on the alert, they retired.

On the 24th, the time allowed for the Amír's answer having expired, we began our return to camp. Having wind and stream in our favour, we glided smoothly down to the village of Jarrak, upwards of eighteen miles, in three hours.

On the 25th we landed at Jarrak, and joined the army, which arrived that morning. Here I had a narrow escape from being drowned. Having to move a heavy box full of my books, I, with the aid of a Sindhí boatman, got it on the edge of two boats; and, as I stood with my legs wide apart, the Sindhí suddenly left me so planted, and unable to move, for fear of losing the box. In this disagreeable and dangerous position I remained for a quarter of an hour, when, just as the boats began to part, and at the moment that I and the box were about to drop into the river, the boatman came back, and, without a word of excuse, asked for a present "suitable," as he said, "to my dignity." I was obliged to suppress my indignation, and give the rascal something to rescue me and my box, though mentally I consigned him to the infernal regions for his impudence.

CHAPTER X.

False alarms—Shír Mohamed—Three officers burnt to death—The Amírs accept the Treaty—The army marches for Shikárpur—Nádir Sháh and the Saiyids of Lakkí—Sehwán—Larkhána—Great cheapness of food—Shikárpur—Bilúchí Robbers—Fath Mohamed Ghorí—Sakhar—Khairpur—Mír Rustam—Marauders—The Náik and the Political Agent—Thank you for nothing—Great heat—The scorpion remedy—More plundering.

Our force remained encamped here for eight days, during which time false alarms of night attacks were often spread. A Sipáhí named Chandídín, of the 5th Bombay Native Infantry, having effected his escape from amongst the prisoners of Shír Mohamed Khán, of Mírpur, brought us news that that chief was on the point of joining the Amírs of Hydrábád against us. On the 29th, Mír Ismaíl Sháh and one of his sons arrived in camp to treat with the authorities.

On the evening of the 30th, three dead bodies of Queen's officers were brought to camp. These men had absented themselves without leave, on a hunting expedition, and the fire having broken out from all sides in a forest, they could not escape.

On the 1st February, Mír Ismaíl Sháh, the Ambassador for the Amírs, announced their submission to the terms imposed by the treaty; and next day Takkí Sháh, son of Ismaíl, was despatched to Hydrábád to obtain their Highness' signatures to the paper.

On the 3rd our camp left Jarrak, and halted at the village of Ismaíl jo Got, eleven miles off, and the next march of nine miles brought us to the village of Kotrí, a small hamlet situated on the right bank of the Indus, opposite to Hydrábád. The Sindhian army that had stationed itself at the opposite bank of the river, marched back to the capital on the 3rd, but we saw a portion of it on its return in haste. The army consisted of about ten thousand men and thirty pieces of cannon, of which seven thousand men and twelve guns belonged to Shír Mahomed, of Mírpur, who had joined the Amírs to afford his aid against the infidel host; but, seeing the English far superior in power, number, and discipline, he retired to his own district, after having sent a very civil answer to the Resident's strong and rigorous letter, drafted out by myself and forwarded to him some days before.

The river begins at this season to rise; its waters, though always muddy, are very wholesome if purified. The mode of purification is very simple. Take a kernel of almond and rub it against the inner side of a pitcher until it is exhausted; fill the pitcher with the water and let it stay unshaken for one hour, and you will then find the water beautifully clear;

have it then strained in another vessel, and drink it to your satisfaction. But if you drink this water unstrained, and especially after eating the delicious fish called pulla, you are sure to get dysentery, which generally proves fatal.

On the 6th the Resident, having received a number of trays of sweetmeats from their Highnesses as an entertainment to all the gentlemen of the camp, had the kindness to send me two of them, containing about eighty pounds of excellent confections, etc. The English, being originally carnivorous, cannot enjoy the taste of our confections, and this quantity, I believe, had come to my share simply for that reason. All my friends, servants, and self, enjoyed the gift of the great man for some days, and returned our thanks to him.

On the 9th, Captain Eastwick was ordered to conduct the army up to Shikárpur, and we made all the necessary preparations for the performance of that duty.

On the morning of Sunday, the 10th, we marched with the army, and halted at the village of Badá, eight miles from Kotrí. Sádikshāh, one of the sons of Ismaíl Sháh, joined us here as an agent on the part of the Amírs to render us his aid in obtaining supplies. We had orders to keep as near as possible to the right bank of the Indus. A dragoon foolishly took his horse to drink apart from the watering place in the river, and sank with the animal, never to rise again. A camel, whilst quenching his thirst, seated itself in about knee-deep of water to cool his body, but no sooner had he done so than he was pulled in by a gigantic force, and carried off by a large alligator. Five private Sipáhís deserted this day from their regiments.

The march of the

11th	was	ten	miles to	Umarpur.
12th	„	nine	„	Gopang.
13th	„	ten	„	Majhand.
14th	„	eleven	„	Suma.
15th	„	twelve	„	Amrí.
16th	„	twelve	„	Lakkí.

Lakkí is a large village of about one hundred huts. It belongs to the Saiyids of Sindh. I visited the shrine of Sháh Sadr here, situated at the foot of a large mountain of Síwistán, at the distance of about three hundred yards from the village. This famous saint originally came from Arabia, and brought thousands of infidels to the light of Islám from the darkness of idolatry in Sindh. His tomb was built here by order of Nádir Sháh, king of Persia, in 1155 A.H. Tradition states that Nádir, in a dream, was invited by this saint to come up to Umarkót where he was to find a very large treasure; and His Majesty, having acted upon the visionary command, discovered the treasure promised to him, and received a very large amount, as a tribute from the Amírs of the time, in addition. His Majesty then bestowed a large sum of money upon the Saiyids of the village, directing them to have the edifice built over the remains of the saint. This they carried into execution at the time. The following inscription at the door of the shrine gives the date of its completion:—

"I inquired of intellect the year of its date.
"Inspiration informed me it is the Paradise of the member of the sacred house." 1155 A.H. 1742 A.D.

All Saiyids of Sindh that are called Lakkí Saiyids, are, I am informed, the descendants of this saint, whose parentage ascends up to the Imám Alí Nakkí. I am therefore inclined to think that the word Lakkí is a corruption of Nakkí, which is the name of the tenth Imám.

The view of the mountains about one mile from this is fine. On the nearest hill there are two springs near one another; the water of one is very cool and limpid, and that of the other very hot.

A banian remaining behind in this march, was overtaken by the Bilúch marauders, who robbed him of his clothes, and inflicted two sword cuts on his arm. The poor fellow came in bleeding: several camels were stolen; the perpetrators of these outrages were Burgoarí, Marrí, and Lagharí Bilúchis, who inhabit this mountain with their asses, goats, sheep, etc., and very seldom visit the neighbouring villages.

17th, 18th, and 19th. Halted to have the heavy ordnance, etc., sent on first. Three camel robbers having been seized, were on the 18th flogged, and had their heads and beards shaved. A European soldier, who stood by me whilst the guilty were undergoing the penalty, observed that he would be happy to receive such punishment every day, except the flogging part.

On the 20th, we marched early in the morning, and reached the Sehwán Pass at ten o'clock A.M. The morning was very misty; it rained and thundered in the night very heavily, which is not a usual thing in India in this month. The pass is nearly half-way between Lakkí and Sehwán, and about two hundred yards long. The difficulty is merely on account of the river's cutting the very foot of the mountain. During your walk on this path you will find yourself in an awkward position, as on your left is the proud, sublime, and steep side of the mountain; and, on your right, down a very deep precipice, you behold with awe the river whirling on. Our engineers, however, widened the path about ten feet wherever they found it too narrow, and thus rendered it practicable for the present. Our whole force passed without any accident, except a poor woman, whose leg bone was fractured in the tumult.

On the 21st we halted, and Sir H. Fane landed at our encampment and had an interview with Nuwáb Mohamed Khán Laghárí, deputed by the Sindh authorities to meet this nobleman on his way here. No one was allowed a seat, except Sir H. and the Nuwáb.

I attended several Darbárs of the Governor-General when at Ajmír, but never found any gentleman, whether sallow or white, underrated as in this extraordinary audience. The English officers of the Bengal side have in general a too good opinion of themselves. Captain Eastwick stood as interpreter in the presence of the two representatives, and I, behind him, euphonizing every now and then his Persian sentences to the Nuwáb. When Sir H. heard me first, he called out, "And who are you, sir?" To this Captain Eastwick replied, "He is my Munshí." Sir H. is a tall, well-made, intelligent, middle-aged man, but he seemed to have had no lessons of politeness. The Bilúch Nuwáb wanted to continue the conversation after business was over, but Sir H. got up and dismissed him abruptly.

The 22nd was a cold and foggy morning. I visited the town of Sehwán which contains about five thousand houses, or fifteen thousand inhabitants. The shrine of Lál Sháh Báz, the famous saint of this place, is a grand one, built in 1148 A.H., and it contains but one tomb, that of the saint. A tiger of large size is kept in a wooden cage at the gate.

Marched on the 23rd to the village of Tartí, nine miles; our force was obliged to cross a branch of the Indus called Aral, near Sehwán. Our engineers made a good pontoon bridge over this river, and the army and baggage crossed over it in the morning. Tartí is a large village, consisting of about two thousand houses, situated near a spacious lake of fresh water.

On the 24th, we had a very troublesome march, on account of the General's changing his mind at a late hour.

On the 25th, I had the honour of a kind visit from Dájí Ghorporé, a nobleman formerly in the service of the late Peshwá, and now one of the officers commanding the Púnah Irregular Horse. I found him to be a gentleman of honourable feelings and extended views.

In the confusion of yesterday, a part of Dr. Rook's baggage was stolen. This being our holiday of Idu'z-zuhá, I was requested by my Mohamedan friends to deliver the sermon, but, being excessively fatigued, I declined. The village of Rokan, where we were, is a large one, and is full thirty miles from Sehwán. The Mulla of the place, being a mere illiterate Sindhí, the Divine service of this holiday was lost, and to me for the first time.

The morning of the 26th was very cold, and the water in our vessels froze during the night. We marched to the village of Ghallu, ten miles. For the last three stages we found the soil brackish. In this district, salt is manufactured in abundance. It is stored in large heaps, covered with the dust, without being burnt, as usual in other countries. On examining it, I found it consisted of more nitric ingredients than the common salt of India.

27th. Sixteen miles to the village of Ghará, six miles beyond the shrine of Pírpanja. This saint belongs to the order of those Mohamedan monks who dress themselves in black blankets and nothing else. This was a long and fatiguing march through the forest, which is not very thick about this part. The custom of wearing caps, gradually diminishing from Sehwán, is nearly out from this stage. Here you will see almost all the Sindhí heads ornamented with white and becoming turbans.

28th. Six miles to the village of Chinna, good road and fertile country all the way. The cold began to diminish.

1st March. This morning the General changed his mind about the halting-place, and caused much confusion. At first, the village of Kamori, sixteen miles, was fixed, which being subsequently changed for Fathpur, ten miles only, many missed the road, and many had to return from Kamorí to Fathpur.

On the 2nd, sixteen miles, to the village of Bakrání, where, on the 3rd, a halt was ordered, not for the Sabbath, but on account of a large branch of the Indus coming across the way, which required the troops to pass by degrees, the stream being nearly six feet deep in the middle.

On the 4th, we crossed the stream early in the morning, and reached the town of Larkhána in about two hours, it being only eight miles from the last stage. Larkhána is a large town surrounded by a mud wall, and governed by an old illiterate man, Pír Abdu'rrahím. Here the army was obliged to halt until the 11th, to make the necessary arrangements for the long hazardous journey through the Bolán Pass into a climate too cold for the natives of India. Many camel drivers, especially those of Kach, refused to go to the cold climate; but, having been well flogged and chastised for refusing, poor fellows, they saw no alternative except submission or desertion. The latter plan was, however, adopted by many, who left their camels to the tender mercy of the swearing soldiers, and took their way home. Here ended, for the present, the duty that Captain Eastwick had to perform, of escorting the army. A young officer, Major Tod, having arrived on the 6th, was to take charge as Political Officer; so Captain Eastwick, leaving me in the camp, and instructing me to afford all the information I could to the Aides-de-Camp or Major Tod, if required to do so, himself proceeded to Shikárpur, to see Mr. W. H. Macnaghten, the Envoy and Minister. On the 9th, Captain Eastwick returned to the camp from Shikárpur, having been appointed officiating Political Agent in Upper Sindh. He consulted me whether he should remain as Political Agent in Upper Sindh, or accompany the Envoy to Afghánistán, this being left to his option. He inclined to the latter service, in the performance of which he would have the opportunity of seeing a new country, and of obtaining experience in the impending battles, and distinguishing himself.

I told him I knew the character of the Afgháns better than any Englishman; that I would neither for money nor love endanger myself in the expedition, the success of which was to me exceedingly doubtful; that I would humbly advise him not to go, unless he was ordered, to Afghánistán, where I doubted not he would fall the first victim to his own energy, zeal, and ardour. Hearing this, he smiled scornfully at my remarks, and observed,—"My friend, life is a lottery; what is the use of living, when you can benefit others and yourself by your death?" I had an excellent answer to his last remarks on the tip of my tongue, but did not like to argue farther, so I cut the matter short by referring to other things. His services, happily for us both, were so required in Upper Sindh, that he had not time afterwards to think of proceeding to Afghánistán.

On the 12th a division of the army marched towards Kandahár, under Sir John Keane, and the other division was obliged to remain till carriage could be procured.

This very evening we also separated ourselves from the army and slept at Chuharpur, four miles from Larkhána, on our way to Shikárpur. We were furnished with a military guard of a native officer and twenty-three rank and file.

On the morning of the 13th we marched eight miles to the village of Naudera. Good road all the way, and the country very populous. The environs of the villages were beautifully surrounded with the palm and mango trees, most agreeable to the sight. We put up in a small garden-house. Naudera is a large village, and belongs to Mír Mír Mohamed, under the management of a rough, but very witty old man, by name Mohamed Khán Siyál (meaning jackal). The art of extracting the palm-juice, which might largely add to the revenue, is unknown in the country. We found the provisions so cheap, that I purchased good fowls for two pice (one and a half farthing) each, the same as you get in London for two shillings. Other things also were proportionably cheap.

On the morning of the 14th we marched sixteen miles to Gohej, belonging to Mír Nasír Khán. This village is larger than Naudera, but many inhabitants had deserted it on account of the Bengal army having passed through it. We got, however, everything we required as cheap as at Naudera.

On the morning of the 15th, we marched sixteen miles, and reached Shikárpur at nine o'clock, A.M. This town is the largest in Sindh, containing about fifteen thousand houses, which are flat-roofed, and some of them two-storied. The city is encircled with mud walls, and has a small fort outside the town. The environs are very pretty, having groves of mangos and palms, etc., all round. The water is from wells. The soil seems to be fitted to grow the poppy and flax, several fields of which we observed in a most flourishing state. About one half of the inhabitants are Hindús of the Khatrí and Lohána clans, and the other half are Muslims. Shikárpur has an excellent market-place, shaded all over from the sun. The Hindú tradesmen of this place talk Persian and Pushtu, as well as their own Sindhí. We pitched our tent near the town for the present, and lived in the enjoyment of quiet and solitude after a month's hard work in escorting the army.

On the morning of the 16th I accompanied Captain Eastwick to the town. He examined the city, the market-place, and the fort, etc., with a scrutinizing glance, and then went to see a state prisoner, a German gentleman. Heard the French language talked for the first time.

On the morning of the 17th I took a walk in the lines of the two remaining Bengal regiments, and the principal camp market (called Sadri Bázár). Felt very sorry to learn that a number of followers and animals perished beyond the desert for want of water. Mismanagement in every department prevailed. Sir A. Burnes, the former Political Agent in Upper Sindh, disbursed large sums of Government money without keeping any accounts. No day closed without seeing some of our people killed or wounded, and some camels carried off by the Bilúchí robbers.

Two very rich and influential Hindú merchants, Chitrumall and Jet Singh, paid their visits to Captain Eastwick this morning. The latter is a very handsome man, well-informed, and exceedingly polite. His sister, having been the beauty of Sindh, was forcibly taken away by Sháh Shúja, whose name is detested by him and by his clan.

On the 18th of March we made preparations for our march, but it having rained much in the night, our tents had become so heavy that we had to wait until they were dry.

An affray took place the day previous, between a party of the Bengal Irregular Horse, guarding camels, assisted by Abdu'ssamad Khán, the manager of the village of Lakkí, and ten Bilúch robbers, who attempted to carry off the camels. In this, three of the banditti were wounded and one killed; the head, having been severed from the trunk, was brought to Captain Eastwick, as a mark of valour on the part of our people.

It was a most disgusting and horrid sight to behold a human head weltering in blood and dust. Thus we abuse the law of nature and cruelly treat our fellow-creatures, to serve our filthy purpose of lucre.

On the 19th we left Shikárpur for Sakhar, and marched in the morning sixteen miles to Mahbúb jo Got, passing the village of Lakkí, about half-way. Lakkí is a large village belonging to Mír Núr

Mohamed. Good road all the way, through dense forest. There was no chance of missing the road, as hundreds of dead camels were lying on both sides as well as in the middle of it; so the best guide for everybody was his own nose.

On the 20th we reached Sakhar, fourteen miles from Mahbúb jo Got. We started at six in the morning, and arrived at eight o'clock A.M. Sakhar was a large city, but now is almost in ruins. It has, I am informed, never recovered the shock it suffered in the last conflict between Sháh Shúja and the Khairpur Amírs. Sakhar is situate on the right bank of the river Indus. Rorí, a large populous city, is on the left, and Bakhar, a fortress in the middle of the stream, upon a small island nearly triangular. This fortress, so much praised by the Persian historians and Sindhís for its impregnability, was lent to the British authorities to keep their stores, etc., until the end of the campaign, but, as I anticipated, the loan turned out irrecoverable.

On the 21st, I was deputed to call upon Fath Mohamed Khán Ghorí, the Minister of Khairpur, who arrived and encamped at the town of Rorí, the day before, by his master's orders, to punish the Bilúch robbers infesting the country between Sakhar and Shikárpur. He is a very old man, about eighty, but his spirit and energy surpass those of a young man. His head is clear, his experience in local affairs great, and his management of the country commended, both by his master and his subjects. I was politely received by the old gentleman, and, after compliments, I brought the subject of the Bilúch robbers under discussion. The old man observed that the Bilúch robberies were even more troublesome to the natives themselves than to the foreigners, and that he was obliged at last to gird on his sword, and proceed with his army to chastise the banditti. I told him the object of my master was to coerce the wild people rather than extirpate them; but I could not help smiling at the old man's remark about his army, etc., as his force consisted of about forty-five foot and one hundred and fifty mounted soldiers. The horses of the latter appeared most lean and miserable. The old gentleman sagaciously perceived the meaning of my smile, and said, "Do not look upon my soldiers and horses with contempt. They are not fat, but fitted for the warfare of this country, and can endure hunger and thirst for three days,—more than your good looking men and fat horses can, in chasing the robbers amongst hills and dales of the land." I did not like to hurt the feelings of the old man, whose grandson appeared to be older than myself; and observed that I had every confidence in the valour and puissance of the soldiers under his command; that I begged his Grace's pardon for my rude mirth, to which I was addicted in consequence of having long been in the society of the English people. We then parted with each other as good friends, with the promise of seeing each other on the next day but one, when he would visit Captain Eastwick.

On the 23rd, he did so, and gained the Political Agent's good opinion in the very first visit.

Large heaps of grain, that had been lying by the river side for the last eight or ten days in charge of the commissariat conductor, not being timely removed, were carried off the night before by an inundation of the river, which was so violent and sudden as to break asunder the bridge of native boats that joined Sakhar to Rorí. Captain Eastwick adverted to the subject in conversation with the minister, telling him that the river, too, bore the character of the Bilúch robbers, and stole away the masses of grain by night. To this old Fath Mohamed replied, very promptly, that he thought the river, on the contrary, acted the part of a friend and adviser to us, in giving us warning not to be careless in a foreign land.

On the 25th, we crossed the river to the town of Rorí, and encamped in a fine garden commanding a beautiful view of both sides of the river, and of the fortress in the middle.

On the 28th, we left Rorí for Khairpur. Started early in the morning, and reached the place at about eight o'clock, A.M., the distance being about fifteen miles. An officer, by name Alí Mohamed, with a party of horsemen, came to receive us three miles out of the town. We pitched our camp in a small enclosure, with a small house, destined for all the European guests who might have occasion to visit the Amír. No sooner had the Political Agent done his breakfast, than two officers of higher rank, namely, Asanand Vakíl and Jetmall Díwán, waited upon him to inquire after his health on the part of the Amír. Captain Eastwick received them with politeness, and told them that he could not make a longer stay than one day, and that he would be glad to see the Amír as soon as convenient to His Highness. They returned with this message to their master, and, in the evening, Ináyatullah Khán, son of the old minister, and Ján Mohamed, came with their retinue, and escorted him to the palace. Mír Rustam Khán rose from his masnad and embraced the Political Agent with Asiatic courtesy. The audience chamber was as plain as that at Hydrábád, but less crowded. The Political Agent was seated next to the Amír on the floor. The Darbár consisted of the following nobles—Mír Zanghí Khán, His Highness' uncle; Mír Nasír Khán, his nephew; Mír Mubárak; twenty Bilúchís; and the two Hindú officers that waited upon the Political Agent in the morning. The object of the conference was, as I found afterwards, to impress on the mind of His Highness the necessity of taking immediate steps to coerce and chastise the several robber tribes of Bilúchís. Mír Rustam promised to do all he could, and professed himself the humble, but sincere, friend of the English. The Amír seemed advanced in years: perhaps about sixty. He was a handsome man, and it was clear, from his conversation, that his mind was noble and devoted to religion. He has eight sons. Khairpur is a large town. The palace is situated in the middle of a mud wall fortress. In the forenoon of the next day, another Darbár of ceremony was held, and the Political Agent was received with all honour. Pleasant conversation, with an admixture of business, continued for about an hour, and then the court adjourned. At the time of parting, when Captain Eastwick was about to bid His Highness, and the family, adieu, the Amír observed: "Now I speak to you as a friend; I have a greater regard for you than any Englishman I have ever seen, for I feel a real pleasure in conversing with you. I believe you are a good Christian, with a heart as pure as a mirror: I therefore esteem you as one of my own sons." Captain Eastwick bowed, and made a suitable reply. We then left the Darbár for our camp, and, after the performance of our daily work, paid a parting visit to the old Amír; and, having chatted half an hour, left him with our best wishes.

On the morning of the 30th, we left Khairpur for Sakhar, which place we reached at nine o'clock A.M. As we marched along, easily and leisurely, I observed, all along the road, *Cassia fistula* trees in abundance.

They are as handsome as the *Mimosa seris*, but their flowers are deep yellow, handsomer than the latter, and their fruits are long spherical beans, about an inch in diameter, and from two to three feet in length. The tree, with its green foliage, yellow flowers, and bunches of ebony stave-like beans pending from its boughs, is a picturesque object. The *Cassia fistula* fruit contains a quantity of sweet pulp, with a peculiar smell, covering its seeds, which resemble the *cytisus cajan*. Physicians of India and Persia use the pulp as an aperient medicine. A dose of one ounce of it, dissolved in hot water, and taken with the almond oil, operates well upon the lower intestines. The Sindhís seem to be ignorant of its good effects, or else they might drive a lucrative trade by exporting it to Bombay, and other places.

On the 2nd of April, 1839, preparations were ordered for our return to Shikárpur. The press of business for the last few days was so great, that I could not leave my desk from sunrise to sunset, and was unable to go out and see anything in the country. I therefore stole an hour of my employer's time, and visited the shrine of Sháh Khairu'd-dín, the famous saint of this place. The tomb is an excellent piece of architecture, built in 1029 A.H., or 1619 A.C.

On the 3rd we left Sakhar, and reached Shikárpur in three easy marches. Here we found the state of affairs worse than ever. Bilúch robbers had the impudence to visit the environs of the city, almost every day, cutting, maiming, and murdering the poor camel drivers, and some of the guards on pasturing duty. Our native soldiers were useless out of the lines, for want of local knowledge. The tall, well-made, and handsome Bengálí Sipáhís have not always a heart corresponding with their outward form.

Here I give an instance of their prowess, displayed by a party of them. On the 6th of this month, thirty-nine camels, belonging to Government, under the pasturing care of a Náik and five Sipáhís, were seized upon and carried off by ten Bilúch robbers in the afternoon. Two of the drivers received sword cuts, and the sight of these bleeding comrades made the rest run to the Agency; and the guards, too, followed their example. The non-commissioned officer then presented himself to the Political Agent, and, after his "present arms," gravely said: "The thirty-nine camels, sir, are carried off by the robbers just now, sir; two drivers are wounded, and all is well, sir." The report of the officer excited my mirth, so much that I left my desk in the room to get rid of my laughter, and then I heard the following dialogue between the Political Agent and the Náik:—

Political Agent.—What were the numbers of the robbers?

Náik.—They were ten, but we discerned a cloud of dust behind them, which indicated a larger number following.

P. A.—Why did you not fire at the robbers?

N.—Because we were dressing our food under a tree; and, seeing the wounded men run, we ran to you!

P. A.—You are very nice soldiers!

N.—I thank your Honour for the good word; I have done my duty.

P. A.—Good word and thanks! I have a great mind to give you a court-martial for your unsoldier-like conduct.

N.—Then we must thank our own bad luck, to get such a reward from your Honour's hand for our faithful services.

P. A.—Leave my presence. Do not utter another word, and do not show me your face again. Right about face! march to the lines.

It was on this occasion that I saw Captain East wick lose his temper, for the first time in twelve years' association. He then immediately ordered a party of the Bengal Irregular Horse, under Núr-baksh Risáldár, to pursue the banditti; but no trace of them was to be found: they were as if swallowed by the earth, with the camels and the spoil. To crown other misfortunes, the heat was now so great, attended with the hot wind, that we felt confident, in case nothing else could destroy us, the heat would very soon. The thermometer in my small hut was 110° in the middle of the day, and 90° in the coolest hours. The six hours after midnight were the only time blessed with cool breezes: but, during the remaining hours, we had a window of Jahannum open towards us: exposure to the sun was certain death. Officers of strong constitution and bulky frames I have often seen leaving for the advance one day, and the next day their sudden death has been reported to us. The natives and the Bilúch robbers could bear the sun famously: they could trot along almost every day from morning till sunset, exposed to the sun, and without eating or drinking, which is beyond the power of our people of India; Europeans are out of the question entirely. I could not account for this great heat; the place being about four degrees northward from Súrat, the climate ought to be cooler than that of Gujurát.

Not being able to suffer the heat any longer, I built a small shed of a prickly bush, very cooling in its property, termed Jawassa in Hindústání, in front of my hut, and employed a water carrier to sprinkle it from morning till evening. This made me comfortable for the time.

On the morning of the 11th, I ordered my servant boy to shake my bedding and put it in the sun for an hour or so, that the moisture imbibed by the quilt might be dried. As soon as the quilt was removed from its place, what did I behold but an immense scorpion, tapering towards its tail of nine vertebræ, armed with a sting at the end, crawling with impunity at the edge of the carpet. I had never seen such a large monster before. It was black in the body, with small bristles all over, dark green in the tail, and red at the sting. This hideous sight rendered me and the servant horror-struck. In the meantime, an Afghán friend of mine, by name Atá Mohamed Khán Kákar, a respectable resident of the town, honoured me with a visit, and, seeing the reptile, observed, "Lutfullah, you are a lucky man, having made a narrow escape this morning. This cursed worm is called Jerrárá, and its fatal sting puts a period to animal life in a moment; return, therefore, your thanks to the Lord, all merciful, who gave you a new life in having saved you from the mortal sting of this evil bed-companion of yours."—"I have no fear of the worm," replied I, "for it dare not sting me unless it is written in the book of my fate to be stung by it." Saying this, I made the animal crawl into a small earthen vessel, and stopped the mouth of it with clay; and then making a large fire, I put the vessel therein for an hour or so, to turn the reptile into ashes, which, administered in doses of half a grain to adults, are a specific remedy for violent colicky pains.

I was informed that the revenues of Shikárpur, together with its dependencies, amounted to about three lákhs of rupees, the net amount of which is divided into seven shares. Four of them go to two Amírs of Hydrábád, namely, Núr Mohamed and Nasír Mohamed, and the remaining three are taken by the Amírs of Khairpur,—viz., one of the three by Mír Mubárak, and the two by Mír Rustam. The shares of the Amírs of Hydrábád are farmed to Jetmall, a very clever and powerful Hindú, for the sum of 14,000 rupees per annum. Jetmall was originally a liquor merchant, but his wealth, talent, and ability raised him to this high station in life. He is a very tall as well as bulky man, and is said to make his supper upon one goat and a bottle of brandy every night.

The revenues of Khairpur, with its dependencies, my friend, Jet Singh, the banker, informed me amounted to about five lákhs of rupees (or 50,000*l.*) per annum, which sum, being divided into five shares, three go to Mír Rustam, one to Mír Mubárak, and the remaining one to other members of the family.

On the morning of the 12th, Captain Eastwick being informed that a large party of Bilúch robbers were lying in ambush about thirty miles off, determined to surprise them. He left the camp at noon with about twenty irregular horsemen, and reached the spot early the next morning, where he found small heaps of ashes—the sign of the outlaws having prepared their meal there—and the dung of their horses, too, lying about. Finding the ashes cold and the dung quite dry, which indicated their having left the place more than six or seven hours before, he returned, disappointed, late in the evening, fatigued and exhausted by the terrific heat.

Seeing now the emergent necessity of raising a local corps to keep the marauders in check, he sent in an application to Government to be permitted to do so; but, as time did not allow him to wait for an answer from the authorities, he at once, on his own responsibility, began on the 15th to enlist Bilúchís, selecting especially the two chiefs of the clans of Khosas and Kahirís, who were at feud with the banditti of the following clans, most notorious at this time for their black deeds.

1. Domkí; 2. Jakrání; 3. Bugtí; 4. Marrí; 5. Mazárí; 6. Laghárí; 7. Burdí; 8. Rind; 9. Birohí.

The first chief that we took into employment was Kádirbaksh Khosa, a very handsome young man, aged about twenty-five, with fifty horsemen. He was to have the command over all the Khosas and others that were to be enlisted through him. My task was a difficult one now, as I had to take down the names and descriptions of the wild men and their wild horses: some of them laughed heartily when I took down their names, looking at their face for their complexion and distinctive marks. Others really took me to be a magician, and tried my wit if I could pronounce their name after an hour by referring to my book, which having done very easily, they returned from my presence with their mouths wide open. They had no idea as to their ages.

Men with grey beards wanted me to believe that they were not more than twenty-five or thirty. I asked one of them if he recollected the elder Mír Fath Alí Khán's expelling the Kalhoras from Sindh? He replied, "That occurred only a few years ago, when I was a young boy and used to go to the fields to pasture cattle with a pellet bow." At such nonsense I could not help laughing, for the event alluded to took place in 1779 A.D., and, accordingly, he must have been full seventy, though evidently not more than forty. He did not like my laughing, and, holding me by the hand, remarked, "My good friend, you seem to be one of the true believers, but, having associated with the infidel Feringees for a long time, you have lost your conscience, and you will therefore never give credit to a Muslim." I begged his pardon, and told him not to concern himself about my laughter, to which bad habit I was unfortunately addicted, and that he would always find me ready to give my belief to the word of my brother Muslims.

On the 26th our secret informers brought us the news of a Persian gentleman of suspicious character having arrived in the city. We immediately repaired to his quarters, and found that two camels were being loaded, and his servants were preparing, for their intended march. We soon found that he was a gentleman having some object in view, which he took care to avoid divulging, by turning the conversation to different topics, and telling us that he was a Dervesh, by name Núr Sháh, and had nothing to do with worldly affairs. Under these circumstances, the Political Agent told him that he must consider himself under arrest until some reasonable explanation of his being in the country was given. These words startled him at once, and he remonstrated against the measure with the characteristic Persian rhetorical fluency; but all was of no avail, and he was taken to the Agency as a State prisoner.

In the afternoon I was deputed to proceed to Khánpur, about thirteen miles from this, to visit Kamál Khán, the chief of the Káhirí clan to persuade him to visit the Political Agent, with the promise of his being employed in the Government service. I was to tell him that the maltreatment which his tribe and himself had experienced from Bijár Khán Domkí, the outlaw, should be taken into consideration. I proceeded with my escort of half a dozen of the Bilúchís, and reached the place late at night, all safe, without having had the honour of an encounter with the robbers. The Bilúchís of my escort were merry fellows, and as soon as they were out of the confines of the cantonment and in the forest, they seemed to have attained to the summit of happiness, and beguiled the way in laughing, talking, and singing. I asked them how it would fare if we were attacked by the robbers. In such a case, replied they, we must attack them in return; and they reassured me in the following words: "Be not anxious about it, my friend; no robber dare touch thy person as long as we six have our heads on our shoulders."

Old Kamál Khán received me with the frankness and hospitality of the tribes of the wilderness. He had two excellent sheep roasted, and some cakes made with clarified butter. Upon these dainties I dined with him and a number of his Bilúch relations. We then performed our prayers, in which, being requested, I stood as leader, and acted my part to the satisfaction of my wild congregation. Before going to bed, which was made of straw, I conversed fully with Kamál Khán on the subject of my mission, and brought to his view the unlimited benefits he was to obtain by his immediately entering our service. He expressed his consent, and said that he and his clan would be happy to serve the English cause, on condition of non-interference with his religion; for he was told by some people that the English would first take the country and then force the people to embrace their religion. I assured him that he need have no fear about that, and should not listen to the stories and fables fabricated by designing persons. I asked him if he had heard of any compulsory measures, towards persons of any religion, ever adopted by the English in India, where they had ruled now for the last one hundred years? In proof of their forbearance, I asked him to see the regiments of the army with his own eyes, in which he would find people of all castes following their own religions without any interference on the part of the Government; and, lastly, I asked him what opinion he had of myself, who had been with the English more than twenty-two years. Hearing this, he put his index fingers upon both his eyes, in token of his believing me with his heart and soul.

On the next morning, very early, we left Khánpur in company with Kamál Khán, and reached the Agency at Shikárpur at eight o'clock A. M. I presented him to the Political Agent, by whom he was taken into the service of the Honourable Company, with his colleagues, on the promise of their ever being faithful to the British interests.

On the 29th, being requested by some friends of the town, I visited a wonderful man there. It appears that nature, deviating from the usual course, gave this man a small trunk, like an elephant, on the right side of his face, beginning from the forehead to his chin. With his left eye only could he see, the other being covered with this superfluous part of the body. He was a young man of about twenty, sound in mind, as he gave rational answers to the several questions I put to him in the Sindhí language.

Another difficulty now made its appearance in the state of affairs. Our disciplined people could not know the newly employed Bilúchís from the robbers.

Whenever they chanced to see three or four of these paid Bilúchís near the camp, parties of twenty or thirty native soldiers rushed upon them, seized them furiously, thrashed them, and brought them into our presence, sometimes wounded, too.

We did not like to rouse the anger of our new lions in taming them, so we proposed to them to wear our belts as a mark of the service; and, with some difficulty, we prevailed upon them to submit to the halter of our bondage.

On the 5th of May, the Political Agent ordered the bay Arab horse of his, that I was allowed to ride, to be lent to Sarwar Khán Loháni, who rode this beautiful animal, and went off with a party of our Bilúch horsemen after the robbers, in the heat of the sun, the thermometer being at 150°, leaving his own horse to enjoy the stable. He returned in the evening with the party, having succeeded (as he pretended) in overtaking one of the robbers only, whose head they severed from the body and brought to the Agent to show their valour. Poor bay horse! he brought his brutal rider back, and no sooner was he unsaddled in the stable than he dropped down dead.

The heat was now insufferably great. I ordered some eggs to be placed in the sun to see the power of the heat, and found them well roasted in about forty minutes.

On the 7th, a party of our Bilúchís, under the command of Misrí Khán Khosa, overtook a gang of robbers, and had a skirmish with them, in which Misrí Khán himself received two wounds on his shoulder and leg. But he succeeded in bringing in four of the banditti prisoners, being of the Domkí and Dashtí clans, the companions of the notorious Ráhman. The Political Agent consulted Díwán Jetmall, the governor of Shikárpur, about disposing of them. The governor gave his opinion that they should at once be despatched by a disgraceful and torturing kind of death. The Political Agent and his English friends agreed in putting these poor devils to death, but they remitted the torture, and ordered their being hanged one by one every day. When I interpreted the horrible sentence to them with a throbbing heart, especially pointing out one of them for the execution of the next day, they stared at me very fiercely, without uttering a word; but the man pointed out carelessly replied, "*Je kí raza Khudah jí*," i.e., "God's will must be done." As for my friend, Misrí Khán, he had his wounds stitched and dressed by our doctor without a sigh or sob, returned his thanks to the medico, and went home unaided and unconcerned about the loss of a large quantity of blood, with which all his dress was wet. At his departure I said I was sorry to see him involved in that misfortune which his own ambition had brought upon him. "Call it not misfortune, man," replied he angrily; "it is honour not obtainable by every man, the marks of which shall ever be indelible upon my person." After this I wished him a speedy recovery, and we parted for the time.

CHAPTER XI.

Zark Domkí—The storming of Khángarh—The new Governor of Shikárpur—Mr. Ross Bell—Abd'urrahmán and his civilized Bride—Seclusion of women, desirable or not—Voyage to Hydrábád—I obtain leave for three months to revisit Súrat—Voyage and journey to Jáfirábád.

Early next morning a detachment of our regiment and some armed people of the governor took one of the prisoners to the other side of the town to be executed. But, alas! destiny led them to take one Zark Domkí, instead of the rightful individual. It made, however, very little difference, as the sentence of death had passed for all of them, and they were to be hung one after another every day. Poor Zark's cup of fate being filled before the others, he proceeded to the place without uttering a word, whilst the rest had some time more in the world.

On the 11th we heard of a fight between a detachment of the 5th Bombay N. I., some Bilúch Horse, and the Khosas of Khángarh. Four of our men were killed, and a Súbahdár and a Mr. Stanley were slightly wounded. The Khosas lost thirty men. Want of knowledge of the language was the cause of this misfortune. All the friendly signals on the part of the Khosas in the fortress were taken to be hostile by our people, as was proved before the Political Agent afterwards. Next morning the wounded and prisoners being brought in, the Political Agent set the latter at liberty, and had the former put under the care of our European physician.

A great annual fair being held at the branch of the river, about one mile from the town, in honour of the inundation, I proceeded to witness the same, and found a great concourse of the natives of both sexes assembled. I had the opportunity of seeing beauties of the Hindú caste unveiled, and I declare I found some of them no less graceful and charming than the nymphs of England. Mirth prevailed everywhere to this degree that, in one of these happy assemblies, I saw an old Hindú with a long flowing white beard, dancing to the sound of the tambourine, played by a handsome lady who assisted the jolly old fellow with her delicate voice, every now and then, in his historical songs. On the 18th, I paid a visit to Jet Singh, the banker. Amongst the jewels pawned to him, I saw a very handsome pair of emerald ear-rings. Each of the two emeralds was somewhat larger than a pigeon's egg, and without a flaw. They were considered worth 20,000 rupees, and were mortgaged to him for 18,000.

Shikárpur had been for two or three days without a governor: Jetmall, the late governor, being told he was to be removed, absconded. In the meantime, an order arrived from Hydrábád, saying he was not to be changed for the present, which having been forwarded by his friends to the place where he was, he made his appearance, and had scarcely returned, when the unpleasant news of his adversary's approach caused his second flight.

Takkí Sháh, eldest son of Ismaíl Sháh, the new governor, arrived on the 26th, and, after taking charge of his office, paid his visit to the Political Agent, to whom he gave some complimentary messages on the part of his masters and his old father the Minister. He expressed his deep regret that the plans of the Court to ensnare his predecessor were unsuccessful; otherwise he would have made the golden bird lay innumerable golden eggs for the benefit of his masters and himself.

On the 6th of June, Mr. Ross Bell, the new Political Agent, arrived. His outward appearance was strikingly handsome. But I soon found this handsome edifice was darkened by pride, ostentation, and vanity. He considered all men below his dignity, and treated the Government servants as slaves.

Mr. Ross Bell's mode of conducting business was strangely different from what I had ever seen. He had no confidence in his subordinates, and they had no feeling of allegiance towards him in the performance of their duty. Lying down upon his sofa, the great man dictated his letters to his cringing Munshí, who dared not seat himself, either on the floor or on a chair, and was obliged to take down word by word, whether sense or nonsense, standing upon his legs, with his inkstand fastened to his waistband. Who could stand such degradation as this? I would not submit to it for the salary of the Political Agent himself: but my friend, Trebania Saha, as well as his colleagues, seemed to enjoy the slavery with open forehead.

One morning after breakfast, Captain Eastwick sent for me to fill up some blanks in his final report of Upper Sindh. He was in the same room with Mr. Ross Bell, who was dictating a letter to his Munshí. I answered several questions put to me, and was in the act of leaving the room, when I heard the great man dictating an erroneous sentence, which his automaton secretary took down exactly, and, reading it out, stood waiting for the next. Thinking that, if the sentence remained, it would prove injurious to the British interests, I could not help speaking out in correction of the error; upon which the great man stared at me fiercely, as if he would devour me up, had it been in his power to do so. But, without caring about his anger, I turned my back and proceeded to my own desk. In the evening, Captain Eastwick told me that Mr. Ross Bell was very angry with me for my interference in his business. I said to him that a sense of duty caused me to correct the mistake.

In the night of the 24th of June, at twelve P.M., I was roused from sleep, and was sent for to the private room of the Agency. I found there Captain Eastwick and Mr. Bell sitting up, with some Persian letters in their hands. I took my seat, and Mr. Bell said something in French, which I guessed was a question as to whether confidence could be placed in me. On receiving a reply in the affirmative, the papers were handed to me to be read and explained. I did as required. I believe the letters were intercepted by some designing dependant of the great man. After I had read out the papers, and the great man had taken some notes, he discussed the subject with Captain Eastwick, in French, for about ten minutes; and then I was ordered to proceed forthwith to Sakhar with a message of importance to Fath Mohamed Khán Ghorí, the Minister.

So, in the morning of the 25th, at one o'clock A.M., I left Shikárpur, and reached my destination in the camp of the Minister at eleven o'clock A.M. I delivered the message, took my breakfast with him, and then, selecting a quiet place to shelter myself and the horse from the sun, I wrote out the report of my mission, and despatched it to Captain Eastwick by one of the horsemen of my escort. I took my rest for about four hours, if rest it could be called, for the thermometer under the tree which shaded me was 116°, and then I started at three o'clock P.M., for Shikárpur; where I arrived, much fatigued, at half-past eleven P.M.

On the 24th of July I was deputed to pay an

official visit to Mír Ismaíl Sháh, the Minister of Hydrábád, who arrived that morning on his way to Calcutta. He had passed eighty-five years, and was actually in his dotage. He had eight sons, all of them holding high and respectable situations under the Government. He was said to have five lákhs of rupees in ready cash in his coffers, and held several villages. So much, I should say, ought to have satisfied him; but no, he was after more and more until he was no more.

On the 29th of July, Captain Eastwick receiving his instructions to return to Hydrábád and resume charge of the Residency there, I made over all the drafts of the letters to my friend, Captain Postans, the Assistant Political Agent, and employed myself in preparation for the happy return to Hydrábád.

I paid parting visits to several friends in the town, amongst whom was Abdu'rráhmán Khán Durrání, the monocular. This old gentleman, according to the English ideas, had attained a great degree of civilization in permitting his wife to see his friends unveiled. I had the good luck of visiting this lady and conversing with her more than once; and this time, having received an invitation, I had the pleasure to dine with her and her civilized husband. This damsel, in her beauty and charm, excelled the fair sex of Shikárpur, and in wit, talent, and ability, surpassed her simple-hearted husband, whom she seemed to lead by the nose.

Seclusion of women from the society of men is considered a fault by the English, but a virtue by us, the true believers. The English leave their women to remain uncontrolled in life, and permit them to enjoy the society of men both in public and private. Poor creatures! naturally weak, how many of them fall victims to the brutal intrigues of men! How many families of high name have been ruined by this unreasonable license! In London alone, eighty thousand females are said to be registered in the black records. If you take an evening walk in one of the quarters of that greatest city of the world, called Regent Street, you will find many ladies of exquisite beauty and high accomplishments, forsaken by their relatives and friends, in the practice and perhaps under the obligation of committing black deeds. Who is to blame for all this? I say, nothing else but the license established by the civilizers.

I do not say that all Mohamedan ladies are virtuous. Virtue and vice are two sisters, the former fair and the latter black; and no nation has ever been or shall ever be uninfluenced by the two ladies. But limits and restraints prescribed by the Mohamedan law and usage in domestic affairs, I am bound to say, at all events prevent increase in vice and decrease in virtue. The time of the Mohamedan ladies being occupied in needlework, in the performance of their religious duties five times a day, in looking over their kitchens, and other household affairs, they have no leisure to think of admirers. Their marriages are arranged by their parents, who are their best friends, and whose experience in worldly affairs must be greater than theirs. Opportunities are in general afforded to the bride to see her would-be husband from a loop-hole or a window before she is married to him; and no matrimonial contract is considered binding, unless the lawfully attested consent of both parties is first obtained, and taken down by the law officer appointed by the Government to solemnize the marriage. Thus many bitter feuds and lasting animosities which poison the minds of contending rivals are avoided, and marriage beds are not only free from contamination, but from the dread of it. In short, seclusion secures women from those delusions and temptations which irritate the mind with fleeting joys, leaving behind the permanent sting of bitter remorse; while, never having tasted the universal triumph and dominion which beauty gives in the circle of Europe, the pang of lost power is not added to the painful sensation of fading charms.

On the 12th of August, 1839, we left Shikárpur for Hydrábád, embarking on board two small flat boats, called *berís,* engaged to receive us at one of the branches of the river Indus, two miles from the town. It was with some difficulty that Captain Eastwick extricated himself from the multitude of his visitors, some of whom ran to pay their respects to him, and overtook us when we were as far as six or seven miles from the town. The very high rise of the water at this season afforded us a beautiful landscape. Three enemies we had to contend with during our voyage,—the heat of the sun, the rats of the boat, and the mosquitos of the river. The first tried his power upon us all day long, the second disturbed our sleep, and the third sucked our blood during the night.

In four days' voyage, by pulling and dragging the boats through the canal, we reached Sakhar once more on the 15th, where, on the next day, I had the pleasure of seeing Captain Eastwick's younger brother, destined to be an assistant to the Political Agent, and found him well acquainted with several Asiatic languages. We made a stay of about one week here, during which time we received the tidings of the capture of Ghasní by Sir J. Keane.

The state of affairs in Upper Sindh seemed to be fast deteriorating. The new Political Agent was mostly engaged in quarrelling, particularly with the Brigadier-General. Such a line of conduct must prove prejudicial to the service.

We left Sakhar on the 24th of August, and reached Hydrábád on the 28th, all safe. We enjoyed hardly five days of peace here, in the very pleasant society of Captain J. D. Leckie, when Captain Eastwick, being attacked with fever, was obliged to proceed to Tatta and thence to Karáchí, leaving me and the baggage at the camp at Tatta. I myself, too, had several attacks of fever, and, not being able to obtain a medical gentleman's aid, I physicked myself with nothing but senna and wormwood infusions, finding the latter plant spontaneously growing here in abundance about the camp.

On the 15th of September we had a hot day, but the evening was nicely cool, and twilight adorned the sky all round with various lively hues, when on a sudden a dark cloud, rising from the south-west direction, spread itself all over, and substituted darkness for the former beautiful scene; and then a very heavy rain began to fall, attended with a severe hurricane, lightning, and thunder. I had seen three tempests within the last four months in Sindh, but this was the father of all. Many officers' tents were torn to pieces and flew away; but my small tent, having the advantage of several iron pegs driven in the stony ground, remained in *statu quo*, though the water, forcing through the entrenchments, rose about two feet high, on the surface of which floated my bed and furniture. This continued for about two hours, and at 8 o'clock P.M., the severity of the weather was luckily changed for calmness, and we went to bed all wet through and through. The weather continued stormy alternately till the 20th.

On the evening of the 28th, I witnessed a horrid sight: a Sipáhí of the 6th Company, 26th Regiment N. I., committed infanticide and suicide. The man was a Marátha, aged about thirty. He lost his beloved wife ten days before, after having given birth to a child, and the poor man had to take care of three children, the first five years old, the second three, and the third the newly-born one, besides having to perform his onerous duties as an English soldier. Overpowered by such miseries, his reason was darkened, and could suggest to him no remedy except putting a period to the lives of the innocent creatures and his own. So at ten o'clock P.M., he first killed the two elder children by cutting their throats, and then shot himself dead. I could not help weeping over the bodies, and the thought of their miserable fate rendered my night an unhappy one.

On the 19th of October, Captain Eastwick returned to Tatta, after five weeks' absence, and then, on the 21st, we left again for Hydrábád to conduct the business of the Residency. Having had to go against the stream, we reached the capital in four days, pulling and dragging the boat. On my arrival, I was sorry to find my friend, Captain Leckie, over-exhausted with fever, and reduced to a skeleton.

On the 29th, I had a very severe attack of fever, which, increasing every day for one week, prostrated my strength entirely, and rendered me so weak that I was unable to move in bed without aid. Captain Eastwick's anxiety for my recovery exceeded that of a father for his son. May God Almighty reward him for his generosity! There was no physician to be referred to. The mixture of senna and wormwood was the only remedy at my command. The disease at last began to abate, after nine days, and then the cooling sherbet of sugar brought on healing effects in three days, and I felt myself quite recovered. But the disease had rendered me so weak that I could not stand up and walk for some days. In the meantime, the month of Ramzán occurring, I was prevented by weakness from observing the fast.

About this time, as I one morning walked out of the Residency compound, a young man with a rough stick in his hand and a portmanteau upon his shoulder, coming up to me, pronounced the formal salutation of a true believer, and inquired if there was a great man in the Residency house, and if he could be seen. I took him to be a rude beggarly traveller, and, giving a rough answer to his query, turned my back. After this he went to the Residency gate, but the guard, seeing his miserable appearance, would not admit him. He then seated himself under a tree, and, taking out a piece of bread from his bag, employed himself in chewing the same. After my walk, I returned to my own quarters, and, when at breakfast, thinking of his deplorable condition, I sent my servant to him with a loaf of bread and some curry, but he was not to be found anywhere. In the afternoon, when I took some papers to Captain Eastwick for his signature, to my great astonishment, I found the same adventurer, in English dress, sitting at the table, and conversing with Captain Eastwick in pure English. I was introduced to him. His name was Curzon, and I found him to be a man of superior education and high qualifications. He knew the Hindústání, Persian, and Arabic languages so well that he even deceived me that morning, when he addressed me, into thinking him a native. He had travelled from Calcutta in the same state, and on the 21st, again he disguised himself in his former garb, and parted with us to proceed to Turkey. I had the pleasure of seeing him afterwards in London, in 1844.

On the night of the 27th, official intelligence of a battle at Khelát reached us. It announced the death of Mihráb Khán, and the capture of his fortress.

Next morning the Amírs were officially informed of this success, upon which they ordered a salute of twenty-one guns to be fired from the castle, and the city to be illuminated in the evening. Private information mentioned that the Amírs were exceedingly sorry to learn of the fall of Khelát, and of the death of the chief, with whom they were not only on terms of intimacy, but to whom they were also related by marriage. Mír Mír Mohamed's father, Mír Ghulám Alí, had married a sister of Mihráb. Such are worldly affairs; a nephew is obliged to order public rejoicings at the death of his uncle.

On the 1st of December, Captain Eastwick had another relapse of fever, which confined him to his bed at once. He held on for a week in hopes of getting better; but the fever rising higher, he became weaker and worse every day. Our return to Karáchí was then determined upon, and in the afternoon of the 8th we left the Residency in charge of Lieut. Whitelock of the 11th Regiment By. N. I. We reached Tatta in the morning of the 10th once more, and Karáchí on the 11th. Our servants, too, were in a condition worse than ourselves. One of my head servants, Hasan, was a large man of strong make, and gigantic stature, and, when in health, I never found him eat less than four pounds a day. But now the fever had reduced him to a phantom of what he was. His native land being Purbandar, I took the opportunity of sending him home by a Sindhí boat sailing for that port.

Under such circumstances, my fears were great. I applied, therefore, to Captain Eastwick for leave for three months, which he granted, and furnished me with the following certificate, and a peon, by name Abdul Karím, to take care of me on my way home:

"My Munshí, Lutfullah Khán, leaves me for three months to visit his family at Súrat. In this world of accidents many circumstances may occur to prevent his return. I cannot, therefore, allow him to depart without recording my deep sense of the value of his services, and the high estimation in which I hold him as a friend and preceptor. I have had opportunities of narrowly observing his character at intervals during the last eleven years, and I can conscientiously affirm that, as a native of India, I have seldom met his equal, never his superior, in liberality of sentiment, in the feelings and manners of a gentleman, in an ardent desire of knowledge, and indefatigable industry in its pursuit.

When the difference of the advantages of an Asiatic and European education is considered, he will bear a comparison with the best of my own countrymen. I can only add that I can never forget my obligations to him, and that, while his character remains the same, I shall always be proud to number him amongst my friends. That health, success, and prosperity may attend him wherever he goes, is the sincere wish of his attached friend,

(Signed) "W. J. Eastwick,
"Assistant Resident in Sindh.

"*Karáchi*,
"19*th December*, 1839."

There was no vessel at this time bound for Súrat; but a Sindhí *battéla*, called Rahmatí, under the Tindal Kásim, laden with dry fish, was about to proceed to Bombay. On inquiring about it, the Tindal engaged to land me at any of the nearest ports. "Kásim," said I to the Tindal, "I would be happy to go on board your vessel, but the smell of your cargo I am afraid would not suit my state of convalescence, and would aggravate the sea-sickness."—"My friend, have no fear about it," replied the gigantic Sindhian sailor, "I shall have the cabin prepared for you, where you shall have no smell of any kind. As for the sea-sickness, if you will have any, it will I am sure do you good, and the sea breeze will greatly contribute to your health."

These and such flattering words persuaded me at once, and I embarked all my baggage on the 19th of December, on board the Rahmatí, without taking the trouble of going to see her first. On the 20th, I parted with my master with a heavy heart, wishing him all success and happiness, and leaving him to the care of the same Supreme Being to whom I looked for my safe arrival at Súrat. Sádik Sháh, the governor, and Náo Mall, the great merchant of Karáchí, gave me the honour of their company as far as the pier-head, where I bade them adieu for the last time, and, getting into a long boat, was soon conveyed on board the Rahmatí.

On reaching the vessel, I was sorry to find it overfilled with dry fish from top to bottom; even the cabin promised to me was not without several bundles of them lying at random. The Tindal was ashore, and there were no persons of consequence to be spoken to upon the subject. I addressed myself to the crew, telling them that I would not remain on board unless they would clean the cabin for me. To this they replied very civilly, that they would do everything in their power for my comfort, but I must wait until the Tindal had arrived. After this I made my bed upon the poop, and, having sprinkled a little lavender all over it, immediately on laying my head upon the pillow I was fast asleep, and did not wake till the morning, when the melodious cries of the sailors, in weighing their anchor and setting the sails, roused me from my dormant state; and, all of us being true believers without exception, jointly pronounced the sacred sentence of our Holy Book, usual on such occasions: "In the name of God, while it moveth forward and while it standeth still, for our Lord is gracious and merciful."

A nice morning breeze floated our vessel swiftly and smoothly, and we were soon out of sight of Karáchí. By the evening of the 21st we were opposite to Ghorabárí. On the 22nd, I could discern the Kach shores by the aid of my telescope; and by the 23rd we came in sight of the Míání Hills and Jagat Point, and passed by them gradually. On the 24th, it being dead calm all day, our progress was very slow. The Tindal had the cabin well cleaned for me, and ordered his people to attend to my commands implicitly. The smell, too, began to be less perceptible every day,—I believe, on account of my nose becoming more and more accustomed to it.

On Wednesday, the morning of the 25th, the Christmas Day of the Christians, we came opposite to Bilwal Patan, and then I could keep myself no longer on board the Rahmatí. I requested Kásim to land me, and he executed my orders as promptly as usual. I parted with him as a friend, and made him a present of a few rupees, which he received very thankfully. I found Kásim Tindal to be a man of high mind, free from avarice, and endowed with a sense of honour; in fact, he was an exception to the general character of the Sindhians.

The governor of this place, on the part of the Nuwáb of Junagarh, I was informed, was still my old friend Saiyid Abdullah Jamadár, who is so highly spoken of by the learned lady, Mrs. Postans, in her travels, and he received me with the usual hospitality. I passed two days with him in shooting and playing chess.

On the 27th, I bade farewell to the good Saiyid, and took my way to Jáfirábád. Having lately sojourned for upwards of three years in Káttiawár, I had acquired a thorough knowledge of every corner of the peninsula, and required no guide to show me the way.

Accordingly I made the following marches:—

Date.	Name of the Village.	Miles.
27th	Dámlej	14
28th	Korí Nár	10
29th	Unah	12
30th	Rohísa	12
31st	Jáfirábád	6

This short journey was something like a pleasant morning walk, in which I shot a few partridges and wild pigeons every day.

On my arrival at Jáfirábád, I was received with hospitality by the Indo-African authorities of the place, the delegates of the Abyssinian chief at Zanjíra, near Bombay. Sídí Mohamed, the governor, assigned me a very nice place in the castle, until a boat bound for Súrat could be obtained. The population of both Jáfirábád and Unah appeared to be increasing at this time. A great difference seemed to have taken place in these towns, from what I had seen two years before. The number of houses now amounted to about 15,000 at each place. On inquiring the cause, the old governor smiled and said, that good government was the only cause of the increase of wealth. How could that be the case, observed I, since Unah belonged to the Nuwáb of Junagarh, whose government he had himself acknowledged to be a tyrannical one. To this he replied that the present governor of that place, Fath Khán, one of the slaves of the Nuwáb, was a good man; and, if he continued in the situation for some years, which was a matter of doubt, Unah was sure to become more populous than Jáfirábád itself.

Jáfirábád is a large town, one of the three estates, viz., Zanjíra, near Bombay; Sachín, with its seventeen villages, near Súrat; and Jáfirábád, in the peninsula, granted by the Peshwá of Púnah to Sídí Abdulkarím Khán, commonly called Ballu Meah, in 1791 A.C. The town has a castle and city walls in good repair, but which are commanded in all directions. The harbour of Jáfirábád is good and safe for vessels of small dimensions. The port carries on a profitable trade with Bombay, Súrat, and other towns on the coast of Gujarát, in exportation of cotton, clarified butter, and cattle, and might become a place of consequence if managed properly.

CHAPTER XII.

The Slave Governor of Jáfírábád—Return to Súrat—Death of the Nuwáb's eldest daughter—I take service with Mr. Pelly—He transfers me to Mr. Langford—The Nuwáb of Cambay and his Salt-pans—Once more a Munshí—The Nuwáb of Súrat dies of cholera—Sequestration of his property—Mír Jáfir Alí, his son-in-law, prepares to proceed to England—Engages me and Mr. Scott as his Secretaries.

THIS year I commenced at Jáfirábád, under the hospitable roof of the Indo-Abyssinian governor of the place, Sídí Mohamed, who was intelligent, well behaved, and well versed in the art of governing his subjects. I had met with three governors, once slaves, inferior to no freemen, within the last twelve months, viz., Anand Khawáss of Joria Bandar, Fath Khán of Unah, and Sídí Mohamed of Jáfirábád. Slaves, when left to their own free will in their conduct, prove better than freemen in general, for their first subjugation teaches them how to act towards their subordinates. But eunuchs are an exception to this rule. The maltreatment received by them in the commencement works so strongly upon their mental faculties, that they are vicious, vindictive, remorseless, and void of fellow feeling and sociableness ever after.

On the evening of the 2nd of January, I took my leave of Sídí Mohamed, and embarked on board a *battéla*, laden with limestone, proceeding to Súrat. On the 10th, I called at the palace, and paid my respects to the Nuwáb and his two sons-in-law. The old gentleman received me with his usual kindness, and examined me narrowly about the affairs of the Amírs of Sindh, and the success of the English in Afghánistán. His Highness appeared to be in the enjoyment of good health, but he was no better in a moral point of view. His companions now were low, mean, and reprobate persons, worse than before, in whose society he passed his time in laughing, joking, and nonsense. He had become addicted to drinking ardent spirits, in addition to the usual dose of opium; and was guided, or rather misguided, in all matters by his Minister, Mohamed Alí Bey. "Yes, my lord," and "Very true," and "Most undoubtedly," were the sentences in general pronounced by his courtiers in replies to his Highness's remarks, observations, and desires, whether right or wrong. After leaving his Highness, when I visited his sons-in-law, they were delighted to see me, and complained about their father-in-law's conduct in life.

On my way to and return from, the palace, I saw the destructive effects of the late conflagration. Nearly one half of the city was turned into ashes. Large naked walls were seen here and there standing upright, the only remnant of sublime edifices and exquisite mansions.

On the 22nd, I learnt that Captain Eastwick was proceeding to Bombay on sick leave. Thus my return to Sindh was rendered unnecessary.

On the 30th of March I attended the grand funeral of the Nuwáb's eldest daughter, Mír Akbar Alí's wife. She died of consumption this morning at five o'clock, at the age of twenty-one. She had had four children, but none survived her. This lady is said to have been the best of the two daughters. Her love for her husband and father was unlimited. The principal cause to which is attributed her untimely death, was the constant maltreatment experienced by her from her rival mother, who, being in power, and in high favour with the old Nuwáb, left no annoyance unpractised towards this unfortunate victim of her malignity. Mír Akbar Alí, having been sent for by the Gaikwár at Baroda, had left ten days before, and could not be present to bid his last farewell to his dear beloved wife. This noble lady had taken in adoption a daughter of a poor Mughal from her infancy, whom she loved like her own child, and had given to her the name of her own great great grandmother, Wiláyatí Khánam. The cries of this young, innocent, and very pretty girl for the loss of her patron mother, moved my sympathy so much that I could not help weeping very bitterly, like one of the relatives and connections, for a long while, until I left that part of the palace to join the procession. Little did I know that this very girl was destined to be my wife seven years after, and to be the mother of my several children.

For five months I continued my old profession of Munshí, when, wishing for Government employ, I went to call upon Mr. Pelly. It happened that as I was going upstairs, a Mr. Major, coming out of his master's room, was going down: he called to me, "For God's sake, don't come up." At first I was thunderstruck at this polite reception of a friend; but, casting my glance at the steps before me, what did I see but a black serpent, about one inch in diameter and four feet long, lying in ambush for a mouse. Mr. Major, being nearest the animal, it assumed a menacing posture towards him; but the bold Christian, taking his nailed shoe off his foot, gave the reptile a blow on its head, which, being inflicted on the vital part, nearly finished it, and then a few more blows from Mr. Pelly, myself, and another servant, rendered it defunct entirely.

My good and noble host then asked me to walk in: I went in and sat with him; but the dictate of instinct made my face pale, my tongue mute, and my heart throb for a little while; then, asking for a glass of water, I drank it, and was relieved from the unpleasant effect of the nervousness. I told Mr. Pelly that want of content and ambition bring many misfortunes upon worldly men; that, not contented with my present income, my ambition brought me thither to ask his favour to give me a situation in the Government service, and, instead of gaining my object, I had nearly lost my life and the object itself both together, The old gentleman, smiling at my remark, observed, "Be not discouraged, Lutfullah, by mere accidents: our life is in the hand of that Almighty Being without whose commands it can be injured by none." He added, it was in his power to give me at present a small situation as English clerk and translator, for thirty rupees per mensem, in his office, and that he would give me thirty more out of his own pocket, if I instructed his daughter and son in the Hindústání language for an hour every morning. This kind offer I accepted at once, and thanked my benefactor for his generous and good act towards me.

On the 19th of December I reached Bombay, to bid farewell to my old master, Captain Eastwick, proceeding to England for the recovery of his health. We were glad to see each other after one year's interval, and conversed for many hours together, when he was free from fever. As he was about to proceed to his native land by the next steamer, I stayed all the time with him, wrote several official letters for him, and superintended his domestic arrangements. On the 1st of January, 1841, when we were about to part from each other, he was good enough to present me with a letter to Mr. Pelly, and with a sum of money and some articles. I told him that I had come to see him, and not to receive presents; but, seeing that my refusal would displease him, I spoke no more to him upon the subject. At noon I hired a good easy carriage for his conveyance to the harbour; and, having carefully put him into it, I seated myself by him and held him fast, as he was shivering with his cold fit. In this state I conveyed him on board the steamer *Victoria*. He was then conducted to the saloon, where, having spread a small thin mattress, I made him lie down upon it; and, no sooner had I covered him with his cloak, than I was ordered to leave the vessel. I then bade him adieu with throbbing heart and tearful eyes, thinking over the difficulties of the long voyage he was to encounter in such a state of ill health.

We poor creatures of limited senses and imperfect understanding are easily overpowered with grief or rejoicing, without thinking of the unlimited power of that Omnipotent Being, before whom it was not difficult to cure the hopeless malady of Job and engulf Pharaoh and his host in the Red Sea.

On the evening of the 5th, at last finding out a boat bound for Súrat, I embarked on board of it, and we sailed in the name of the Lord. The wind not being in favour so much as was required, we reached our destination on the evening of the 11th, all safe, but greatly fatigued by the effect of the jolting and shaking. On the 12th, I attended the office and delivered the letter of Captain Eastwick to Mr. Pelly, who had the kindness to give me an extract of the same, under his own signature, and promised to promote me on the first opportunity. I resumed my office duties again as usual, and on the 4th of February, Mr. Pelly prepared to proceed on his tour in the Konkan Zila; and, having ordered a part of his establishment, inclusive of myself, to go along with him, I got in readiness and joined him, on the morning of the 5th, at the Súrat Bar, on board his vessel, and was received by him with great kindness. We had an excellent passage, and reached Karanjá, the place of our destination, on the 7th. Entering Bombay harbour, and leaving that town to the left, we landed at the foot of the opposite hill, from which spot across to Bombay Castle is about three miles.

On our landing at Karanjá, I found a few small huts, with inhabitants half naked. Three places were called houses: the first was the Government distillery; the second, the dwelling house of the Pársí in charge of the same; and the third was a caravansary, lately built by Mohamed Alí Rogey, the Nákhudá, a respectable inhabitant of Bombay, whose philanthropy and charitable feelings had, I am informed, induced him to build this place for the accommodation of travellers.

Karanjá, with its environs, is a very nice healthy

climate, influenced by the sea breeze from three sides. In this good place I sojourned peacefully for a period of about two months.

On the 30th of March, Mr. Pelly making his preparations to proceed to the Nílgiris, he ordered me and the other clerks of the establishment to join Mr. Langford, his substitute, at Bandra. All the members of the establishment, particularly myself, were very sorry to lose the generous, noble-minded, and good master, Mr. Pelly, who knew the merit of all. On his departure, he gave me an excellent certificate, a note addressed to his successor, and a handsome present in money.

The next day I crossed to Bombay in the morning, took my breakfast, and hired a couple of carts, one for my luggage and servant, the other for myself, and proceeded on to Bandra, which place we reached at about eleven o'clock A.M. On starting from Bombay, my rascally servant, Rahím, deserted me, under the pretence of going to buy some provisions from the bázár: I waited for him one full hour, and searched for him everywhere in the market, but he was not to be found, so I had to help myself in loading and unloading the carts and making myself comfortable in the journey. At Bandra, I put up in the small Pársí inn. The daughter of the Pársí landlady was a very pretty young woman: she had a charming countenance and a fascinating air. Begin you to converse with her, and you will immediately find your heart pierced through by her sweet subduing glances: in fact, she was a lady called by the English a civilized woman, and I considered it my good luck to eat and drink from her sweet hands.

In the evening, I accompanied the head clerk up to the house on the hill, to pay our visit to Mr. Langford, and to receive his instructions about ourselves. We sent word that we were waiting to pay our respects; but the servant returned with the answer, "Wait till you are sent for." After two hours' anxious expectation, admittance being granted, we went into the presence, and, after making our bows, the head clerk was questioned if there was any business of emergency which required immediate attention. On his reply in the negative, we were dismissed abruptly, and ordered to be in Súrat within ten days. Not having had the honour of exchanging a word with the new master, I presented Mr. Pelly's note of recommendation to him, which he reluctantly took from my hand; and, casting a cursory glance upon it, he destroyed it, and told me that he had no more to say to me than what he had just spoken to the head clerk, and that Captain Jacob had lately given him some information about me. I did not like this curt answer, with the air of arrogance, and had a great mind to tender my resignation on the spot; but the head clerk, who stood by me, reading my emotions from my forehead, pinched my hand to stop my tongue, which prevented me. So I bade

Mr. Langford a good night, without uttering another word. On our way home, I told my friend Beyzanjí, the head clerk, that, after this visit, I felt disgusted with the Honourable Company's Service, in which one is required every now and then to be cringing before new masters. "Don't you see," said I, "that Mr. Langford says that he had heard about me from Captain Jacob, who, I am sure, has no favourable opinion of me; so I should expect no promotion in this department."—"But why should you be alarmed?" replied Beyzanjí; "Mr. Langford cannot be always the head of the establishment: he is only acting for Mr. Pelly."

Our conversation ended with our arrival at the inn, where we were received by the fairy, the landlady's daughter, with an open, sweet, smiling countenance, which made me forget all cares. We took our dinner, served by her fair hands, made arrangements about our starting early in the next morning, settled about the hire of the carts for the next stage, and went to bed as comfortable as at home.

Early in the morning of the 1st of April, we left Bandra for Súrat, and travelled on easily, changing our carts at every stage; we reached our destination on the 8th, all safe. On the 20th of November, I was ordered by Mr. Langford to accompany him to Cambay, where he required my aid in the proposed arrangements with the Nuwáb, as to the salt-pans of that district.

On the 24th, I left Súrat for Cambay with the clerks of the establishment, on board the Government schooner, and reached that port in the morning of the 28th. Immediately on our arrival here, Gopálbhái, the head man of the native establishment, and myself, received instructions to wait upon the Nuwáb, and to confer with him about the business, and prepare him to acquiesce in Mr. Langford's desires without any further discussion. My companion and myself then put on our court dresses and, at about half-past ten o'clock, proceeded to the Court. His Highness having been previously informed of our intended visit, we were duly received by an officer of the State and presented to him in the great hall, opposite to a large reservoir. We found the Nuwáb, a stripling of about eighteen, sitting upon his State cushion, with a bolster behind him. He had only four persons for his courtiers, seated to the right, at a little distance from him. These were gentlemanly looking men. There was another person sitting in the window of the hinder gallery behind a blind screen, close to His Highness's cushion, watching strictly what was going on in the Court. We could discern a human figure, but did not know who and what he was until afterwards, when we were informed that it was the uncle, whose daughter was married to the young Nuwáb, and who always watched him very carefully, and managed both his public and private affairs. Upon the whole, the

Court, although it was void of all Asiatic pomp, yet had sufficient dignity for State occasions.

We took our seat in front of His Highness, and, after mutual inquiries about health, silence for a little while prevailed. My colleague, although high in the service, not being versed in court etiquette and language, whispered to me to explain the subject of our mission. I then gave the Nuwáb Mr. Langford's compliments, and began my speech, commencing with praises of the enormous power of the British Government and its just and proper use in the hands of its authorities. I then came round to the matter of the salt-pans of his district, and tried my best to impress upon his mind that it was impossible to prevent the salt being undersold and the revenue defrauded under the old system carried on by his people, and that the management of the pans must, therefore, devolve upon the British functionaries. The man seemed to hear what was said to him, but he would neither say yes nor no, nor even shake his head to show his approbation or disapprobation. At the end of my speech, therefore, I was obliged to put an interrogative sentence, telling him that, if he disapproved of the plan suggested, he would oblige us by saying so at once, that we might inform Mr. Langford, who would adopt another mode to remedy the evil. "You are right," observed His Highness at last; "think not that I disapprove of all you have said; I shall see Mr. Langford this afternoon, and settle the matter with him at once." Thus having obtained what we wanted, we took our leave of him and returned to our lodging in the factory.

On my return I drew up a report of our visit and presented it to Mr. Langford, who highly approved of it. He told me that, as he required me no more in the district, I had better return to Súrat by the boats that had brought us hither, and were going back by the next tide; that I had given him all the satisfaction he required in the performance of my duty during his charge of the office, and that I should have my promotion by the first opportunity. I thanked him for these soft and civil words in my behalf, and prepared myself immediately for the return. Our voyage back to Súrat was a speedy one, and on the 1st of December I rejoined the office at that place; but hearing that Mr. Langford was going to move us to an unhealthy station, I sent in my resignation.

Being now free from the office slavery, which took up seven hours every day for only thirty rupees per mensem, I conveniently allotted my time to my English pupils; amongst whom I had the pleasure to have Mr. C. J. Erskine, a young man of extraordinary talent and ability, whom I liked much. So industrious was he in pursuit of knowledge, that in a few months he passed in three languages, *i.e.*, Hindústání, Persian, and Gujarátí;

and he paid me very liberally, in fact, far beyond my expectation. Although I was better off in my pecuniary affairs at this time, yet certainty of expenditure and uncertainty of income rendering me uneasy, I thought of having a permanent situation, and, with this view, I wrote to Mír Sarfaráz Alí. On the 13th of April, I was regularly engaged to instruct one of this nobleman's sons in the English language for an hour every day, on a small salary; but the young nobleman, my pupil, seeing afterwards that one hour's time was not sufficient, increased my salary to fifty rupees per mensem, with free table and carriage. I then gave up all the English pupils except Mr. Erskine.

His Highness the Nuwáb was also glad to see me with his only son-in-law now in Súrat, the other having gone to Baroda after the death of his wife. He gave me a nice copy of Goldsmith's Natural History, presented to him by an English friend, and asked me to translate it for him into Persian at my leisure hours, promising to reward me very handsomely for my labour. This offer I accepted with great pleasure. I wrote about two hundred pages, every sheet of which, as soon as I finished, was taken by His Highness, read with avidity, and carefully kept.

On the evening of the 7th of August I received a note from Mír Jáfir Alí Khán, requesting me to attend immediately, as the Nuwáb had been taken very ill with cholera, on his return from seeing the steamer *Carnac* for the first time. Instantly, on the receipt of this unwelcome note, I ran to the palace, and on my arrival near the room where his Highness was, I saw Dr. J. Tawse leaving it with some instructions, and the Pársí Native Agent following him. I entered the room and saw His Highness in a bad state, his face changed, his eyes sunk deep, and his voice low; in fact, I found him beyond the reach of remedy. Besides, his being under the care of his philosophical minister and his sapient young attendants ensured his speedy departure from this world. I felt deeply for the poor old man, thinking that all his state, wealth, and dignity were now unable to save him. I whispered my idea to my young master, taking him aside; but he did not like to hear what I spoke to him, and, instead of resorting to some precautionary measures, began to cry like a child. Seeing that it was no time for advice, I soothed the young man by telling him that he must not allow himself to be overpowered by grief.

In the meantime, it being announced that the Nuwáb's favourite wife and his daughter were coming down to see him, we left the room clear for the ladies of the palace. The visit of these children of weakness and simplicity caused the old man to lose a part of his remaining senses. At four o'clock, P.M., death at last relieved him from all his pains and anxieties. The poor old man died thus suddenly at the age of fifty-nine years, after enjoying his nominal Nuwábship about twenty-one years.

His young son-in-law's grief, confusion, and distress were at this moment inexpressibly great. I prevailed upon him, however, to write an express letter to his father at Baroda, whose experience and timely aid he so particularly required at this critical juncture. After this, at my earnest request, he sealed the Treasury Rooms, with the account books and records, etc. At dawn we broke the seal of the treasury again to take out some money for the funeral expenses, but to our astonishment we found in the money chest nothing but a vacuum, though the sum of 8,333 rupees, 5 ánás, and 4 pices of the Nuwáb's monthly pension had been received from the Collector's Treasury only two days before. The Minister's pretended grief for the loss of his master was so great that he could not say how the money obtained its wings, and flew away in so short a time, and his subordinates' mouths were closed. The rooms were then locked and sealed up again, and Mír Jáfir Alí got from his own banker five hundred rupees for the funeral expenses. It is a most remarkable thing that a man, having an income of nearly two lákhs per annum, had not at the time of his death sufficient money in his treasury to defray the charges of his own first stage to the other world.

On the decease of the Nuwáb, the descendants of

his great great grandfather and his repudiated wife prepared to take their revenge upon the surviving family of the deceased.

Petitions on the part of the conflicting parties, reviling and abusing each other, were sent in to Government. It was considered advisable that Mír Sarfaráz Alí should proceed to Bombay, taking me along with him to represent the claims of his son and daughter-in-law, and her children, to Government, in person. So on the 3rd of October I left Súrat for Bombay, in company with the old gentleman, in whose most agreeable and valuable society I passed two months. I drew up two petitions to Government for him, of which he approved very highly, and he conferred a handsome reward of five hundred rupees on me. Also he wrote a very flattering note in his own handwriting to my address, which I preserve on my records as a mark of his favour. He visited the Honourable the Governor three times, and then received an answer from Government, assuring him that justice should be done in due time. Upon this we made preparations for our return to Súrat, and came back to that city on the 1st of December. A few days before our return, the property of his late Excellency was sequestered by the Government Agent, and the parties remained anxiously expecting the final orders of the supreme Government, and building their castles in the air.

On the 28th, I was officially requested by the

magistrate of Súrat to attend forthwith at the Political Agent's court at Rájkot as a witness. I had accordingly to proceed thither, and was detained six weeks, to my great annoyance and pecuniary loss.

To return to the late Nuwáb's affairs: fourteen months after his late Excellency's death the supreme Government of India sent its dreadful order through the Bombay Government, by which the title of the Nuwáb became extinct, the pension ceased, and only such members of the family as were in indigence were entitled to any support from Government. The ears of my young employer, and of all the members of the family, were quite stunned to hear this arbitrary order. Mír Jáfir consulted with his elders, and it was suggested that he should proceed to Bombay, and represent his grievances to Government in person; and that, if he failed to succeed, he should then repair to England. So, in accordance with this advice, he prepared to proceed to the Presidency by land, and requested me to accompany him. A lucky hour having been fixed by our astrologers for the departure, again, in the latter part of the month of December, we left Súrat for Bombay. We proceeded on, shooting and hunting all the way, and finished our pleasant journey and the month of December both together. For about five weeks we stayed at Bombay, during which time Mír Jáfir Alí Khán waited upon the Honourable the Governor thrice in person, and sent in his memorials to Government; but no decisive answer being obtained, he made up his mind to proceed to England. He engaged the services of an Englishman, Mr. T. J. A. Scott, and of myself, as his secretaries and interpreters for the trip, and passed his agreements to both of us. We then returned to Súrat on the 4th of February to make our final arrangements for the long trip to England, and on the 12th of March, 1844, we left our homes and friends for the other end of the world, *viâ* Ceylon. We chartered the steamer *Sir James Carnac*, as far as that island, and thence we had to embark on board the large steamer *Bentinck*, belonging to the P. and O. Company.

CHAPTER XIII.

The voyage to Ceylon—Christian quarters and the Unclean Animal—Cingalese Gentlemen—Aden—Ass-equipages—The Kaba on the move—Eve's burial-place—Selfishness of John Bull—Grand Cairo—Mohamed Alí—Mrs. Larking—Arabic the Language of the Húrís—Alexandria—Did Umar burn the great Library?—Gibraltar—Arrival at the Mother-bank.

In the afternoon of the 13th we got over our official and private business in haste, and early the next morning, sails and engine being put in motion, off we went in the most holy name of the Omniscient Being, an atom of whose unlimited wisdom is the source of all our sciences from eternity to eternity. On the 4th we came in sight of Vingorla. On the 15th we saw Gowa, the Portuguese settlement. On the 16th we passed by the Pigeon Island, and in the evening we got in sight of Mangalúr. On the 17th, passing by Kalikot, we made Cochin by dusk. On the 18th, at three o'clock A.M., we had to contend with very rough weather, so much so that it not only prostrated all our companions, but the crew of the steamer too seemed to be in distress. Poor Captain Duverger, a Frenchman, who commanded the vessel, walked up and down on the deck all the time, cigar in mouth, and the effect of the forbidden liquor in his head. He passed by me every now and then as I sat squatted by the side of his walk, embracing one of the awning posts, and told me, "My friend, tell His Highness and your companions to be manly, and not quake for a capful of wind." Got in sight of Cape Komorin this evening. The last rock of old India looked well and picturesque. The weather continued as harsh as the day before, and the night and the next morning were as bad as the preceding day. I myself, too, began to feel very uncomfortable, and tired of being tossed up and down. Captain Duverger told me that we were opposite the Gulf of Manár and Adam's Bridge, where storms always rage, and that we were about to get over our difficulties. His prophecy proved true, and on the morning of the 20th we were blessed with the beautiful sight of Point de Galle, in Ceylon, at a distance of about forty miles.

The beautiful view of this precious island became more and more enchanting as we approached. At last we cast our anchor in the harbour, and were immediately surrounded by the black natives, the Cingalese, so-called from the ancient name of their land, Singaldíp. The language of the natives sounded to me a harsh jargon, without distinction of syllables or periods, something like gravel put into a copper vessel and shaken; but they spoke English well enough. Seeing marks of the tides at the landing-place, I inquired the cause, and was informed, to my great surprise, that there was no ebb and flow of the tides perceptible in that part of the island. We were overtaken by the evening dusk before we got over our confusion and bustle of landing. In the hurry, an English hotel being recommended for our short sojourn, we proceeded thither and put up comfortably.

Early in the morning, to our great astonishment and disgust, we beheld a herd of unclean animals running, grunting, snorting, and roaring about our rooms. This abominable sight at once made us anxious to quit the Christian roof as soon as possible; and, on inquiry, we found that there were several houses of Muslims in the town; one of them, the property of a very nice gentlemanly man, by name Maka Murker, was obligingly lent to us, and we immediately migrated to that place, and were gladdened by the hospitality of our good host. The Christians of this time, in reforming themselves, have reformed their religion too. They eat and drink and do what they like under the acts of their Parliaments, without any regard to the Old and New Testaments, *vide* Leviticus, chap. xi. ver. 7; Matthew, chap. v. ver. 17, 19.

The animals of this island are not dissimilar to those of India, with some exceptions, in which I would number the elephant. This animal, from what I have seen here, appears to me far handsomer than those the Indian forests produce; besides, white and brown elephants, which are rare in India, are common in this land.

The following day we were honoured with a visit from five native gentlemen, fine looking men, of a brownish shining complexion, in costume of the ancient fashion, long robes and circular turbans nicely zoned. They were introduced to us as Ministers and State-officers of the former governing power of the island. The power is now annihilated in *toto*, but these are the marks of the ruin of the kingdom, from which one might trace its origin. From the conversation that took place, I conclude that these gentlemen were intelligent and well-informed. The religion of the country is Buddhism. The dead, if laymen, are buried; if priests, are given to be consumed by fire. The prevailing diseases of the island are leprosy and elephantiasis.

On the morning of the 22nd I had a kind invitation from a Mohamedan native gentleman, by name Ahmad Labbe, to breakfast with him at his country house, situated in a cinnamon garden, about three miles from the town. At eight o'clock in the morning, I set out and travelled in a coach for about half an hour in the country, all over verdant, and ornamented with beautiful trees, passing every now and then by aqueducts and rivulets of fresh water. I must not call this a travel, as it was somewhat better than a morning walk into a garden, refreshing the soul. On my arrival at the garden-house of my host, I met with a very warm reception from him. Ignorance of each other's dialect obliged us to converse in English, in which my host seemed to be well versed. For a little while he took me along with him, and walked in his magnificent garden, and pointed out a variety of the spice-trees, besides cinnamon, such as those of the cardamons, the cloves, the nutmeg, and the bread-fruit, etc., to my great satisfaction. After this pleasant and instructive walk, we came to the table, which I found laid with several well-seasoned dishes. In the meantime, another good-humoured young gentleman, a relative of the Labbe, by name Tambe Sáhib, joined us, and all three of us sat down to breakfast. My host took upon him to make tea for all, and, to my great astonishment, instead of sugar and milk—the usual auxiliaries of that beverage—he added a good quantity of salt, pepper, and clarified butter to it. So the cup of tea sent to me had more the appearance and taste of a black dose than anything else. Not wishing to displease my friends, I sipped it a little with my food, feigning to like the taste; but, unfortunately, my taking it sparingly being attributed to my requiring more of the ingredients, another large quantity of them was added as a special favour to my cup, and, whether I liked it or not, I was in a most friendly manner compelled to swallow it. Nausea at the heart and burning sensation from the tongue to the stomach overpowered me for a little while; but I endured them well, and, I must say, it was a reward for my hypocrisy, which I well deserved. After the breakfast was over, I was taken to another apartment, where, kalyúns being brought, we had a hearty smoke, and conversed a little more on the subject of the Indian Government, and then I parted with my noble friend and returned home. The rehearsal of what had taken place excited much laughter of my companions at home, but I cared not for it, as I had obtained a piece of experience at the cost of a dose, which did me no harm, but operated as medicine twice or three times.

In the morning of the 25th, hearing a terrible noise at the harbour, we ran and got upon the rampart to find out the cause, when, to our great delight, we discerned the large steamer *Bentinck* forcing its way through the sea, with its four tremendous wheels at work, making a dreadful noise, and sending up its smoke to the sky. Upon the whole, the sight of this exceedingly big sea monster will give you an idea of a roaring Satan making its appearance to devour up all that may come in its way. On the 26th, we embarked on board this large vessel, bidding adieu to the beautiful island of Ceylon. We were introduced to the commanding officer, Captain Kellock, a nice gentlemanly man, of a size proportionable to the vessel he commanded. Our cells—or cabins, in the sea language—were shown to us; luckily they were in the second of the four stories that the ship contained. The vessel, although very large, we yet found too much crowded, there being no less than three hundred passengers on board, besides the crew. At half-past two o'clock, P.M., the anchor was weighed and the steamer started with its gigantic force, wending its way as fast as possible. All of us were made very comfortable on board the vessel, through the attention of the good captain and officers. I must say that all the passengers who go by the P. and O. Company's steamers are more comfortable than at home. The English people, from what we saw of them on board the *Bentinck*, are first-rate eaters and drinkers; almost all of them ate and drank four times, five times, and even some six times a day. I must confess that we ourselves had not a bad appetite, and were amply furnished with every article of food we required, and made comfortable in every respect.

On the 2nd of April we came in sight of the island of Socotra, as predicted the day previous by a number of birds called bostons flying in that direction in the afternoon. This bird seems to be gifted with a wonderful power of flight over the seas. The island of Socotra was not less than two hundred miles distant from the spot where we saw them the day before. Hence it might be concluded that the bird, leaving the island in the morning and returning to it in the evening for its rest, must travel about five hundred miles a day. Praise to the power of the Omnipotent Being! in one stroke of whose mysterious pen, innumerable dexterities and arts can be seen, if one has an attentive eye and comprehensive mind. I witnessed another wonder in this part of the sea,—the flying fish. From one of these flocks that happened to go across our steamer, three flying fish having fallen upon the deck, I seized upon one; and a near view of the animal showed that it was a pretty little creature, and that nature had furnished it with two pairs of wings, one to be used in the water and the other in the air. Besides, when it was fried, I found it to be a very delicious food.

On the morning of the 4th we came in sight of Aden, and let down our anchor in its harbour at half-past one o'clock P.M. The distance reckoned from Ceylon is 2,215 English miles, So far, our voyage was, upon the whole, a very pleasant and very comfortable one. We had smooth and calm water almost all the way from Ceylon. After our arrival, the ship's company got permission to go to the land, if they liked; so we landed at once and placed ourselves on the lap of Mother Earth after eight days' separation. There is no such thing as a wheel-carriage known in Arabia; we had, therefore, no alternative left but to hire some asses for our short travel to the town of Aden, six miles from the harbour. Some uses in one country are abuses in another. For instance, ass-riding in India is a sign of public disgrace. There you will see nobody riding a donkey except those who, for heinous crimes, are sentenced to be paraded on the back of that animal. But in Arabia, and perhaps in all other countries, ass-riding is considered no disgrace. The head of our party, Mír Jáfir Alí Khán, who weighed something more than seventeen stone, was thought too heavy to be carried by an ass; besides, he could not be persuaded to ride one, as he lifted up one of the animals upon both his hands to show the Arab owner that it was impossible for him to be carried by a beast that could be lifted up by himself. In the meantime, a muleteer came in, running as if after a wild goose chase, and tendered the use of his fat mule to the bulky rider, who readily accepted the offer, and paid the man well; and then we cantered on to the town. Town you may call it, if you like, as long as you have not seen it; but, when you have done so, I am sure you would call it a haunt of evil spirits. It is no town, nor even a village, but a few miserable huts situated in the middle pit of the barren hills, circling round in the shape of a natural fortification, the diameter of which is about three miles.

As a military post I dare say it is not a bad place, if they were to build a suitable gate, and a few bastions; but in all other respects, in my opinion, the name Aden, denoting Paradise, given to this place, is altogether contrary to its qualities. This name must, I believe, have been given to the place upon the same principle as we give the name Káfúr, or Camphor, to our African slaves. There is no sign of vegetation here as far as you can see. There is no fresh water, except in one small well, under the Government guard, the water of which is sold for high prices. I suppose I may not say anything about the animal productions of a place where there is no water nor vegetable. The inhabitants are wretched and mean-looking people, bareheaded and barefooted, having nothing to cover their body except a small piece of linen. There were only three or four persons who seemed to honour their heads with turbans; one of them was Edrúsí Saiyid, who acted as priest to these wretches, and led their prayers in the small mosque, apparently going fast to decay. We put up under a shed belonging to an Indian retailer, and, having prepared and eaten our dinner, all of us went to bed and slept undisturbed very soundly, and did not get up until very late the next morning, when the hot rays of the sun, penetrating through the partition, obliged us to rise. After the ablution and breakfast we thought of returning to the steamer; but, it being Friday, the day of our Sabbath, it was agreed upon that we should not leave Aden before the performance of our Divine service at noon in the mosque of this place. At the appointed hour we proceeded to the sacred place of worship, whence the Holy Mecca, the rendezvous of the prayers of the Muslim world, was not too far; attended to the sermon nicely delivered by the Saiyid aforementioned, and, having performed the prescribed duties, we left Aden for the harbour, which we reached in time, and embarked.

So, in the evening of this day, the 5th of April, at half-past six o'clock, the anchor was weighed, and off the steamer went on its way. In the morning of the 6th we passed through the Bábu'lmandab, and entered the Bahr i Kulzúm, by the English called the Red Sea. By ten o'clock we came opposite to Mokka, and then passed several small islands on the left side. This day, in the afternoon, I found, by the mariner's compass, that the Kaba, the criterion point of our prayers, began to incline to the East. I mentioned the fact to my Muslim companions, who, instead of believing me, laughed at me heartily, and said that too much reading in English books most certainly had made my religious feelings too weak. "How could it be possible," said they, "that the Kaba, the most sacred house of God, which is the centre of the universe, should change its position!"—"He must have taken a glass of wine with his English friends," observed another, jokingly, "and what he says, therefore, cannot be sound." In the meantime, my third friend, the old physician, changed his posture, and, addressing himself to his young master, remarked, "Did your Highness ever hear such nonsense? A man with a sound mind would never say that the Kaba changes its position." All these remarks I heard with patience without saying a word, and established my truth by another *bonâ fide* proof. The Arab pilot, taken by the captain from Aden, stood to say his afternoon prayers to the direction mentioned by me. "How is this," said I to my friends, "that this Arab turns to the direction I pointed out?"—"We daresay he is a Jew; we shall, however," said they, "ask him some questions, through the medium of another interpreter, and satisfy ourselves upon this subject of importance." They did so, and got a good reward for their folly. In the first place the interpreter, a young Frenchman, laughed at them for the questions they put, and, secondly, the rough Arab gave them a scolding answer, and told them that they would soon see at Suez and Cairo all the true believers direct their prayers to the due east. "If you Indians," growled he angrily, "believe in the same God and the same prophet as they do, please follow their example; if not, prepare yourself for hell fire." In the evening we came in sight of the lights of Jeddah, the celebrated port where all the Indian Muslims disembark first, and whence they proceed on to the holy city of Mekka for the performance of their pilgrimage. As for the derivation of the word Jeddah, which signifies grandmother, I have read in some book that when our first parents were thrown from the blissful region under the wrath of God for their transgression, Adam was destined to fall at Ceylon and Eve at this place. They then wandered about for some years in the wilderness, and had at last the pleasure of meeting each other in the holy land of Jerusalem. The old lady, it is stated, at the concluding part of her life, requested to be conveyed to the same place where her feet first touched the earth. This being done, she departed this life, and was interred at this place, whence it had been called Jeddah from time immemorial. I have been informed there is a tomb of enormous length in the vicinity of this town, consecrated up to this time in the name of Mother Eve.

The 7th and 8th of April pássed comfortably; but on the 9th, we found the sea to be rough in consequence of the northerly wind, which is said to be generally too strong and troublesome in this part of the globe. It continued the same until the evening of the 12th, when we reached the port of Suez, 1,300 English miles from Aden. After our arrival at the bar of this port, we transhipped ourselves into an Arab sambruk to be landed at the town. This long boat being hired by ourselves, it contained nobody but eight of us Indians and the English secretary, Mr. T. J. A. Scott, with his wife and child. Much cold and great inconvenience we experienced in this small boat. The water having ebbed, it grounded every now and then; and, at the dusk of evening, it became so tempestuous, cold, and chilly, that every one of us was seized with trepidation. Mír Jáfir Alí

Khán was worst off, through his own imprudence in leaving his cloak on board the steamer. I offered him mine, but he politely declined the offer, telling me that it was too small for him, so it would be worse than useless to deprive me of the benefit without relieving him from the cold. At the same time, he suggested to me that there were two blankets without any owner lying about the place where Mr. Scott sat, and one of them had been taken for Mrs. Scott, so the remaining one might be brought to him. I proceeded thither to fetch it, but Mr. Scott prevented my doing so, telling me in a very rough manner, as if we had never known each other, that he was the first person to seize upon the blanket, and he would not allow his father Peter to take it from him until he had done with it. I told him that I did not want it, but that his master required it very badly. "I would not," replied he, "for the world kill myself for others, you may tell my master." But there was no need of telling the master, as he overheard and understood what passed between us. This showed clearly that selfishness was the general character of John Bull.

At half-past seven o'clock in the evening we reached the pier at Suez, and were conducted to the inn, where, thanks to God, we got a nice comfortable room, good dinner, and clean beds. After the hardships we had suffered in the afternoon, seeing some oranges that were brought from Cairo and sold at the door of the hotel, I bought a few, and found them excel, in sweetness and flavour, all fruit of that kind I had ever tasted in my life. My companions, too, extolled the fruit very highly, and not only devoured all that I had bought, but purchased a good lot of them to supply our wants on our way in the desert.

In the afternoon of the 13th we left Suez; our luggage and servants were loaded on the camels, and ourselves were furnished with light carriages, called vans; each of these vehicles held four persons, and the fifth was the Arab driver. It was lucky that four of us were put in the same van without making a heterogeneous mixture of the English with us. We proceeded on in the cool of the night, partly conversing and partly dozing and drooping with sleep. At midnight we reached the stage house, where we slept comfortably till morning; and then, after taking our breakfast, set off again and reached Al Misr, commonly called Grand Cairo, on the evening of the 14th. It was a most enchanting scene to see, just at the verge of the wilderness, the lofty edifices and the golden spires of the domes and palaces shining brightly over the houses of the population of this city, the capital of Egypt.

The houses of the city are built in the ancient Arab manner, within courtyards, confused and crowded, and the streets are very narrow in some places, hardly admitting two persons to go abreast. Men and women are strong, robust and fair; and the eyes of the Egyptian ladies are remarkably handsome and most enchanting. Donkey riding is considered no disgrace here; you will see even ladies of rank and dignity, when tired of walking in the streets, beckoning to the donkey man for his animal, who instantly attends to the call, and the fair creature, getting upon its back astride, canters on to her destination. The language of business is Arabic, and that used at Court and in families is peculiarly Turkish. So much for the city of Grand Cairo.

On our arrival here we put up in the house of a native Christian physician, and passed a very comfortable night after the fatigue of our journey. On the morning of the 15th, our young master, among others, had the pleasure of receiving a visit from Mr. J. Tibaldie, the head director of the Transit Company, a man of rank, wealth, and talent, perhaps of French origin, but well qualified in the English, French, and Italian languages. This gentleman proposed to Mír Jáfir Alí Khán to pay his respects to Mohamed Alí Pasha in the afternoon at his garden house, called Shubra, to which he agreed.

This morning I asked leave to go and see the Pyramids, one of the wonders of the world; but, to my great dismay, I was refused, under the plea that I could not be expected to return by the afternoon, when my services of interpreting to the Pasha would be urgently required. I prevailed, however, upon my employer to grant me two hours, and, riding a swift ass, I proceeded to visit the tomb of Imám Mohamed Shafaí, the author of the third orthodox sect of the Muslims, which is situated about one mile to the east of the town. On my arrival there I was actually in tears to find that the ashes of this renowned reformer, or rather founder of the third sect of Islám, were neglected within the sight of a Muslim Prince. The vault was half-decayed and the tomb inside broken, bent down, and overgrown with prickly bushes. I cared not, however, for the external worldly ornament, and said my prayers over the sacred ashes of the saint, and returned home in full satisfaction. The birth of this extraordinary holy man, histories inform us, took place at Ascalon, in Palestine, in the year 767, A.C., or 150 A.H. He was carried to the holy city of Mekka during his infancy, where he was educated. He was gifted with such a capacity that, when fifteen years old, he composed several books on Mohamedan jurisprudence, of incomparable excellence. He came to Egypt in 814, A.C., or 199 A.H., and five years after that, left his transitory abode for the blissful regions.

In the afternoon, being furnished with equipage, we proceeded to the Royal Garden House of Shubra, in company with Mr. J. Tibaldie. After going about two miles, partly in and partly out of the city, we reached the Garden, and, meeting with ready admittance, we entered it, and found the place to be a paradise on earth. The flower and fruit-trees were in beautiful order, loaded with blossoms and fruits, nicely reared with perfect horticultural art, and the avenues, paved with white and black pebbles, represented Persian carpets, spread in straight lines everywhere. On entering the palace, we found it to be a massive edifice of alabaster, having an excellent reservoir in the middle. The ceilings were masterly worked in basso relievo, and the pillars, single and solid pieces of the same stone, polished to the lustre of a mirror. We were conducted by a state officer, splendidly dressed, to a spacious room at the northern corner, and there we saw the old famous prince, Mohamed Alí Pasha, plainly attired in a red Turkish cap and a blue cloth coat descending to his knees; and then, being introduced to him, each of us touching His Highness' right hand with his, kissed it, according to the Turkish form of compliments, and then seated ourselves on the divan, in line to the right of the old prince. Two pairs of valuable Cashmere shawls were then presented by Mír Jáfir Alí Khán, and were kindly accepted by His Highness. Now three heads and tongues were employed to interpret, *i. e.*, I explained my young master's expressions to Mr. Tibaldie, in English, and Mr. Tibaldie to His Highness' principal dragoman (or interpreter) in French, and the interpreter to His Highness in Turkish. The mutual compliments were but very short, and then my young master began addressing himself to His Highness in the usual flattering mode of the English princes. He observed that he had always heard about the well-regulated good government wisely constituted and personally conducted by His Highness; that he thanked heaven he had now an ocular demonstration of the same, and found that all he had heard was nothing but truth. To this the old Pasha replied, "Something is done, but a great deal more remains to be done." After this, His Highness put several questions on the system of the English Government in India, which were duly replied to in short but comprehensive answers. The coffee then being ordered, was brought in, and, being presented to each of us, we rose in turns, and, kissing our own hands to His Highness, as a Turkish homage, we drank it in the same way as an Englishman drinks his friend's health, and then getting our leave, returned home well satisfied with the interview with an extraordinary man, who, although an unlettered soldier once, yet had raised himself to the summit of sovereignty, like the European Cromwell and Buonaparte and our own Haidar and Ranjít.

Mohamed Alí was of middle stature, and slender but compact in make. His complexion was nearly fair, and his head well-shaped. His forehead was high and broad, having a plurality of horizontal wrinkles, that appeared and disappeared according to the working of his mind. He had an oval face, fringed with a short white beard, expressive features, an aquiline nosé, and black penetrating keen eyes set deep under arched eyebrows. His deportment in general was grave, disclosing the mental energy which distinguished him; but he seemed to have a lively disposition and fascinating manners upon the whole, combined with the air of authority. He was about eighty years of age, and very nearly one-half of that time he had been the ruler of Egypt.

On the 16th we got on board one of the small steamers appointed to convey passengers to Alexandria by the Nile. We sailed down smoothly and comfortably. The scenery on both the banks was beautiful all the way. We saw several alligators, in the act of running after their prey, rushing on in the water, regardless of the noise that our steamer made. These monsters seem to be endowed with an enormous power by nature; they swam both with and against the stream with equal velocity.

At noon on the 17th we reached the celebrated port of Alexandria, the metropolis of Egypt, and the former emporium of the East, and disembarked at the garden-house of Mr. J. Tibaldie's sister, Mrs. Larking. A tall, handsome, well-made, and well-behaved gentleman assisted our landing from the steamer, and then we had the pleasure of knowing him to be Mr. Larking himself. This very polite and hospitable Christian, who does honour to the English name, received us all like his own brothers, and conducted us to his nice house, commanding a view of both the river and the city. On entering his hospitable roof we had the pleasure of being introduced to Mrs. Larking, a lady consummate in beauty and noble in mind, which gift and quality deserve to be painted and eulogised by a skilful artist and a vivid-minded poet, and not by a poor writer like myself. In short, all of us were as comfortable as at home. This beautiful damsel, it appears, knew several languages; but she conversed in two, *i. e.*, she talked with her husband in French, and with us, as well as with her own servants, in pure Arabic. This was the first time that I saw and heard a fair mouth scattering pearls of eloquent phrases in that scientific language. She had an excellent accent, and expressed her delicate ideas in a most charming manner. I confess that, in conversing with her, I considered myself having the felicity of confabulating with one of the gazelle-eyed nymphs of Paradise who, our religion teaches us, speak no other language but the Arabic. I conclude Mr. Larking to be the luckiest man in Egypt, being blest with seven goods—good health, good wife, a very nice, good child, good disposition, good fortune, good name, and good luck; and I wish him all happiness throughout his life. An early dinner being ordered, we had the pleasure of dining with this good pair, and then, in the afternoon, being supplied with a carriage, we were conducted through the city of Alexandria to another garden-house, belonging to Mr. Thurburn, the father-in-law of good Mr. Larking. Here we were comfortably lodged for a short time, expecting the steamer that was to take us on to England.

The next day we had the pleasure of seeing the old gentleman, Mr. Thurburn, at his own house. He received us with unfeigned attention, and treated us with sincere courtesy during the visit; and, on our leaving, gave strict orders to his servants to see that we were comfortable in every respect, and to attend to all our commands during our sojourn in his nice garden-house. In the evening, being invited to dine with another son-in-law of Mr. Thurbun, by name Mr. Straunary Tossizza, the Greek Consul, we went to his house. On our arrival, we found the house sumptuously furnished like a palace, fit for a prince to reside in. Here we were also received by our noble host and his beautiful wife and her younger sister. These two fairies, I must say, surpassed their sister, Mrs. Larking, in their incomparable beauty. The house was decorated with all kinds of rich articles; and the guests were treated with such real courtesy and politeness as never can be met with from the Christians in India. We returned home after ten o'clock, P.M., over-filled with feelings of gratitude towards our noble hosts.

For six days we had to stay at Alexandria, during

which time I went my rounds within and without the city, at my leisure, for an hour or so every day in search of information.

Many Christian writers, either on account of their want of knowledge, or from an unfounded prejudice against the true faith (except Gibbon and other eminent authors), accuse our Caliph of the unpardonable crime of having ordered the contents of the famous library that once adorned this city to be used as fuel for the five thousand baths which are said to have been here. It is something like Dr. Smith, who, in his "Epistles de Moribus ac Institutis Turcarum," no less than thrice mentions the Mohamedans visiting the tomb of their prophet at Medina, and once speaks of his being born there, the reverse of which is true. So, too, Dr. Philip Prince, in his "Universal History," page 57, observes: "A Mohamedan, amongst other observances, must wash himself thrice a day," instead of five times a day. Writers of events, I beg to observe, ought to be void of all partiality, and ought to have a thorough knowledge of the nature and character of the subject they undertake to explain. In the first place, they ought to have known that Mohamedan tenets teach all true believers to hold papers of all kinds sacred, and never to touch them even with their feat, nor allow them to be thrown into an unclean place, as they may contain the name of the Almighty Allah—contrary to the custom of the Christians of the present age, who have no regard even for their Bible, and would use its leaves, if damaged in any way, as useless paper. Secondly, it is quite absurd to think the same Caliph would commit such an act of insanity, who, on his visit to Jerusalem as a conqueror, ordered the great University there to be repaired at the public expense, and who would not say his prayers within the Grand Temple of that holy place, for fear of its being spoiled by his soldiers in following his example. Besides, the General Amrú, who was a lover of science and literature, and a man gifted with poetical talent, would by no means make himself an instrument of such an act of irrational madness.

In the afternoon of the 24th, at two o'clock P.M., we parted with our noble, hospitable, and good Christian friends, and, embarking on board the large steamer, *Great Liverpool*, we bade adieu to the port of Alexandria. With regard to the room and attention, we found ourselves more comfortable and more attended to than on board the *Bentinck*. The fact is, that the more you proceed on towards England, the more you find the English people endowed with politeness and civility. On leaving the harbour of Alexandria, our large steamer, with its 167 passengers, glided on the sea smoothly with its usual force. All the company were in excellent spirits, it being calm and peaceful. On the 26th, we discerned the island of Candia—something like a flake of brilliant cloud—about sixty miles off, covered with snow. And on the 28th, we reached Malta, at half-past twelve o'clock, P.M., a distance of 830 miles from Alexandria, in four days. Here, the steamer requiring to be coaled, we stopped one day.

On the afternoon of the 29th, again the gigantic engine of our steamer was set in motion, and she forced her way onward with an additional velocity, obtained by setting sails. We left the harbour of Malta at one o'clock, P.M., and, by the evening, we passed the beautiful island of Sicily, having in view Mount Etna, with the tremendous volcano shooting out from its summit. It is a beautiful scene, both during day and night.

On the afternoon of the 4th, at three o'clock, P.M., we reached the famous port of Gibraltar, a distance of 825 miles from Malta, in four days; and the same distance more now remained for us to traverse to England, the place of our destination. A slight accident to the boiler of the steamer detained us here for a day, during which, the passengers being allowed to go on shore, we also took the opportunity of going to the town and seeing this wonderfully strong place, once belonging to the true believers and now one of the British possessions. I confess I was actually struck with amazement, awe, and admiration to see the incomparable fortress of Gibraltar. It is the most impregnable fortress in the world that nature and art have formed in a single solid rock standing in the sea, commanding the entrances of the

Atlantic Ocean on one side, and the Mediterranean on the other; keeping, at the same time, the continent of Spain in awe, to which it joins itself by an isthmus. It looks over the Mount Abyla, on the opposite shore of Africa, as its companion, standing in the same majestic attitude. The sides of the rock of Gibraltar are excavated in the forms of galleries; and guard-rooms, range above range, with loopholes for the muzzles of large cannons, directing destructive fire upon all points of the compass, render this stronghold the most formidable in the world. In the year 712, A.C., this invincible fortress, being conquered by the Muslim General, Tàrik bin Zyád, along with the province of Granada in Spain, its former name, Calpe, was changed into that of Jabalul-Tárik, whence the present appellation of Gibraltar. For about 780 years it remained under the sway of the Muslims, and was then lost through the short-sighted policy of King Abu Abdullah and his predecessor, 1492, A.C., together with all the Muslim possessions in the country. The Kings of Spain then became its owners, and continued in possession of it for a period of 212 years, when, in the year 1704, fortune gave it to the English, the luckiest nation in the world, who are the rightful possessors of it up to the present day. The population of this town is said to be about 7,000 inhabitants, of the English, Jewish, and Portuguese castes, exclusive of the garrison soldiers, about 2,000 in number.

By the evening of the 5th, the boiler being mended, the anchor was weighed, and we proceeded out to sea. The calm of the sea, the genial society, and the attention of the good captain and his noble officers to our wants, rendered our voyage most pleasant, and on the 10th of May, at night, the anchor was cast at a spot called the "Mother-bank," where the steamer was to be quarantined for some days, until the passengers should be declared to be in perfect health and free from the signs of the Egyptian plague. Early in the morning, a friend of mine, Mr. Renell, of the Bengal Service, coming to my cabin, roused me up from sleep, telling me that there were some native girls to be seen near our vessel. It was too cold for me, a native of India, to get out of my bed so early, though it was the morning of the 11th of May, the hottest month in our climate; but the temptation caused me to wrap myself up in my cloak and attend immediately to my friend's call. Upon going upon deck, I beheld that our steamer was moored in a purgatory-like situation. On the left we had a beautiful view of the main land, and on the right we had the Isle of Wight, a magnificent hill with its white cliffs reflected in the sea. At the same time, there were lying several small boats near our vessel, which, among other spectators, contained several fresh and fair damsels of England, of very dazzling beauty, so it appeared to me at least.

To be quarantined, after such a long voyage, and

to see everything good and marvellous about you, without being permitted to have any intercourse with it, is a state most disagreeable to man. Three tedious, long, and dull days we passed in this state of tantalization on board the steamer; when, on the morning of the fourth, to our great delight, we found our boat moving towards the land in view, and, in about one hour's sail, she entered the Southampton Dock, all safe, thanks to the Almighty God!

CHAPTER XIV.

Land at Southampton—London—Kind Friends—Mr. Latham—Mr. Pulsford—The sights of London—The Opera—Mr. Baring—Lord Ripon—Return to India.

On the morning of the 14th of May, at seven o'clock, we landed near the Custom House, whence our baggage passed without the difficulty and loss of time customary in India, and we put up in a very nice inn, called the Union Hotel, which commanded a view of both the sea and the town. Our party, it appears, was looked upon by the curious natives as one of the seven wonders of the world. Luckily for myself, I had purchased a Turkish dress at Cairo, and thereby found myself safe from being stared at. As for my companions, they, except Mír Jáfir, were impatient to go to the bázár; and, immediately after breakfast, they proceeded to the market-places in their simple Indian dresses, where they were not only gazed at by all with curiosity, but followed by a crowd. Being annoyed at this, they returned home without being able to buy anything, and with a mob at their heels. Before they entered the door of the hotel, they turned right about face, to see their unwelcome audience, and a shout of "Hurrah!"

resounded from all directions. "Over-curious white devils," exclaimed our doctor, Badru'd-dín, very angrily to me; "they have no respect for caste or age: I have a great mind to pelt stones at them." —"Don't you do so, Hakím Sáhib," said I to the old doctor, "or you will bring evil on yourself and the hotel: these people don't fear any one. It is true, they are over curious, but, after all, they have done you no harm: let, therefore, well alone."

On the morning of the 15th, we proceeded by rail to London. Seating ourselves in these fairy vans, we proceeded on most comfortably in this unfatiguing journey. Beautiful, but momentary, were the views of the country, green and watered with silvery brooks; and magnificent were the sights of the villages, towns, and parishes that presented themselves to our eyes during our progress. The objects appeared and disappeared successively in most delightful forms, until we reached our destination. The doors of the carriage then being opened, we alighted in a very spacious yard, all paved with black stones.

In a few minutes, two nice carriages, drawn by horses of gigantic make and power, being brought near, we got up into them and drove into the far-famed City of London. Street after street, and square after square, that we passed through for about three-quarters of an hour, were all paved, clean and regular, thronged with the busy inhabitants of both sexes, almost all the females good-looking, and the males well-made and active. Palaces of nobles and dukes are distinguished by their large porticos and superior construction. In one of them I saw two well-dressed men with ashes sprinkled over their heads; and, thereby concluding that some death might have occurred in the house, I told Mr. Scott, who sat by me, that a mournful event might have been the cause of the dust on their heads; but the young man laughed at my beard, and said it was the old custom still preserved by some of powdering their hair. Upon the whole, one might imagine that this vast city, whose population is no less than twenty lákhs of inhabitants, contained the riches of the whole world. Surrounded by such wonders and curiosities, we travelled on to a quarter termed Brook Street, and alighted at a magnificent house, called Mivart's Hotel.

Supplied with all kinds of luxuries suitable to princes, we lived in this inn for three days; and then our chief, being frightened at the enormous charges, of about two hundred rupees per diem, engaged a private lodging, No. 7, Sloane Street.

Here we settled after our long voyage from the middle of the globe to the end of the world, where the sun appears, far to the south, as weak as the moon, and the polar star nearly vertical; where the country all over is fertile, and the people ingenious, civil, and active; where the language, customs, and manners are entirely different from our own; where, in fine, the destiny of our sweet native land lies in the hand of some twenty-five great men. It cannot be, I am sure, without the will of that one Supreme Being that this small island, which seems on the globe like a mole on the body of a man, should command the greater part of the world, and keep the rest in awe.

On the 16th, I had the pleasure of seeing my old friend and patron, Captain Eastwick, after three years and a half, and he took me along with him to his own house.

We passed a week in quietude at home,—I mean my chief and his other attendants; as for myself, I had no rest, even when at home, having the onerous task of acting as secretary and interpreter to all. None of them knowing the language of the country, I was required to be the medium of their business, barters, and negociations, with the natives. During this time I had the pleasure of gaining the acquaintance of two gentlemen of high station in life, namely, Alfred Latham and R. Pulsford, Esquires, the first a great merchant, and the second a member of Parliament; and, through the kindness of these two good gentlemen, I had the satisfaction of obtaining much information, and seeing many places free of charge.

On the 24th we were taken by our kind friends to see some of the famous places in the town. The first objects that engaged our attention were the enormous bridges in the city, especially the iron bridge, and the swinging bridge. It astonished us greatly to see large masses of cast iron regularly fixed and nicely cemented together in these useful fabrics. The country, we felt convinced, must have some inexhaustible mines of this metal, which is so necessary for man; for, besides these bridges, iron appears to be used very profusely. No house seemed to be without iron railings, iron bars, and some houses are even roofed with iron, and some gardens hedged with iron bars. After about half an hour's drive here and there, we were conducted to St. Paul's Cathedral, an edifice that, in my opinion, has not its equal in the world.

What I disliked most was the multitude of statues and images, all of them scientifically sculptured it is true. I know they are not worshipped, according to the Protestant tenet: but a temple dedicated to sacred purposes, whether humble or majestic, ought to be plain, so as not to withdraw the attention of the congregation from the sermons and preachings. After seeing this grand cathedral, we proceeded on to a subterraneous passage called the Thames Tunnel.

On the 25th our kind friends, Mr. and Mrs. Latham, invited us to the Italian Opera. In the evening, at about eight o'clock, we repaired to this house of entertainment, and found it to be a large palace of substantial construction, erected upon rows of pillars of cast iron. The interior is built up in rich and splendid style. Five tiers of small rooms, called the boxes, for the spectators to sit in, wide enough to hold four or five persons in each, are built up one above another, running in semicircular lines, one end of which begins from one corner of the stage hall, and ends at the other. The boxes and the chairs therein are lined and cushioned with rich damask. The seats of Her Majesty and the royal family are to the right side of the stage. Our seat was just opposite to the stage, in the same line with the royal seats. We sat comfortably for about half an hour, looking at the grandeur of the place, and remarking upon the convenience of the gas lights, which brightened or dimmed at pleasure. Hundreds of lamps at one time were reduced to the dimness of night, nearly depriving the vision of its free exercise, and, at another, they were made at once to shine as bright as daylight. At half-past eight the curtain was pulled up, and two very handsome ladies, very indecently dressed, and an old man, representing their father, appeared on the stage. They sang, I fancy, some historical ballad, in conjunction with the instrumental music, and danced very expertly. Whilst the females whirled round in their dancing, their short gowns flew up to the forbidden height. Tantalizing the assembly it appears was their principal aim by such a violation of decorum. We enjoyed the music well, but could not understand a word of what was said.

Having gained acquaintance with a number of respectable inhabitants and great men here, we were almost every evening invited to partake of their hospitable entertainments, and passed our evening hours delightfully in the enjoyment of their good society. As for myself alone, when I had no invitation to accompany my chief, I proceeded to the theatres, generally to the Haymarket Theatre and the Lyceum, sometimes alone, and sometimes in company with my friend and pupil, Captain T. Postans, whom chance had brought here with his amiable and learned wife.

On the 27th I dined and passed a happy evening with Captain and Mrs. Eastwick, who had invited a party of their friends and relatives to meet us. On the 28th, having had an invitation to the fancy ball house, we proceeded thither in the evening, and were highly gratified by seeing persons dressed in various costumes of different countries. One gentleman in Persian dress actually deceived us, as he passed by; not only his dress, but his manners, too, appearing to us those of a Mughal. My chief's brother-in-law accosted him and, after formal salutation in Persian, asked him how he did, and how long since he had left Shíráz? But the man, instead of answering him in that language, smiled and spoke in English, which betrayed him to be an Englishman wearing a false beard, better a than true one in every respect.

On the 30th I accompanied my chief to the East

India House in Leadenhall Street. They call it a house, but it is a palace, containing a great number of apartments and halls, all well furnished. It is the place where the destiny of my sweet native land lies in the hands of twenty-four men, called the Honourable Directors of the Honourable East India Company, who are the principal movers of the string of the machine of Government in India. On our arrival, we were conducted by two state ushers to a room in the middle of the palace, where we found the chairman, with his deputy next to him, sitting on their chairs. The chairman's name was Captain John Shepherd, and that of his deputy Sir Henry Willock. Both of them appeared to be grave and intelligent persons; the latter spoke Persian well. By these gentlemen we were received politely. The conversation first began in Persian with Sir Henry Willock, who, finding it somewhat irksome to explain our meaning every now and then to the chairman, let down the burden of interpreting on me; so I went on, partly explaining the ideas of my young chief, and partly coining some out of my own head, whatever I thought expedient to serve the interest of my client. The result of the conference, gathered from the remarks of these two great men, was that my chief's coming to this country to obtain justice was an imprudent act, as he might have obtained it in his own country by simply writing to them, without undergoing the hardships of a long voyage and incurring heavy expenses. Little did they know that a despotic stroke of the pen of Lord Ellenborough, their own Governor-General in India, deprived my chief of his rights, and so compelled him to proceed to England to seek for justice.

After about half an hour's conversation we took our leave of these great men, who are the fountain-head of all the affairs of India. We were then, by a kind friend, taken up stairs, where we saw the Honourable Company's museum, which is a great collection of rarities from all parts of the world, and had the honour of being introduced to three men of learning, viz., John Shakespear, the author of the Hindústání Dictionary; Professor Wilson, the first-rate Oriental scholar; and Colonel W. H. Sykes. Knowing the first-named gentleman to be the author of a book in our language, I addressed to him a very complimentary long sentence in my own language. But, alas! I found that he could not understand me, nor could he utter a word in that language in which he had composed several very useful books. There is no doubt but the second gentleman, the professor, was a learned man, as his conversation with us demonstrated his high acquirements at once. The third gentleman, we were informed, was one of the directors, as well as a member of the Royal Asiatic Society. He was a tall, thin, and handsome-looking man, in appearance more like a noble Arab than an Englishman. His previous long residence in India, it appears, had made him quite conversant with our manners, languages, and feelings. So this accidental interview with him produced a genial delight in our hearts, and his civility, complaisance, and kindness, attracted our minds at once to seek for his friendship. During my stay in London, I had often the honour of seeing him, and conversing with him; and he was always particularly kind towards me. I found him to be a man of sublime mind, endowed with high attainments, considerable ability, and acute understanding.

This evening, Mr. Latham kindly took me to the Royal Institution. On my arrival, I was introduced to three or four noblemen, whose names I have quite forgotten; but they treated me like their own brother, made me sit near, and explained to me what I could not understand. The fact is, that in England, you will find those that are highest in rank are the politest in society. The lecture was ably delivered on anatomy—which has been a favourite study of mine for many years past—by Professor Faraday; and I declare, what I learnt in hearing this one lecture I could not have acquired in one year's hard labour with my books. Mr. Latham further was so good as to obtain permission for me to be admitted whenever I liked, free of charge. Besides, he kindly promised to speak to the superintendents of the St. George's Hospital and the College of Surgeons, who would kindly send for me, whenever a dissection might take place in those institutions most beneficial to mankind.

On the 1st June, we were introduced to a nobleman, by name Colonel T. Wood, and met with a kind reception at his house, from himself, his wife—a lady of high rank—and his two daughters, exquisite in beauty, and adorned with the accomplishments obtained from high education. After this, we paid another visit to the East India House; and were taken thence by Mr. Pulsford to the British Museum and the Zoological Gardens, with which we were highly delighted.

On the 2nd, it being Sunday, the whole city appeared to be in a very dreary and dull state. No shop was open, and no carriages, cabs, or omnibuses were to be seen running to and fro as usual. But all the inhabitants were richly and neatly dressed within doors. Our English servants, too, having already performed last night what was required of them to-day, dressed themselves very smartly, and went away to the place of their worship. Sunday is called the Sabbath, and it is scrupulously held sacred, just the same as Friday with us, and Saturday with the Jews; though the word Sabbath, both in Hebrew and Arabic, signifies Saturday, and not Sunday. This being not a day of business, we took a long drive to the two places called Highgate and Hampstead, and being gratified with the fresh air and scenery of the town and the country, returned home in the evening.

On the morning of the 3rd we paid our visit to a learned man, by name Dr. Bowring, and derived much benefit concerning our business by conversing with this able man. In the afternoon we visited the House of Lords, and the Parliament, and heard the question of the duty on sugar most ably discussed.

On the 4th I received an invitation to visit the St. George's Hospital, through the recommendation of Mr. Latham, where I was received with great attention and kindness by Dr. Cutler and Mr. Prescott Hewett, and was kindly taken by the latter, along with himself on going round, to see all the patients in the hospital, and then was allowed to participate in the fresh dissection of a subject expired only two days before. Here I became convinced that a great part of what I had studied in "Galen's Anatomy" in Persian and Arabic was founded upon fancy and conjecture, and that it was impossible for anybody to acquire a thorough knowledge of this most useful study for mankind, without the practical course of dissection.

On the morning of the 5th we proceeded to see the Ascot races, a few miles from town. We beheld a great concourse of people assembled to see what horse would win, and what horse would lose. Almost all the spectators, I am informed, lay wagers among themselves; and these races are to be the cause of gain and loss of large sums of money amongst the inhabitants. The English racers are the best animals I have ever seen. We cared but little for the amusement, but gained a grand object by taking the trouble of coming to this place; that is, we were blessed with a near sight of our gracious Sovereign, and her husband the Prince, to whom we made our profound bows, which were very politely returned by her Majesty and her illustrious Consort. It appears that our dresses, our faces, and our obeisance, without taking off the turbans, attracted the attention of the Royal pair, and of the nobility in their cavalcade; but it was all without the vulgar curiosity of common people. Those who are crowned with greatness by the grace of the Almighty, their minds are also endowed with greatness,

On the 7th we paid a visit to the Institution-house of the Civil Engineers, and had the pleasure of an interview with Mr. Walker, the President, and Mr. C. Manby, the Secretary of the Institution, both men of great ability.

In the evening of the 8th, having been invited, we proceeded to the Asiatic Society, and had the pleasure of hearing a very able lecture on geology, delivered by Dr. Falconer. After which, Lord Auckland, our former Governor-General, made a speech, which we could not understand, as his lordship used a language too high for a foreigner to follow him; so this speech, acting as a narcotic dose upon our brain, we conversed with other lords and nobles that happened to be near us.

On the 9th, it being Sunday, we took another drive to the village of Richmond, about seven miles from the town, with an English friend.

On the 10th, we attended the meeting held at the Society for the Encouragement of Arts, Manufactures, and Commerce. The assembly was presided over by Prince Albert himself. We had the honour of getting seats next to the Duke of Sutherland, and His Grace conversed with me in a very polite and friendly manner, whenever his attention was not required to the meeting. On the arrival of the noble President, all present rose up to pay him their respects; and we also made obeisances in our own Asiatic manner; and the Prince, returning his compliments to all, very gracefully took his seat on the high chair placed in the middle. The artificers and manufacturers then, one by one, presented their patent articles to the Prince, and described them minutely. The things presented met with the approbation of the President and members, and the makers received their applause, and subsequently, perhaps, some reward in money too. After this, we went down-stairs to inspect a large collection of the specimens of various kinds of articles, formerly patented; and, in going our round again, we had the honour to meet the Prince, to whom we made our profound bows; and His Royal Highness very gracefully addressed my chief, asking him the usual first question of every Englishman, "How do you like this country?" The answer given through me, was, that we liked it much. The next question was, "What did we admire most in England?" I boldly but respectfully answered, on the part of my chief, that the civility of the people of high rank and station was the thing most admirable to us; which answer, producing a slight smile on the Royal face, His Highness walked on. Thus ended our accidental interview with a Prince whom fortune has aided to ascend the summit of the highest authority in the world.

In the afternoon we saw the Chinese Exhibition; and, at night, proceeded to another fancy ball, which we found superior to the former.

Not being fully satisfied with our former visit to the British Museum, on the 11th we repaired to that place again, and had the satisfaction of seeing what remained unseen in our previous visit. We then proceed to see Westminster Abbey, and found it to be a lofty edifice of great beauty and splendour finished in the ancient Gothic style. It is said to have been built by Henry III., one of the former kings of England, in 1221 A.C. The pavement of the choir of this sacred place attracted our attention first, being a rich mosaic of innumerable pieces of jasper, porphyry, alabaster, lapis lazuli, and serpentine marbles, all varying in size, and skilfully arranged. The portico, termed Solomon's gate, leading into the northern cross, presents a magnificent view to the observer. This sacred place, too, is not destitute of the images of the great men of England, but they are not so numerous as at St. Paul's. The abbot, a very polite young man, of great ability and talent, took us to the west door, whence we had a most beautiful view of the inner body of the convent, which impressed us with awe, caused by the loftiness of the roof and the range of columns by which the whole edifice is supported. The double ranges of the coloured glass windows of the two upper galleries, based upon the arcade of the aforesaid pillars, freely admitted beams of light to the whole abbey without glare. After going through all the convent, the abbot took us to a large hall, where coronations of the Kings of this land take place. The great chair upon which they are seated, seems to be a very old-fashioned one; and we could not leave the hall without touching this high chair, the seat of empire. We then were taken by the good abbot to his own residence, near the Abbey, and each of us was treated with the best of beverages a glass of water. After this, having conversed with our host for a while on the subject of his cross, and our crescent of the ancient time, my chief went home, and I was taken by Captain Postans, to visit a great man, the Honourable W.B. Baring, Secretary to the Board of Control.

On going to the house, we were kindly received by the Secretary, a young man of about thirty. He put several questions to me regarding the Government in India, and I answered them according to my humble opinion, of course in favour of my own country, which answers seemed not to agree with the spirit of our host. My friend, Captain Postans, talked with him for a while, and we took our leave.

On the 14th, we went to an evening party at Lord Ashley's. His lordship and his beautiful lady received us with great courtesy. Here we had the pleasure of being introduced to Viscount Jocelyn and his wife, the loveliest of English beauties. After a little while I had the honour of playing at chess with this nymph of Paradise. I played two games with her, and allowed myself to be beaten both times to please her.

On the 19th, I attended the Court of Proprietors, assembled in the India House, and had the satisfaction of hearing an able speech from Mr. Sullivan, tending to the welfare of both the rulers and the ruled of India.

On the 25th, we had the honour of paying our visit to Lord Ripon, President of the Board of Control. This Minister received us with the courtesy natural to the nobility of England; but, feeling his pulse with regard to our business, we found his lordship to be a very stiff and different man altogether.

On the 27th, we went to an evening party at Major Jervis's house, in the company of several beauties and great men, amongst whom I found Colonel Miles, the same Arabic scholar whom I had the pleasure of seeing at Víra, twenty-four years before. I told him there was a great difference between the two places of our meeting; and he remarked, that the difference was not only in places, but in time. I paid him another visit at his own house, which he never returned, thinking, perhaps, that he was still in India, and not in the land of freedom, where all are equal.

On the 28th, we proceeded to Regent's Park to see a wonderful place called the Diorama. On our arrival at this place of incantation, we were conducted by the keeper into a room as dark as an infidel's heart, and were kindly seated upon chairs. I say kindly, for, having placed ourselves at his disposal, he might have maltreated us in this dungeon with impunity, if he liked. In the meantime, our sense of hearing was gratified with distant music, and then a beautiful scene of a frosty morning gradually presented itself to our deceived vision, in which we saw a rough clownish vegetable vendor at the river side, having landed his large parcels of cargo in a tremendous heap, himself shrivelled with the weather, sitting half-asleep in his boat, and his wife and a child sleeping on the bundles. The motion of the water of the river was nature itself, and by the side of the stream there appeared a magnificent palace, whose inmates were engaged in various employments. In the meantime, the sun shone brilliantly and extended his rays all over: and then the evening came on, the scene changed, so much so that the vegetable seller was metamorphosed into a pretty woman, the stars became visible, and the moon rose, casting her serene light over the scene. The palace, too, appeared illuminated with lamps and chandeliers. And the scene then gradually vanished, and the first darkness again prevailed, in which the distant music once more allured our attention. After a little while, the light of morning again began to appear, and in about one minute the interior of a grand church presented itself to our view, first vacant, but in another minute filled with the congregation. The morning then turned to day, and the day, in a few minutes, into evening, and then night came on, and then to our great delight we were helped out by the keeper from this house of false magic. The secret of this place was that the house was partly blocked up and partly orificed with windows, turning on a pivot, and the windowed part coming in contact with perspective paintings, placed behind large magnifying glasses, formed this optical deception. But how the water moved, how the sun, the moon, and the stars appeared and disappeared, how the objects were transformed, and the times changed, was still beyond my comprehension. Thus, half-satisfied and half-puzzled, we returned home. Some of my companions would have the house to be under the power of evil spirits.

On the 29th, I received permission to visit the College of Surgeon's in Lincoln's Inn Fields, and met with a kind reception from the superintendent, Professor Owen, who gave instructions to his assistants to show me all that I should like to see, and describe everything in full. I walked round the several stories of the house, and inspected human bodies, both whole and in parts, arranged in regular order for the benefit of the students, who, by this help, can easily, in a short time, ascend the summit of the science of anatomy in both theory and practice.

On the 1st of July we paid a visit to the National Gallery. From this place we proceeded to a theatre, where Herr Döbler, a juggler, exhibited his arts. We admired very highly his performances, in making an automaton shoot at the mark with its gun, in producing pigeons from dry fish, destroying watches, burning handkerchiefs, and then producing them safe, and similar tricks. But, after all, our Indian jugglers are superior to these Europeans. In the first place, the latter are furnished with all suitable materials for their performance, with the advantage of the stage-house, which can be darkened or lightened at pleasure; whereas the poor Indian juggler stands in an open plain before the public, and performs such tricks as giving his snake to his mongoose, who devours it before all, the animal's mouth being seen stained with blood; and then the man pulls out the reptile, all alive, from the tail of the mongoose. An Indian juggler stabs his own child and cuts the throat of his wife before your eyes: you see the blood issuing from the wounds, and then you find that all is sleight of hand. I myself once contracted a friendship with a Bráhman juggler, by name Lálbhatt, who pretended to have had a divine inspiration from his goddess, and performed such tricks as in former ages would have surely been taken for miracles. Once I took my two European friends, Dr. J. Patch and Dr. W. Leggett, to the place where this wonderful man sojourned, at Súrat. The two doctors were greatly astonished to see the man clapping his hands, and producing a quantity of cardamom and betel nuts; asking one of my native friends to hold fast his own emerald ring in his hand, which in two or three minutes vanished from his hand, and was found upon the lower dress of Dr. Leggett; and similar wonders.

The first week of July passed pleasantly in comparative idleness. In the afternoons I took a walk to Kensington Gardens, not far from our quarters, where I sat peacefully for an hour or two, looking at the beauties of nature.

On the 10th, I accompanied my chief to the Polytechnic Institution, Regent Street. Among other things the diving bell amused us much. I undertook to descend into the water by this extraordinary vessel, while my chief and companions would not only not venture to descend, but dissuaded me very strongly from undertaking the trial, telling me that it was an act of great imprudence to endanger life in such useless sport. Turning a deaf ear to such remonstrances, I hastened to the brink of the water, and pronouncing my Bismillah (in the name of the most merciful name of Allah) I got into the bell with four Englishmen. Upon our entering, we found a commodious seat, and then the bell being let down into the deep, we felt a queer compressing sensation in our ears, but that was all the inconvenience we experienced. We saw a patch of the water on one side, where the bell was left open near our feet; but the vacuum of the vessel being filled up with the air, with which we were constantly supplied by means of a communicating tube between the inner part of the bell and the outward atmosphere, prevented the water from rushing in. On reaching the bottom we saw the pebbles and gravel, and then were pulled out again from the dangerous deep to the open air of the world.

On the 11th, we proceeded to the Court of Justice of this city; and, on our arrival, were received with kindness by the Lord Chancellor, and were requested to take our seat near the high chair of his lordship, on the right side of the Court. His lordship, perhaps being hard of hearing, gave me, as interpreter, a chair at his elbow, and my chief sat at a little distance. The case before his lordship at the time was that of an Indo-European, Colonel Dyce Sombre, an unlucky man, who had lost his large fortune by falling in love and entering into a marriage contract with an English lady of rank. After a little conversation, not wishing to take up his lordship's valuable time, we took our leave of the Court, and proceeded to return a visit to another nobleman. Then, in company with our shipmate and very obliging friend, Colonel Stratton, of the Madras army, we waited on Prince Soltikoff, a young man of very high talent and great ability. He showed us a portfolio containing beautiful drawings of cities, castles, and vegetable productions of various countries in Asia, worked by himself, which showed great knowledge of drawing. Upon the whole, he was an amiable, fine-looking man, not in the least elated with the pride of birth.

The next day I was ordered by my chief to wait again upon the Russian Prince, and invite him, on his part, to Astley's Theatre, where he had engaged a box. I proceeded forthwith to execute my orders, and delivered over the message to the Prince, who accepted the invitation for the night. There was a tall, well made, and very handsome young Englishman in the room at this time, who seemed to take interest in my conversation with His Highness; and the Prince, observing this, introduced me to him, pronouncing my name to him and his name—Lord John Elphinstone, the late Governor of Madras to me. I was glad to make acquaintance with this nobleman, as my little conversation with him clearly showed that his cultivated mind corresponded with his outward appearance.

In the evening, the Prince having arrived in time, we proceeded to Astley's Theatre, and the performances that we saw there were most admirable. The horses of this theatre understood man's language and music, for they turned and returned, ran and stopped, at the words of command and notes of the music. Upon one horse, whilst cantering, a very pretty young damsel, with a smiling countenance, jumped from the ground and stood upon the saddle, urging the animal to speed. In the meantime, one of the performers threw an ivory ball at her, which she caught with alacrity, and playfully tossed it up and caught it repeatedly, as if the atmosphere was under her command, and placed it in her hand quite safe whenever she threw it up. This was not all; but, in every turn, she caught an additional ball from the performer, and went on tossing it up, until she had received seven; and all she tossed up and caught invariably in both hands with wonderful dexterity. Every one of the seven balls appeared continually to be in motion at the miraculous touch of her hand; and the horse ran its round as fast as possible, whilst the fairy stood upon it, with her smiling lovely countenance, unshaken. After, this, the warfare and the political affairs of China were acted upon the stage; and all ended in a laughable farce.

On the 17th, having heard of a wonderful dwarf's arrival from the country, we went to see him at his lodging, and found him to be but 16lbs. in weight, and 28 inches in stature, aged thirteen years. He was free from all the dwarfish deformities, such as a curve in the calf-bones or vertebræ, or a lump upon the back, etc. He was called the General Tom Thumb; and, by receiving rational answers to our questions from him, we found his reason to be quite sound. He was dressed in a military uniform, with a cocked hat upon his head and a small sword buckled to his side, which gave him a most ludicrous appearance and excited the laughter of his visitors, especially when he sang love songs and danced with a girl, somewhat bigger than himself, in a very lively manner.

On the 24th, being invited to spend the day with Mr. A. Latham at his country house in the suburbs of Windsor, we proceeded thither by the first train early in the morning, and reached the famous Windsor, twenty-two miles west of London, in something less than an hour. The town is well populated, and situated on a pleasant site by the River Thames. Our good host having obtained permission, we entered the magnificent castle, and had the satisfaction of seeing the palace inside, and the ancient church. We then proceeded to Mr. Latham's house, and passed a very happy day under his hospitable roof.

On the 31st we were invited by our friend R. Pulsford, Esq., to take a whitebait dinner with him at Greenwich, so we proceeded thither at noon in his company on board one of the small steamers running to and fro on the river Thames, and arrived in about half an hour. We put up in a nice inn at the river side, and partook of our friend's hospitality. The town of Greenwich is situated at the bank of the river, five miles east of London, and is very populous. It is noted for its magnificent hospital for decayed seamen, its beautiful park, and for its astronomical observatory on the summit of a hill, whence all the English seamen reckon their first meridian of longitude.

The beginning of the month of August passed in business until the 14th, when, whilst walking in the bázár, I was informed of the arrival of some Americans in the Egyptian Hall. I went in, and, having paid a piece of silver as a fee to the owner, I saw my fellow creatures, nine in number, in their uncivilized rude state, dressed in skins, feathers, and straws, made up and interwoven by themselves. Their complexion was copper-coloured, their appearance wild, their body proportionate, excepting the arms, which were too slender. They spoke a jargon, in sound resembling Maráthí, and a young Englishman interpreted their ideas, which were simple and chaste in their nature. They painted their foreheads and bodies somewhat like the Hindús. This day I received a handsome present of a valuable telescope from R. Pulsford, Esq., as a token of friendship, which I very reluctantly accepted. I prize the keepsake, however, very highly, it being from a gentleman who took much interest in the welfare of my native land and myself.

On the 26th, the news of the birth of a prince to our gracious Sovereign at Windsor having been telegraphed, I was, according to our Asiatic customs, ordered by my chief to carry a letter of congratulation to the Castle. So again I proceeded to Windsor, delivered my letter to the secretary, and, receiving his reply, returned home in the afternoon.

On the 27th, having obtained a letter of introduction to Lord Bloomfield commanding at Woolwich, we proceeded thither early in the morning, accompanied by Captain T. Postans. We sent the letter to the great man, and were informed that we would be received in the afternoon at his lordship's residence. In the meantime, an officer was deputed to remain in attendance upon us, and to show us over the different departments. So, by the kindness of this officer, we had the satisfaction of seeing the instruments of the British wealth; and the use of them was explained most minutely to us.

It was Sir Charles Forbes who procured us this

attention at Woolwich; and, from the time of our arrival, we were helped through difficulties in a most friendly manner by this good baronet, who was one of the staunch patrons of India.

Now, my chief having received answers to his petitions from the Court of Directors, and, in the beginning of September, having obtained assurance from the Chairman that his business would be satisfactorily settled in India, we had nothing to detain us in England, except the gratification of the pleasures of my young chief; upon whom, with much difficulty, I prevailed to leave this city of enchantments as soon as possible, and our passage was taken in the mail steamer that was to leave the shores of England on the 3rd proximo. So we had one whole month, free from the burden of business, to bid farewell to our friends, and to see something more that remained unseen. Amongst our new friends in London we had also the pleasure of having a true believer in Saiyid Amínu'd-dín Al Alí, commonly called Alí Effendi, the ambassador on the part of the Sultan of Constantinople to the Court of England. We had the honour of several interviews with this noble minister of the Sovereign of Islám. My chief made him a present of a very valuable Indian sword in token of his most sincere regard and profound respect. On the 12th of September, we paid our parting visit to him, and his Grace would not allow us to leave him without a mark of his friendship. He gave my chief a very valuable volume of a Turkish book, and a similar one to myself, endorsed by himself. And then, after a long conversation about the Indian Government, we took our leave of him, assuring him that our services at all times were at the disposal of the Islám Government whenever they were required.

I may now sum up the character of the English, by saying they are entirely submissive to the law and obedient to the commands of their superiors. Their sense of patriotism is greater than that of any nation in the world. Their obedience, trust, and submission to the female sex are far beyond the limit of moderation. In fact, the freedom granted to womankind in this country is great, and the mischief arising from this unreasonable toleration is most deplorable.

I must now leap over the course of ten years, from 1844 to 1854, during which time I experienced many vicissitudes; to enter into the particulars, I require another volume, which I intend to fill when I am master of my own time, retired from the service of Mír Játir, and peacefully sitting at my own desk at home.

In short, on the 3rd of October we left England, and on the 12th of November we reached Bombay, thanks to the Almighty Alláh, all safe, where we stayed for a fortnight, during which time we got over the official business, in paying visits to the Honourable the Governor, delivering the letters to him, both from his friends and from his superiors, and seeing other friends at Bombay. My chief then proceeded to Súrat by sea and I by land, and I reached sweet home once more on the 5th of December, 1844, A. C. My dear wife, my God bless her soul! was delighted to see me after this long journey, and I was twice as much delighted to see my only sincere friend in the world and my beloved partner in pleasure and adversity.

It is quite evident that the pecuniary circumstances of my chief and myself were improved by having proceeded to England, in proportion to our individual capacities. But a severe misfortune at the same time lurked behind the invisible curtain of destiny, to inflict a deep and unhealable wound upon our hearts. His dear wife, the source of his aggrandisement and wealth, departed this life on the 9th of January, 1845, of consumption; and then, on the 15th of January, 1847, my dearest wife, too, having had an attack of the cholera, left this world for the next. My grief for this severe and irreparable loss was so great that I thought of renouncing the world at once. But my friends and companions, especially my chief, blindfolded me again, and led me into the worldly delusions by degrees, and again I gave in my neck to be yoked to the waggon of worldly cares.

On Monday, the 12th of July, 1847, again I entered into the marriage contract with Wiláyatí

Khánum, the adopted daughter of Najíbu'nnissa-begam, eldest daughter of the late Nuwáb of Súrat; and by this lady I am blessed with four children, three girls and one boy. May God bless them all! My domestic cares are now aggravated, my years advanced, and my income inadequate to cover the expenses of a large family. But I resign myself to the will of that Omniscient Being, whose omnipotent power first creates the food and then his creatures destined to live upon it. Amen!

THE END.